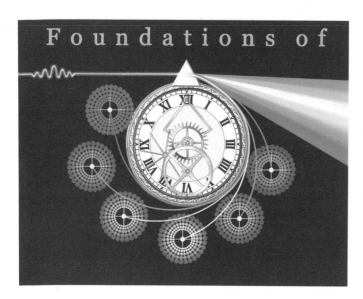

Foundations of

Physical Science

with Earth and Space Science

Investigations

Tom Hsu, Ph.D.

FIRST EDITION
CPO Science
Peabody, Massachusetts 01960

The cover colorfully combines illustrations of the forces of nature studied in the various fields of the physical sciences. Here, the "evolving tapestry of conceptual thinking" begins with water. Water droplets dance with the planets including our own watery planet and Saturn with its icy rings. Water reappears in the combustion reaction of methane, as the substance on which plants depend, as pounding waves, and, on the back cover, as the darkening clouds of a coming storm. From this cycle of water, a modern bicycle rolls into a graphical interpretation of white light split into its rainbow of wavelengths and a fiber optic. You may lose yourself in many of these images which represent hundreds of years of scientific and technological innovation. Nevertheless, that our innovations are inextricably woven into and from the natural world is illustrated by the images of Earth and the spiral connection between the DNA helix and a bicyclist ever-moving forward. On the back cover, images from physics, chemistry, and earth and space science move around a chambered nautilus seen through the windows of the Golden Rectangle. We at CPO Science with Bruce Holloway, the spirited illustrator of the cover, hope these images will inspire your interest and excitement about the discovery of science.

The CPO Science Development Team

Foundations of Physical Science with Earth and Space Sciences - Investigations
Copyright © 2003 CPO Science
ISBN 1-58892-060-7
1 2 3 4 5 6 7 8 9 - QWE - 05 04 03

CPO Science
26 Howley Street,
Peabody, MA 01960
(866) 588-6951
http://www.cpo.com

Printed and Bound in the United States of America

CPO SCIENCE DEVELOPMENT TEAM

Tom Hsu, Ph.D. – Author

Ph.D., Applied Plasma Physics, Massachusetts Institute of Technology

Nationally recognized innovator in science and math who has taught in middle and high school, college, and graduate programs. Personally held workshops with more than 10,000 teachers and administrators to promote teaching physics using a hands-on approach. CPO was founded by Dr. Hsu to create innovative hands-on materials for teaching math and science.

Lynda Pennell – Educational Products and Training, Vice President

B.A., English, M.Ed., Administration, Reading Disabilities, Northeastern University; CAGS Media, University of Massachusetts, Boston

Nationally known in high school restructuring and for integrating academic and career education. Has served as the director of an urban school with seventeen years teaching/administrative experience.

Thomas Narro – Product Design, Vice President

B.S., Mechanical Engineering, Rensselaer Polytechnic Institute

Accomplished design and manufacturing engineer; experienced consultant in corporate re-engineering and industrial-environmental acoustics.

Scott Eddleman – Curriculum Manager

B.S., Biology, Southern Illinois University; M.Ed., Harvard University

Taught for thirteen years in urban and rural settings; nationally known as a trainer of inquiry-based science and mathematics project-based instruction; curriculum development consultant.

Laine Ives – Curriculum Writer

B.A., English, Gordon College; graduate work, biology, Cornell University, Wheelock College

Experience teaching middle and high school, here and abroad, and expertise in developing middle school curriculum and hands-on activities.

Mary Beth Abel Hughes – Curriculum Writer

B.S., Marine Biology, College of Charleston; M.S., Biological Sciences, University of Rhode Island

Taught science and math at an innovative high school; has expertise in scientific research and inquiry-based teaching methods.

Erik Benton – Professional Development Specialist

B.F.A. University of Massachusetts

Taught for eight years in public and private schools, focusing on inquiry and experiential learning environments.

Irene Baker – Senior Curriculum Writer

B.S., Chemistry, B.S., Humanities, MIT; M.Ed., Lesley University

Experience is in scientific curriculum development, in educational research and assessment, and as a science consultant.

Bruce Holloway – Senior Creative Designer

Pratt Institute, N.Y.; Boston Museum School of Fine Arts

Expertise is in product design, advertising, and three-dimensional exhibit design; winner of National Wildlife 1999 Stamp Award.

Polly Crisman – Graphic Designer and Illustrator

B.F.A., University of New Hampshire

Graphic artist who has worked in advertising and marketing and as a freelance illustrator and cartoonist.

Patsy DeCoster – Professional Development Manager

B.S., Biology/Secondary Education, Grove City College; M.Ed., Tufts University

Curriculum and professional development specialist. Taught science for twelve years. National inquiry-based science presenter.

Matt Lombard – Marketing Manager

B.S., Salem State College

Oversees all marketing activities for CPO Science. Expertise in equipment photography and catalog design.

CPO SCIENCE EQUIPMENT DEVELOPMENT

Greg Krekorian – Production manager

Roger Barous – Floor manager

Shawn Green – Electronics specialist

Kathryn Gavin – Quality specialist

Agnes Chan – Industrial engineer

David Zucker – Industrial engineer

Dexter Beals – Electrical engineer (Beals Dynamics)

Dr. Jeff Casey – Physicist

Thomas Altman – Light and optics specialist

TECHNICAL CONSULTANTS

Tracy Morrow – FrameWork consultant

Julie Dalton – Copy editor

Mary Ann Erickson – Indexing

James Travers – Graphic designer

David Rosolko – Graphic designer

John Mahomet – Graphic designer

Kelly Story – assessment specialist

Mike Doughty – intern, Endicott College

Jennifer Lockhart – intern, Endicott College

CONTENT CONSULTANTS

Dr. Jack Hass – Professor Emeritus, Gordon College, Massachusetts

Terri Gipson – Associate Director of Space Sciences, St. Louis Science Center, Missouri

Dr. Robert Pockalny – Assistant Marine Research Scientist, University of Rhode Island, Rhode Island

Dr. David Guerra – Chair, Department of Physics, St. Anselm College, New Hampshire

James Sammons – Writer/Developer, Sammons' INK, LTD, Rhode Island

David Bliss – Teacher, Mohawk Central High School, New York

Thomas Altman – Teacher, Oswego High School, New York

Gary Garber – Teacher, Boston University Academy, Massachusetts

Catalina Moreno – Teacher, East Boston High School, Massachusetts

John Yonkers – Retired Adult Educator, Madison-Oneida Board of Cooperative Education Services, Verona, New York

David Buckley – Teacher, Mohawk Central High School, New York

Kent Dristle – Teacher, Oswego High School, New York

REVIEWERS

Bell, Tom
Curriculum Specialist
Cumberland County Schools
North Carolina

Chesick, Elizabeth
Head of Science Department
Baldwin School
Pennsylvania

Curry, Dwight
Assistant Director of Physical Science
St. Louis Science Center
Missouri

Gharooni, Hamid
Program Director, Math & Science
Madison Park Technical-Vocational High School
Massachusetts

Inman, Jamie
Physics Teacher
North Carolina

Lamp, David
Associate Professor
Physics Department
Texas Tech University
Texas

Leeds, Susan
Science teacher, eighth grade
Howard Middle School
Florida

Lowe, Larry
Physics and Electricity Teacher
Masconomet Regional High School
Massachusetts

Madar, Robert
Senior Consultant and Trainer
Impact Consulting
Oregon

Nelson, Genevieve M.
Head of Science Department
Germantown Friends School
Pennsylvania

Ramsay, Willa A.
Science Education Consultant
California

Schafer, Susan
Principal Investigator
College of Engineering
Texas Tech University
Texas

Scott, Janet
Curriculum Specialist
Durham Public Schools
North Carolina

Sewall, Les
Science Education Consultant
Georgia

Tally, Michael
Science Supervisor
Wake County Public Schools
North Carolina

Texas, Leslie A.
Senior Consultant and Trainer
Impact Consulting
Kentucky

Thompson, Gaile B.
Director of Science Collaborative
Region 14 ESC
Texas

Woodring, Kathleen
Physics Teacher
Industrial High School
Texas

USING ICONS TO LOCATE INFORMATION

Icons are symbols that have meaning. They are small pictures that convey meaning without words. In the CPO program we use icons to point out things such as safety considerations, real-world connections, and when to find information in the reference pages, complete a writing assignment, or work in a team. The chart below lists the icons that refer to instruction and safety and the meaning for each one.

	Reading: you need to read for understanding.		**Real-world connections:** you are learning how the information is used in the world today.
	Hands-on activity: you will complete a lab or other activity.		**Teamwork:** you will be working in a team to complete the activity.
	Time: Tells how much time the activity may take.		**Economics:** you are learning about how science impacts the economy.
	Research: you will need to look up facts and information.		**Formula:** you are reading information about a formula or will need to use an equation to solve a problem.
	Setup: directions for equipment setup are found here.		**Use extreme caution:** follow all instructions carefully to avoid injury to yourself or others.
	History: you are reading historical information.		**Electrical hazard:** follow all instructions carefully while using electrical components to avoid injury to yourself or others.
	Environment: you are reading information about the environment or how to protect our environment.		**Wear safety goggles:** requires you to protect your eyes from injury.
	Writing: you need to reflect and write about what you have learned.		**Wear a lab apron:** requires you to protect your clothing and skin.
	Project: you need to complete an assignment that will take longer than one day.		**Wear gloves:** requires you to protect your hands from injury due to heat or chemicals.
	Apply your knowledge: refers to activities or problems that ask you to use your skills in different ways.		**Cleanup:** includes cleaning and putting away reusable equipment and supplies, and disposing of leftover materials.

INVESTIGATION TEXT

Investigations are hands-on activities that accompany the student text. For each section of the text, you will complete a hands-on activity, answer key questions, and find results. The Investigation Manual is a soft cover book containing investigation activities that accompany each section you are reading. Sometimes you will read the student text before doing an Investigation activity, but usually you will complete the Investigation before you read the section.

The Investigations are the heart of the CPO program. We believe that you will learn and remember more if you have many opportunities to explore science through hands-on activities that use equipment to collect data and solve problems. Most of the Investigations rely on the use of CPO equipment to collect accurate data, explore possibilities and answer the key question. The equipment is easy to set up, and your teacher will help you learn how to use the equipment properly.

FEATURES OF THE INVESTIGATION

Key Question: Each Investigation starts with a key question that conveys the main focus of the learning. This question tells you what information you need to collect to answer the questions at the end of the Investigation.

Data Tables: Data tables help you organize and collect your data in a systematic manner.

Learning Objectives (Goals): At the top of each Investigation are the learning goals. These statements will explain what you will have learned and can do after completing the investigation.

Brief introduction: This information helps you understand why the exercise is important and, in most cases, how it connects to other sections you have read or will be reading.

Icons and Section title: The icon reminds you of the unit that you are studying and the section title. This section title corresponds to the reading in your Student Edition.

Numbered Steps: The Investigation sequence numbers point out the sequence of steps you will need to follow to successfully complete the Investigation. These steps highlight specific stages of the scientific method such as: following directions, completing hands-on experiments, collecting and analyzing data and presenting the results. The Applying Your Knowledge step asks you to reflect on what you have learned.

Illustrations: The illustrations support your understanding of the Investigation procedures.

Fill-in answer sheets: Your teacher will provide you with answer sheets to fill in the data tables and the written responses and may collect your information. You can also use the sheets to reinforce your reading in your student text.

INVESTIGATION PAGES

Section title reference from the student text

Section number referenced from the student text

Unit topic

Icon representing unit topic

Key question

Major learning objective for the investigation

Explanation of investigation content

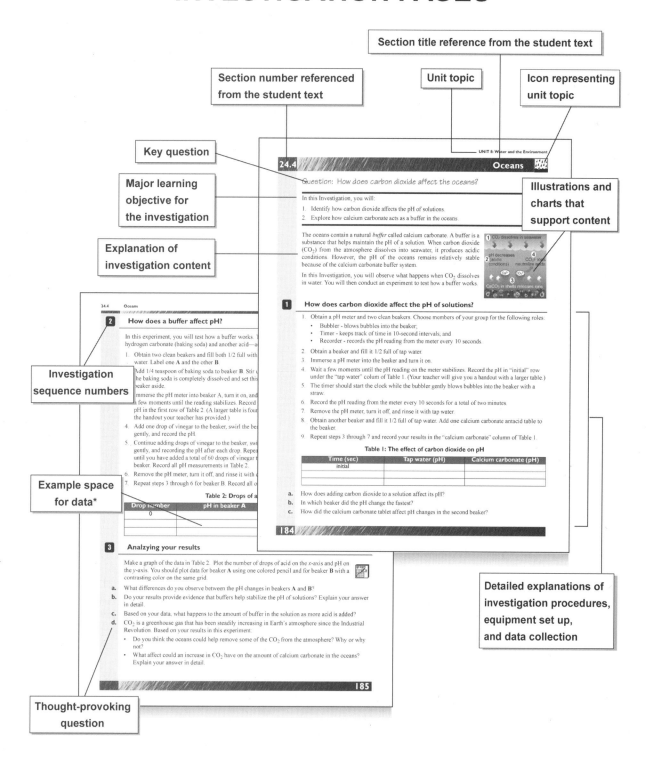

Illustrations and charts that support content

Investigation sequence numbers

Example space for data*

Detailed explanations of investigation procedures, equipment set up, and data collection

Thought-provoking question

* Note: All data and answers to questions will be written on a separate fill-in answer sheet

SAFETY

In scientific investigations, you often work with equipment and supplies. These are fun to use, especially because they help you make discoveries. However, using equipment and carrying out certain procedures in an investigation always require safety. Safety is a very important part of doing science. The purpose of learning and discussing safety in the lab is to help you learn how to be safe at all times.

The Investigations that you will be doing as part of the CPO Integrated Physics and Chemistry curriculum are designed to reduce safety concerns in the laboratory. The physics Investigations use equipment that is stable and easy to use. The chemistry Investigations use household supplies and chemicals. Although these chemicals might be familiar to you, they still must be used safely.

You will be introduced to safety by completing a skill sheet to help you observe the safety aids and important information in your science laboratory. In addition to this skill sheet, you may be asked to check your safety understanding and complete a safety contract. Your teacher will decide what is appropriate for your class.

Throughout the Investigation Guide, safety icons and words and phrases like "caution" and "Safety Tip" are used to highlight important safety information. Read the description of each safety icon carefully and look out for them when reading your Student Edition and Investigation Guide.

◈	**Use extreme caution:** follow all instructions carefully to avoid injury to yourself or others.
⚡	**Electrical hazard:** follow all instructions carefully while using electrical components to avoid injury to yourself or others.
👓	**Wear safety goggles:** requires you to protect your eyes from injury.
🦺	**Wear a lab apron:** requires you to protect your clothing and skin.
🧤	**Wear gloves:** requires you to protect your hands from injury due to heat or chemicals.
🪣	**Cleanup:** includes cleaning and putting away reusable equipment and supplies, and disposing of leftover materials.

Safety in the science lab is the responsibility of everyone! Help create a safe environment in your lab by following the safety guidelines from your teacher as well as the guidelines discussed in this document.

Table of Contents

1.1

Time and Distance

Question: How do we measure and describe the world around us?

In this Investigation, you will:

1. Learn to use electronic timing equipment and photogates.
2. Use units of time in calculations and conversions.
3. Learn to read dimensioned drawings and measure quantities in metric and English units.
4. Investigate the accuracy, precision, and resolution of a scientific instrument.

1   Using the timer as a stopwatch

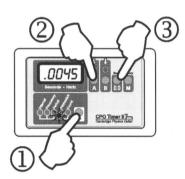

1. Set the timer to **stopwatch**.
2. Start and stop the stopwatch with the "**A**" button.
3. Reset the stopwatch to zero with the "**O**" button.

In science, it is often important to know how things change with time. The electronic timer allows us to make accurate, precise measurements of time. The timer performs many different functions. The first function to try is **stopwatch**. Use the button (1) to move the light under the word stopwatch.

A stopwatch measures a **time interval**. The stopwatch is started and stopped with the "**A**" button (2). The display shows time in seconds up to 60 seconds, then changes to show minutes: seconds for times longer than one minute.

The time it takes a signal to go from your brain to move a muscle is called **reaction time**. Reaction time varies from person to person and can be affected by factors like tiredness or caffeine intake.

Practice taking measurements with the stopwatch; then estimate the approximate reaction time of an average student.

2   Using the photogates

A photogate allows us to use a light beam to start and stop the timer. When the timer is in interval mode, it uses photogates to control the clock.

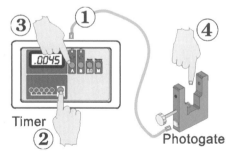

1. Connect a single photogate to the "**A**" input with a cord.
2. Select **interval** on the timer.
3. Push the "**A**" button and the "**A**" light should come on and stay on.
4. Try blocking the light beam with your finger and observe what happens to the timer. Note: The photogate has a reaction time much shorter than your finger. Because it is used for so many measurements, you need to figure out how the photogate and timer work together. Try your own experiments until you can answer the following questions.

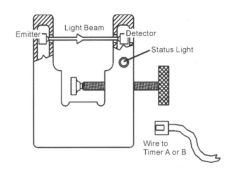

a. Exactly what do you do to start and stop the clock? Be very specific in your answer. Someone who has never seen the photogate before should be able to read your answer and know what to do with the light beam to make the clock start, and what to do to make it stop.

b. If you block the light beam several times in a row, does the time add or does the timer start at zero every time you break the beam? Your answer should provide observations that back up what you say. For example, "the timer does _____ because_____." Fill in the blanks with what you think based on what you observed.

3   Using the timer with two photogates

You can connect two photogates to the timer in interval mode. The second photogate connects behind the "B" light. Notice that the "A" and "B" buttons turn the "A" and "B" lights on and off.

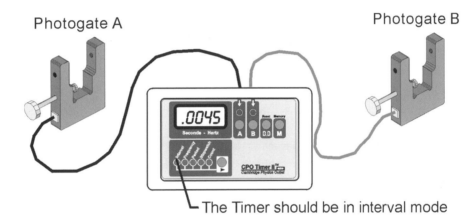

The Timer should be in interval mode

Conduct experiments to determine what stops and starts the stopwatch for each of the different combinations of lights. Write your observations as if you were trying to teach someone else how the timer works.

"A" Light On   "B" Light On   Both "A" and "B" Lights On

a. What starts and stops the timer when only the "A" light is on?

b. What starts and stops the timer when only the "B" light is on?

c. What starts and stops the timer when both "A" and "B" lights are on?

d. Does the timer still make measurements when there are no lights on?

e. What happens if you go though photogate A once and through photogate B multiple times? When answering this question, you might want to think about a race where all the runners start together but you want each runner's individual time to finish the race.

4   **Reflecting on what we learned**

a.   *Resolution* means the smallest interval that can be measured. Try
using one photogate to determine the resolution of the timer. Give
your answer in seconds and tell how your observations support your
answer.

b.   The words *accuracy* and *precision* have special meanings in science
that are a little different from how people use these words every day.
The word *accuracy* refers to how close a measurement is to the true
value. The word *precision* describes how close together repeated
measurements are. When measurements are precise they are close to
the same value. It is possible to be precise but not accurate. Which is
likely to be more precise: time measurements made with a stopwatch
or measurements made with photogates?

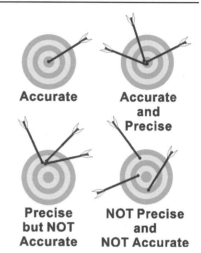

Accurate   **Accurate and Precise**

Precise but NOT Accurate   **NOT Precise and NOT Accurate**

5   **Dimensions and diagrams**

Think about how often you have to describe how big something is or where something is. It is often
said that a picture is worth a thousand words. Because pictures are so much better at describing
location or size, a language of pictures has developed to communicate length or position. Learning to
read diagrams is important in science. It is also important in everyday life because diagrams explain
how to put together almost every product you buy that requires assembly.

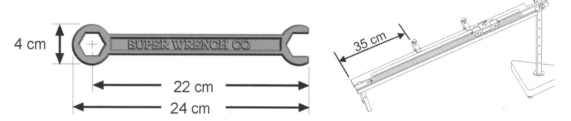

Drawings with little lines and arrows indicate distance or size. The lines, arrows, and numbers are
called *dimensions*, and they tell you how big and where things are. In the example, the length of the
wrench is 24 centimeters. The center of the hole in the wrench is 22 centimeters from one end. The
round end has a diameter of 4 centimeters. In the second example, the photogate is placed 35
centimeters from the end of the ramp.

Measure the dimensions of the car and the photogate as shown on the diagram. Write the dimensions in
the appropriate boxes.

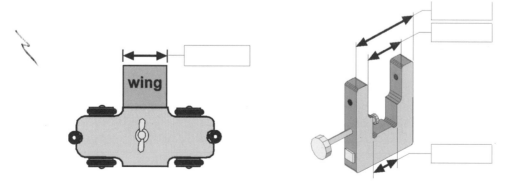

6 Measuring metric lengths

a. Use the metric ruler to make measurements of each of the following dimensions. Write the measurement in centimeters in the appropriate box. You should be accurate to the nearest millimeter (0.1 centimeters).

b. The word **precision** describes how close repeated measurements of the same quantity are. For example, saying measurements are precise to 0.5 cm means the measurements were within +/- 0.5 cm of the average of all the measurements. Compare your results for measurement **b** (see below) with the results from four other students. Fill in the blanks: The average measurement for **b** is _____ centimeters. This measurement is precise to _____ centimeters. This means the measurements are within +/- _____ centimeters of the average.

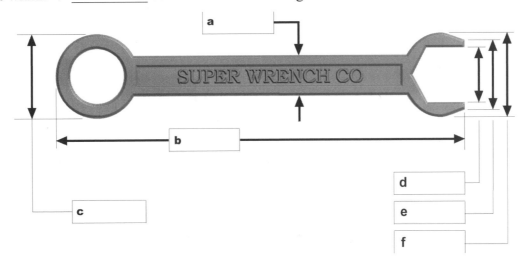

7 Measuring English lengths

a. Use the English ruler to make measurements of each of the following dimensions. Write the measurement in inches in the appropriate box. Your measurement should be taken to the nearest 1/16th inch.

b. Compare your results for measurement **b** (see below) with the results from four other students. Fill in the blanks: The average measurement for **b** is _____ inches. This measurement is precise to _____ inches. This means the measurements are within +/- _____ inches of the average. (Note: Convert the fractions to decimals to identify the precision of your measurements.)

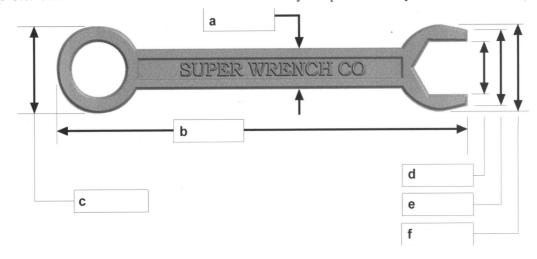

1.2   Investigations and Experiments

Question: How do we ask questions and get answers from nature?

In this Investigation, you will:

1. Use the electronic timer and photogates with a car and ramp.
2. Identify the variables that influence how fast a car travels down a ramp.
3. Learn how to design experiments that provide good scientific results.

We do experiments to collect evidence that allows us to unravel nature's puzzles. You can think of an experiment as asking a question about the universe: "What would happen if I did this?" If your experiment is well planned, the results of the experiment provide the answer you are looking for. If your experiment is not planned correctly, you will still get results but you may not know what they mean. In this Investigation, you will experiment with speed and the angle of a ramp. Only by paying careful attention to the variables can you make sense of your results.

1   Setting up the experiment

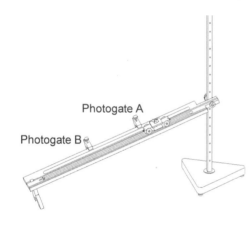

Photogate A

Photogate B

The faster you go, the shorter the time it takes to reach your destination. With two photogates you can measure time very accurately.

Set up the ramp and car as instructed by your teacher. Each group in the class will have a different ramp angle. The angle is determined by which hole in the stand you use to attach the ramp.

Put two photogates on the ramp so that you can measure time for the car. Plug the photogate closest to the top of the ramp into input A of the timer and the other photogate into input B.

a. Look around the class and note which hole each group is using for its ramp. With your group, make a prediction as to which group will have the fastest car, and therefore the shortest time from A to B. This prediction is your group's hypothesis. Write down this hypothesis so you can compare it to your results.

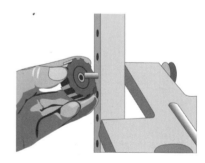

b. Roll the car down the ramp and record the time it takes to go from photogate A to photogate B. Be sure you look at the timer reading with the A and B lights on.

c. Compare your results with other groups'. Did the times that everyone measured agree with your hypothesis about how the angle of the ramp would affect the speed? Why or why not?

d. Is there a better way to test whether increasing the ramp angle makes the car go faster? Explain how you would redo this experiment so the results make sense.

2   Variables in an experiment

Variables are the factors that affect experimental results. In part 1, each group did the experiment with too many differences, instead of only the angle of the ramp. That made it hard to compare results. In an experiment, you have to keep everything the same, and only change one variable at a time. If you only change one thing at a time, when you get a result you know it was caused by the variable you changed.

What variables will affect how fast the car moves down the ramp? List all the variables discussed by your group.

3   Doing a controlled experiment

In this part of the Investigation, you will repeat the time measurements of the car, but as you will see, each group will attach the photogates in the same way. This will allow groups to more accurately compare results.

1. In the table, record any variables you think should be controlled to make the experiment a comparison of how cars behave on ramps of different angles. Write values for these variables in the table. These values will not change during the experiment.

2. Develop a good technique for rolling the car down the ramp so you get three times that are within 0.0005 seconds of each other.

3. Using your new technique and setup, record the time it takes the car to travel from photogate A to photogate B.

Once you have your new results, compare them with the results of the other groups.

The two distances you need to control

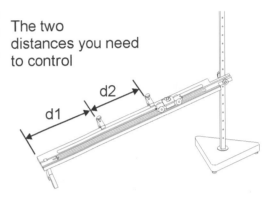

The values for the variables in the experiment

Variable	Chosen value

a. Did your times agree with your hypothesis about how they would change with the angle of the ramp?

b. In one or two sentences describe why this experiment was better or worse than your first experiment. Your answer should talk about cause and effect relationships and variables.

4   Applying what you learned

a. It is often easy to confuse cause and effect. When we see something happen, we think up a reason for why it happened, but we don't always get the right reason. If you drop a piece of paper and a steel weight at the same time, which one hits the ground first? If the paper is flat, the steel always hits first. Why does the steel hit first? Is it because heavier objects fall faster, or is there another reason? In your answer give at least one other reason why a steel weight might fall faster than a flat sheet of paper.

b. Plan and perform another experiment to test the effect of one of the other variables on the speed of the car. Create a data table and a procedure for controlling the variables you don't want to change.

Speed

Question: What is speed and how is it measured?

In this Investigation, you will:

1. Learn how to calculate the speed of a car traveling down a ramp.
2. Compare speeds in different units.

In this Investigation, you will precisely measure how fast a car moves down a ramp and learn how to calculate its speed in different units.

1 ## How is speed measured?

Suppose you run a race. How do you describe your run to a friend? Saying that you ran for 20 minutes would not be enough for your friend to know how fast you went. What your friend needs in order to know how fast you went is your **speed**.

You need two elements in order to describe your speed:

* The **distance** you traveled.
* The **time** it took you.

Examples of speed	Calculating speed	
A sprinter running 100 meters in 10 seconds (speed is 10 m/sec).	**a.**	Use the distances and time values in the examples to calculate speed. If your answers are correct, then you understand how to calculate speed.
A person driving a car 50 miles in 1 hour (speed is 50 mi/hr).		
A fish swimming 10 feet in 15 seconds (speed is 0.67 ft/sec).	**b.**	Your hair grows 0.4 millimeters per day. What is the speed of hair growth per week? Per hour?

2 ## $\frac{a}{b}$ Calculating the speed of the car on the ramp

1. Set up the car and ramp with two photogates that are one foot apart. Measure the distance from the lower edge of one photogate to the lower edge of the next photogate.

2. Measure the distance between photogates in centimeters and record the value in the table on the next page.

3. Measure the distance between photogates in inches and record it also.

4. Make sure that the timer's A and B lights are both on. Roll the car down the ramp and measure the time it takes the car to go from photogate A to photogate B. Record the value in the table under Time from A to B *in all three rows*, since they are all the same time.

Measure distance from lower edge to lower edge.

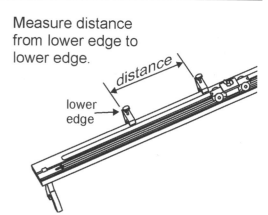

Speed, Distance, and Time Data

Distance from A to B	Time from A to B (sec)	Speed
(feet)		(feet/sec)
(cm)		(cm/sec)
(inches)		(in/sec)

Calculate the speed of your car in ft/sec, cm/sec, and in/sec and write the results in the table.

a.   Which is the fastest speed of the three, or are they all the same speed?

b.   Is it possible that a speed of 254 and a speed of 100 could be the same speed? Explain why you think so and why giving a speed as 254 would not be a very good answer.

3   Experiments with downhill motion

Design and conduct three experiments using the car and ramp. Each experiment should look at one variable that you think will have an effect on the speed of the car. Describe what you will change and how you will determine the speed of the car in each of your three experiments.

Each experiment you do should be described in the following way in your lab notebook. You may use the Sample Lab Record and Data Table below as a guide.

Hypothesis: A sentence describing what you think your experiment should demonstrate.

Procedure: A few sentences describing how you did your experiment.

Measurements: Data that you took including your calculations of speed.

Conclusions: Answer the following questions in your conclusions: What was the outcome of the experiment? Did the outcome support your hypothesis or suggest a different hypothesis?

Be prepared to give a brief presentation to the rest of the class.

Sample Lab Record:

Hypothesis:

Variable to be tested:

Procedure:

Conclusions:

Sample Data Table:

Trial	Experimental Variable	Distance	Time	Speed
1				
2				
3				

Using a Scientific Model to Predict Speed

Question: Can you predict the speed of the car at any point on the ramp?

In this Investigation, you will:

1. Determine the speed of the car at different points as it rolls down the ramp.
2. Make a speed vs. position graph with your collected data.
3. Predict speed at any point on the ramp by using your graph.

What happens to the speed of the car as it rolls down the ramp? You can answer this question by measuring its speed at different points. By making a graph of the car's speed according to its position, you can see how speed changes. This graph can be used to predict how fast the car will be moving anywhere on the ramp. Record your observations and data from the Investigation in your notebook.

1 | Finding the speed of the car at different points along the ramp

Using two photogates far apart gives you a measure of the average speed of the car between the photogates. The car could be going faster at the lower photogate and slower at the upper one. To get a true picture of how the speed of the car changes, you will need to measure the speed with one photogate.

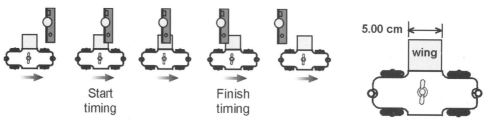

Remember, with one photogate the timers measure the time that the beam is broken. As the car passes through the photogate, the light beam is broken for the width of the wing. The speed of the car is the width of the wing (distance traveled) divided by the time it takes to pass through the light beam (time taken). The advantage to this technique is that it is easy to move a single photogate up and down the ramp to make measurements of the speed at many places.

$$\text{speed} = \frac{\text{width of wing}}{\text{time through photogate}}$$

1. Select between 5 and 10 locations along the ramp to measure the speed of the car. The places should be at regular intervals such as every 10.0 centimeters.
2. At each location record the position of the photogate and the time through the light beam. The distance traveled will be the same for every position since it is the width of the wing.
3. Calculate the speed of the car using the car wing length (5.00 cm) and the time measurement. Record this value in the table.

Speed, Position, and Time Data

Position of photogate A (cm) from top of ramp	Time from photogate A (sec)	Distance traveled by car (cm) Wing width (5.00 cm)	Speed of the car (cm/sec)

2 Graphing and analyzing your results

a. Do you notice a trend in your measurements? How does the speed of the car change as it moves down the ramp?

b. Graph the speed of the car vs. position. Place speed of the car on the *y*-axis and position of photogate A on the *x*-axis. Add labels to each axis and title the graph.

c. What does the graph show about the speed of the car?

3 Using your graph to predict the speed of the car

a. Choose a spot on the ramp where you did not measure the speed of the car.

b. Use your graph to find the predicted speed of the car at that distance. Record your predicted speed.

c. Place the photogate at the distance you selected in step A and record the time it takes for the car to pass through the photogate.

d. Use the wing length (5.00 cm) and the time to calculate the speed. Record the actual speed.

e. How does the predicted speed compare with the actual measured speed? What does this tell you about your experiment and measurements?

4 $\frac{a}{b}$ Calculating percent error

a. Find the difference between the predicted speed and the actual, calculated speed.

   Predicted speed – Actual speed = Difference

b. Take this difference and divide it by the predicted speed, then multiply by 100.

   (Difference ÷ Predicted speed) × 100 = Percent error

c. Use the percent error to calculate percent correct.

   100 – Percent error = Percent correct

Position and Time

Question: How do you model the motion of the car?

In this Investigation, you will:

1. Model the motion of the car with a distance vs. time graph.
2. Measure the slope of your distance vs. time graph at 3 different points.
3. Determine the relationship between slope and speed of the car.

In this Investigation, you will rely on information you have learned from working with the car and ramp to help you model the motion of the car with a distance vs. time graph. By measuring how long it takes the car to reach different points on the ramp, you be able to create a picture of the car's trip down the ramp.

1 ## Setting up the experiment

1. Put photogate A near the top of the ramp, but not so high that the car breaks the light beam before you let it go. Keep photogate A in this spot for the whole experiment. If you move the gate, your experiments won't be as accurate as they could be.
2. Put photogate B lower than photogate A, so the car rolls through photogate A and then through photogate B.
3. Move photogate B to between 5 and 8 different places along the ramp and record the position and times for each place.

2 ## Understanding and using Table I

As you measure the time it takes the car to travel to different positions, you will record your data in the table 1. The table headings are explained below.

☑ Keep good records; you will use the data you collect in the next two Investigations.

Distance from A to B: Measure and record the distance from photogate A to photogate B.

Time from A to B: This is the time it takes the car to travel from A to B. Record the time from the timer with both A and B lights on.

Time at A: Record the time from the timer with the A light on.

Time at B: Record the time from the timer with the B light on.

Speed at A: This is the speed of the car when it passed through photogate A. Calculate this by dividing the width of the wing (5.00 centimeters) by the time through photogate A.

Speed at B: This is the speed of the car when it passed through photogate B. Calculate this by dividing the width of the wing (5.00 centimeters) by the time through photogate B.

3   ## Collecting and recording your data

- Release the car the same way each time to get good results.

- Move photogate B in equal increments (i.e., every 5 or 10 centimeters) so that your data will be easier to graph.

- Remember that both light beams on the timer should be clear before you press reset.

- Be careful at the bottom of the ramp. If the car bounces up when it hits the end, it may bounce back through the light beam. You will not get accurate results because your time will be wrong.

Table 1: Car and ramp data

Position on ramp	Distance from A to B	Time from A to B (t_{AB})	Time at A (t_A)	Time at B (t_B)	Speed at A	Speed at B
	(cm)	(sec)	(sec)	(sec)	(cm/sec)	(cm/sec)
1						
2						
3						
4						
5						
6						
7						
8						

4   ## Graphing and analyzing your data

a.   Make a distance vs. time graph using your data. Plot the time from A to B on the *x*-axis and the distance from A to B on the *y*-axis. At this point, do not connect the data points on the graph. Be sure to label the axes and title the graph.

b.   Is the graph a straight line or a curve?

c.   Does the graph get steeper as the car rolls farther, or does the graph keep the same slope the whole way? What does your answer tell you about the speed of the car at different times along its roll down the ramp?

d.   Pick two points near the bottom of the graph and two more near the top of the graph. Draw two triangles and calculate the speed from the slope of the graph. Is the value you get consistent with other speed measurements you have made with the car and ramp?

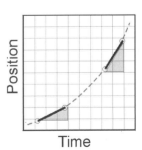

Question: How is the speed of the car changing?

In this Investigation, you will:

1. Determine the rate of acceleration of the car on the ramp through a calculation.
2. Determine the rate of acceleration of the car on the ramp using a graph.

For this Investigation, you will examine the data you collected from Investigation 2.2 with the car and ramp. Using your data, you will determine the rate of acceleration of the car in two ways: through calculation using an equation, and with a graph by taking the slope of the line.

Before beginning the Investigation, define the term "acceleration" in your own words. It may help you to think about flying in an airplane. When a plane is accelerating, you feel its motion. For example, you feel the motion of the plane when it is taking off, but not much when you are flying at altitude.

1 Measuring acceleration

Acceleration is the rate at which the speed changes. For the car on the ramp, the change in speed is the difference between the speed at photogate B and the speed at A. The change in time is the time from A to B. You can calculate acceleration by dividing the change in speed by the change in time.

$$acceleration = \frac{speed\ at\ B - speed\ at\ A}{time\ from\ A\ to\ B}$$

1. Put photogate A about 30 centimeters from the top of the ramp and photogate B another 20-30 centimeters farther down. Leave both photogates in the same position for the rest of Trial 1.

2. Set the ramp at the same angle as you used for the last Investigation so you can compare the data.

3. For Trial 1: With the timer in interval mode, roll the car down the ramp and record the three times (t_A, t_B, and t_{AB}) in the table.

4. Calculate the speeds at points A and B, and the acceleration of the car from the acceleration formula above.

5. For Trial 2: Move the photogates to a new position and repeat the procedure to measure the acceleration.

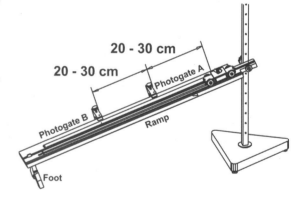

	Trial I	Trial 2
Time A		
Time B		
Time A to B		
Speed at A		
Speed at B		
Acceleration		

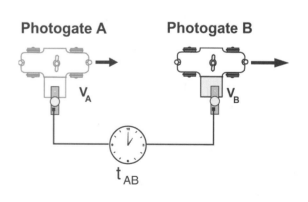

2   Graphing speed vs. time

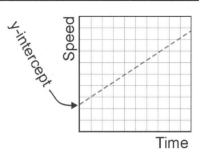

a.   Make a speed vs. time graph. **Use your data from *Investigation 2.2 Position and Time* (Part 3)**. Plot the speed at photogate B on the *y*-axis. Plot the time from A to B on the *x*-axis.

b.   Is your graph a straight line or a curve?

c.   The place on the speed vs. time graph where the line crosses the *y*-axis is called the *y*-intercept. On the speed vs. time graph for the car and ramp, the *y*-intercept represents something about the car. What is the *y*-intercept of your speed vs. time graph? (Hint: The *y*-axis is speed.)

d.   Does the car accelerate as it rolls down the ramp? Justify your answer. Remember that acceleration is defined as a change in speed over time.

3 $\frac{a}{b}$ Calculating acceleration from the slope of the line

In a speed vs. time graph, you are showing the change in speed over time. The slope of the speed vs. time graph is equal to the *acceleration* of the car.

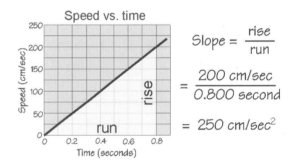

a.   Using your speed vs. time graph, calculate the acceleration of the car from the slope of the line. Refer to the graphic to the right for an example of the calculation. Show all of your work.

b.   Is the acceleration of the car changing as it moves down the ramp? Explain your answer using what you know about the slope of a straight line.

4   Reflecting on what we learned

a.   How does the acceleration you measured compare with the acceleration you calculated from the graph of speed vs. time? If there are differences, try to think where they might have come from.

b.   Give the car a gentle push up the ramp from the bottom. The car will go up, slow down, and come down again. Is there a place in the motion where the speed of the car is zero? Is there a place where the acceleration is zero?

c.   Can you think up two configurations of ramps and cars that show the following properties:
(1) Higher speed but lower acceleration.
(2) Lower speed but higher acceleration.
You should discuss this with your group or the class. You can also test out your ideas, or draw them in sketches. (Hint: The car may not always be in the same place!)

3.1   Force, Mass, and Acceleration

Question: What is the relationship between force, mass, and acceleration?

In this Investigation, you will:

1. Measure the force on a car as it starts to roll down the ramp.
2. Compare the force on the car as the angle of the ramp is changed.
3. Calculate the acceleration of the car as the angle of the ramp is changed.
4. Explore the relationship between force and acceleration.
5. Derive Newton's second law of motion.

It takes the application of force to get an object moving. As early as Aristotle's time, in the third century BC, philosophers were seeking the relationship between force and motion. It was not until 2000 years later (1686) when Newton published the **_Principia_** that this riddle was solved by his second law of motion. In this Investigation, you follow in Newton's footsteps and figure out the relationship between force, mass, and acceleration.

1   Thinking about force

To examine the relationship between force, mass, and acceleration, you will use the car and ramp because it is easy to measure acceleration. In this Investigation, the variable that you will change is the force on the car. You want to find out how changing the force affects the motion. Before you begin the experiment, answer the following questions.

a. What are the ways you can change the amount of force acting to pull the car down the ramp? Keep in mind that force is something which has the ability to change motion.

b. How will you vary the force on the car for this experiment?

2   Measuring the force on the car

1. Set up the car and ramp. Add one weight to the car.
2. Tie a short piece of string to the eye on the car. Make a loop in the other end of the string to attach to the force scale. Using a short piece of string will help you measure force accurately.

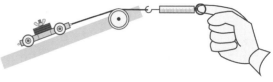

3. Read the scale while letting the car roll slowly down the ramp a short way. The scale measures force in units of newtons. Measuring while rolling down partly corrects for the effects of friction.

3   ## Conducting the experiment

1. Put photogate A about 30 centimeters from the top of the ramp and photogate B another 20-30 centimeters farther down. Leave both photogates in the same position for the rest of the experiment.

2. Measure the amount of force on the car using the method described in Part 2. Record your results in newtons in Table 1 (see below).

3. With the timer in interval mode, roll the car down the ramp and record the three times (t_A, t_B, and t_{AB}) in Table 1.

4. Using a balance, find the mass of your car.

5. Calculate the speeds at photogates A and B, and the acceleration of the car (see acceleration formula below). Write your results in Table 1.

6. Add another weight to the car and repeat steps 2 through 5. Get data for 1, 2, and 3 weights.

7. Change the angle of the ramp and repeat steps 2 - 6.

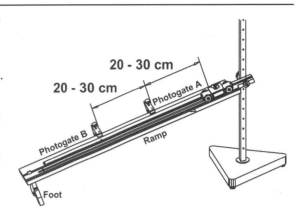

$\frac{a}{b}$ **Calculating acceleration**: The acceleration is calculated by dividing the change in speed by the change in time:

$$acceleration = \frac{speed\ at\ B - speed\ at\ A}{time\ from\ A\ to\ B}$$

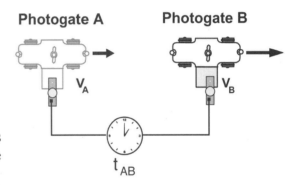

Table 1: Force and acceleration at different ramp angles

	No. of wts.	Force (N)	Mass (kg)	Time A (sec)	Time B (sec)	Time A to B (sec)	Speed A (m/sec)	Speed B (m/sec)	Accel. (m/sec²)
Angle 1	1								
Angle 1	2								
Angle 1	3								
Angle 2	1								
Angle 2	2								
Angle 2	3								
Angle 3	1								
Angle 3	2								
Angle 3	3								

4   Analyzing the data

a.   List three observations you can make about the data from looking at Table 1.

b.   The relation between force and motion is simple but not obvious. Can you see it from the data table? Write a sentence to describe your ideas about the relationship between force and motion.

5   Combining force and mass

In order to identify the relationship between force, mass, and acceleration, you must first make a line graph of the data. Since a graph can only show two numbers, we will be mathematically grouping the force and mass values. Different combinations of force and mass will be graphed on the x-axis and acceleration will be graphed on the y-axis.

a.   Circle the combination of force and mass that has been assigned to your group. The different combinations of force and mass that we will test are:
(1) force ÷ mass
(2) mass ÷ force
(3) force + mass
(4) force × mass

b.   Transfer your force and acceleration data from Table 1 to Table 2 below. Add the mass data to this table. Using this data, make the calculations for your group's force and mass combination. Add these calculations to Table 2.

c.   We use graphs to find relationships. One or more of the graphs should show a pattern we can understand. If we find a pattern in the graph then we know the relationship between the variables from that graph is the one we want.

d.   [graph] Use the data in Table 2 to make a graph that shows the relationship between force, mass, and acceleration. Plot your group's combination of force and mass on the x-axis. Plot acceleration on the y-axis. Be sure to give a title to your graph and label the axes.

Table 2: Force, Mass, and Acceleration Data

a (acceleration) m/sec^2	F (force) N	m (mass of the car) kg	force and mass calculation:

6   Analyzing all of the graphs

Direct relationship
Straight line

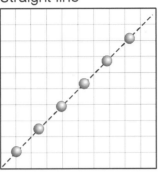

Inverse relationship
Straight line

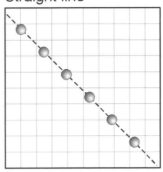

No relationship

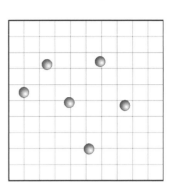

Direct relationship
Curve

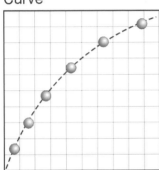

Inverse relationship
Curve

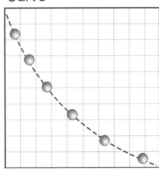

Examine all four graphs generated by your class. For each, indicate a pattern, if any, that you observe for the questions below:

a.   **force ÷ mass:** Is there a pattern? If so, what is it?

b.   **mass ÷ force:** Is there a pattern? If so, what is it?

c.   **force + mass:** Is there a pattern? If so, what is it?

d.   **force × mass:** Is there a pattern? If so, what is it?

7   Newton's second law

Based on this experiment, what is the correct mathematical relationship between the variables force (F), mass (m), and acceleration (a)? Write the equation and explain how you arrived at your answer.

Weight, Gravity, and Friction

Question: How does increasing the mass of the car affect its acceleration?

In this Investigation, you will:

1. Explore how added weight affects a car's acceleration.
2. Discuss and learn whether or not heavier objects fall faster than lighter objects.
3. Investigate friction and how friction affects motion.

So far in this unit, you have learned that the car accelerates as it moves down the ramp. That is, its speed increases over time. In Investigation 3.1, you explored what happened to the acceleration of a car when more force was applied to it.

The force that you used in Investigation 3.1 was gravity. Gravity pulls all objects toward the center of Earth with a force we call weight. The more mass an object has, the greater its weight. If you increase the weight of the car, how will acceleration be affected? Do heavier objects fall faster than lighter ones?

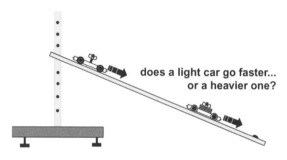

does a light car go faster... or a heavier one?

1 **Do you think adding weights to the car will change its speed?**

a. You can add up to three weights to the car for this experiment. Weights are attached to the top of the car using the wing nut.

b. Roll a car down the ramp with different amounts of weight and watch it, without using photogates. Does the change in mass seem to make a difference in the speed?

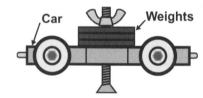

Car   Weights

❖ **Safety Tip: Keep your fingers away from the ramp when the car is rolling. Especially, keep your hands away from the bottom of the ramp until the car stops.**

2 **Testing your hypothesis**

It is difficult to know for sure that the car is going faster (or not) without making measurements. Set up the car and ramp with two photogates. The photogates should be about 20 centimeters apart. Set the angle at the seventh hole from the bottom of the stand.

You will want to measure the mass of the car with no weights, and with one, two, and three weights. On the data table, record the masses and the speeds at which the car rolled between the two photogates.

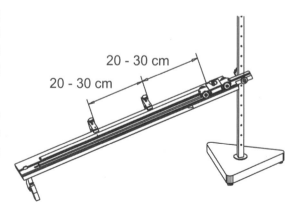

20 - 30 cm

20 - 30 cm

Mass and Speed Data

Mass (g)	Distance from A to B (cm)	Time from A to B (sec)	Speed (cm/sec)

3   Graphing and analyzing the data

a.   Make a graph of speed vs. mass using your data.

b.   Which is the dependent variable? On which axis does it go?

c.   Which is the independent variable? On which axis does it go?

d.   From your graph, what can you say about the effect of increasing mass on the speed of the car? Did the speed change by a lot or by a little? Did the mass change by a lot or a little?

4   Friction

Try the following experiment. Take a steel weight and a flat sheet of paper. Drop them both and the steel weight will hit the ground before the paper every time. Next, crumple the sheet of paper and do the experiment over. They should hit the ground about the same time.

a.   The crumpled paper has the same weight as the flat sheet of paper. What is the explanation for why the crumpled sheet fell fast and the flat sheet fell slowly?

b.   The car has friction, even though the wheels have ball bearings. Can you think of a way to increase the friction in the car? See if you can create enough friction so the car does not accelerate, but keeps the same speed from one photogate to the next.

5   Thinking about the results

Suppose you have a jar of 1,000 marbles. If you lose one marble, it is hard to notice because 1 out of 1,000 is a small change. If you only had 5 marbles in the jar, you would immediately notice if one were missing because 1 out of 5 is a much larger change.

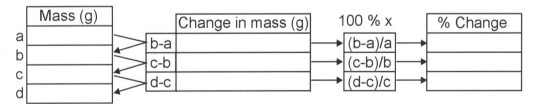

a.   We often express change in percent. One out of 5 is a change of 20 percent ($1/5 \times 100\%$). The percent change is the change divided by what you started with, times 100 percent. Calculate the percent change for the weight experiment.

b.   Does the percent change have anything to do with how much the speed changed as you added the second and third weights?

3.3 Equilibrium, Action, and Reaction

Question: What is Newton's third law of motion?

In this Investigation, you will:

1. Learn how Newton's third law of motion applies to the physics of how objects work.
2. Use your understanding of Newton's third law to find the forces in a system.

In this Investigation you will learn that Newton's third law of motion explains the physics of common objects and activities. All forces come in pairs and that means whenever we push something, there is a reaction pushing back on us.

1 Setting up a system with action and reaction

You will need a car and ramp setup, some string, and some weight as shown in the diagram. Add weight and (or) change the angle of the ramp until you get the car balanced so it moves neither up nor down the ramp.

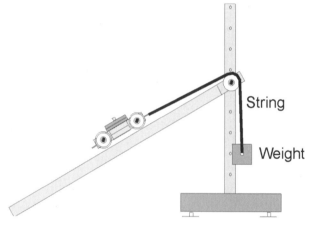

String

Weight

a. The car wants to roll down, and the weight also wants to fall down. Draw a sketch showing the forces that act on the car and the forces that act on the weight.

b. Since nothing is moving, the acceleration is zero. What does this tell you about the forces acting on the car and on the weight?

c. Suppose you added a little more hanging weight. What would happen to the system? In your answer you should discuss balanced and unbalanced forces.

d. Suppose you took away a little from the hanging weight. What would happen to the system? In your answer you should discuss balanced and unbalanced forces.

e. On your force sketch, label the action and reaction forces acting on the car and on the weight.

2 Equilibrium at constant speed

Set up the ramp on the lowest hole in the stand. Using the foot, you can make the ramp completely level. When the ramp is level, gravity does not act to pull the car one way or the other. Attach two photogates to the level ramp about 20 centimeters apart.

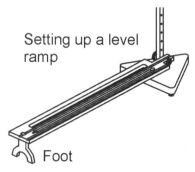

Setting up a level ramp

Foot

Give the car a push and use the photogates to tell whether it is speeding up or slowing down. Raise the foot end of the ramp until you can roll the car through both photogates and get the same time through each one. If the time to go through each is the same, then the speed is also the same.

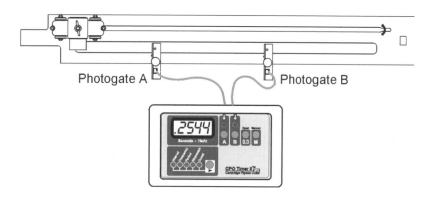

To check the time, you want to look at the time through A and the time through B, with only one light on at a time.

a. Earlier you learned that there is always friction when things are moving. If the speed is the same at A and B, then the acceleration must be zero. If the acceleration is zero, the net force must also be zero. Explain how your process of shimming up the ramp created equilibrium of forces.

b. If friction acting on the car is the action force, what is the reaction force and what object does it act on? (Hint: The object is not moving.)

3 Using Newton's third law to explain the physics of common objects and activities

a. List five objects you use on a day-to-day basis. List five activities you do on a weekly basis.

b. Next to each item on your lists, write down how the activities you do and the objects you use illustrate Newton's third law of motion. Identify an action force and a reaction force for each object and situation.

Examples of the third law

Daily objects	How the third law applies	Weekly activities	How the third law applies

4 What did you learn?

a. Write Newton's third law in your own words.

b. Imagine if Newton's third law of motion was just like a law made by your government. Also, imagine there is going to be a vote tomorrow on whether to keep Newton's third law or change the universe so we did not always have an equal and opposite reaction to every action force. Think up one strange scenario that might happen if the universe changed so that the third law were not true. You may wish to do this as a project jointly with your group.

Question: How do simple machines work?

In this Investigation, you will:

1. Build a simple machine using ropes and pulleys.
2. Measure the input and output forces of simple machines.

Would you believe that a small child could lift an elephant with only muscle power? It's true! You could do it by building a simple machine out of ropes and pulleys. In this Investigation, you will learn how to build machines that allow you to lift large weights with small forces. You will also learn how to measure the input and output forces of these machines.

1 Identifying input and output forces

Watch a demonstration of a simple machine made with ropes and pulleys.

a. What is the definition of a simple machine?
b. With your class, brainstorm additional examples of simple machines. For each machine you come up with, identify the input and output force.

2 Setting up the ropes and pulleys

1. Attach four weights to the bottom block. Use a force scale to obtain the weight of the bottom block after you attach the weights and record the weight. Weight of bottom block: _____ N.

2. The output force of this simple machine will be used to lift the bottom block. Attach the top block near the top of the physics stand. The yellow string can be clipped to either the top block or the bottom block. Start with the yellow string clipped to the bottom block.

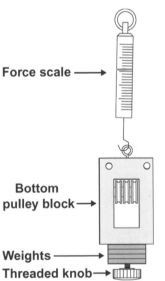

Force scale →

Bottom
pulley block →

Weights →
Threaded knob →

Why all the strings?

*   The yellow string will be used to move the bottom pulley block with the weights up and down. You will pull on one end of the yellow string. There is a clip at the other end of the yellow string for attaching to the pulley blocks.

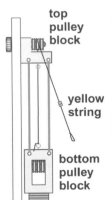

top
pulley
block

yellow
string

bottom
pulley
block

*   The yellow string may have several strands that directly support the bottom pulley block. These are called the supporting strands.

*   The pink string is the safety string. It holds up the bottom block while you rearrange the yellow string.

   ◆ **Safety Tip: Don't pull sideways or you can tip the stand over!**

3   Investigating the ropes and pulleys

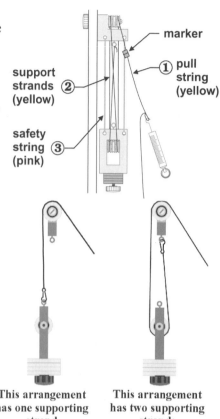

1. Clip the end of the yellow string to the bottom pulley block. Pass the string over the middle pulley of the top block. Use the marker stop (cord stop) to hook the force scale to the string.

2. Measure the force it takes to slowly lift the bottom pulley block.

3. This arrangement has one strand supporting the bottom pulley block. Record the force in the table below in the row corresponding to one strand.

4. Take the yellow string off and clip the end to the top block next. Pass the string around the middle pulley in the bottom block and back over the middle pulley in the top block.

5. Move the marker and measure the force it takes to slowly lift the bottom pulley block. Record this force in the row for two supporting strands.

6. Rearrange the yellow strings so that you get three, four, five, and six supporting strands. Measure and record the force it takes to lift the bottom pulley block for each new setup.

This arrangement has one supporting strand

This arrangement has two supporting strands

Number of support strands	Force to lift bottom pulley block (N)
1	
2	
3	
4	
5	
6	

a. As you add more supporting strands, what happens to the force needed to lift the bottom block?

b. How does the amount of input force required to lift the bottom block change with the string arrangement? Can you identify a mathematical rule?

4   What did you learn?

a. How are all simple machines alike? How is a lever different from a machine made with ropes and pulleys? (Think about input and output force.)

b. What is the relationship between the number of strings on the ropes and pulleys, and the amount of input force required to lift the bottom block?

4.2 The Lever

Question: How does a lever work?

In this Investigation, you will:

1. Use a lever and describe its parts.
2. Analyze how a lever manipulates force.
3. Explore the concept of equilibrium in simple machines.

How can you lift up a car – or even an elephant – all by yourself? One way is with a lever. The lever is an example of a simple machine.

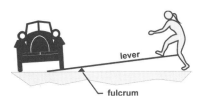

1 Setting up the lever

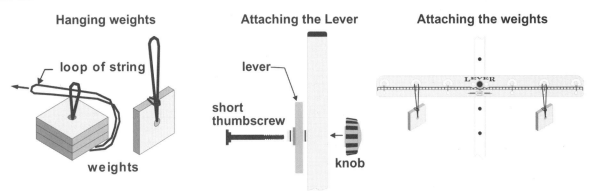

1. Use loops of string to make hangers for the weights. You can put more than one weight on a single string.
2. The weights can be hung from the lever by hooking the string over the center peg in the holes. Make sure that the string is all the way around the peg!

2 Levers in equilibrium

a. The lever is in equilibrium when all the weights on one side balance all the weights on the other side. Hang the weights as shown below. Does the lever balance?

b. What variables can be changed to balance a lever?

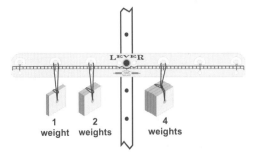

3 **Trying different combinations to balance the lever**

Make different combinations of weights and positions that balance. Use the chart below to write down the numbers of weights you put in each position. If you want to conduct more than four trials, write your results on a separate sheet of paper

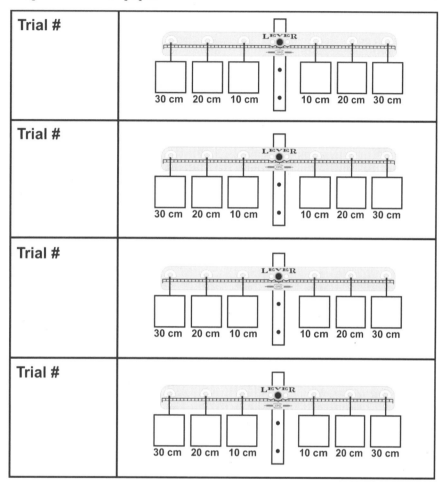

4 **Determine the mathematical rule for equilibrium**

Using the data in the chart above, determine a mathematical rule for levers in equilibrium. Think about the variables in the experiment: input force, output force, length of input arm, and length of output arm. First, make some calculations, then write your rule as an equation.

5 **What did you learn?**

a. Draw a lever that has mechanical advantage. Label these parts: fulcrum, input arm, output arm, input force, and output force.

b. There are two ratios that can be used to determine mechanical advantage in levers. What are the two equations? What is the relationship between the two equations?

c. In a lever, you can increase the amount of output force by increasing the length of the input arm. When you do this, what must decrease in order to increase output force?

4.3 | **Designing Gear Machines**

Question: How do gears work?

In this Investigation, you will:

1. Build machines with gears and deduce the rule for how pairs of gears turn.
2. Apply ratios to design machines with gears.
3. Design a gear machine to solve a specific problem.

Many machines require that rotating motion be transmitted from one place to another. The transmission of rotating motion is often done with shafts and gears. When one or more shafts are connected with gears, the shafts may turn at different speeds and in different directions. Since they act like rotating levers, gears also allow the forces carried by different shafts to be changed.

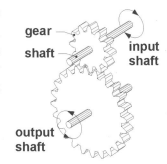

1 **Two gear machines**

1. Set up machines with two gears with different numbers of teeth as shown in the diagram.
2. Count the number of turns of the input gear it takes to make a whole number of turns of the output gear (such as one or two full turns). Write the data in the table below.

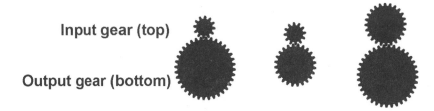

Table 1: Teeth and turns for 3 gear machines

Input Teeth	Input Turns	Output Teeth	Output Turns

2 **Deducing the rule for gears**

From your data, derive a mathematical formula which relates the turns of the input gear to the turns of the output gear. The rule also must include the teeth in each gear. State your rule using four variables: Input Teeth, Input Turns, Output Teeth, and Output Turns. This rule is called the *law of gearing* and is the basis for designing machines that use gears.

3 ## Complex gear machines

Many machines require large gear ratios. For example, a clock has a gear ratio of 1:60 between the minute hand and the second hand. This ratio could be made with one pair of gears where one gear was 60 times larger than the other. It can also be done with two pairs of gears in a much smaller and more economical design.

1. Set up a compound gear machine with at least 2 pairs of gears.

2. Use the table to work out the gear ratio.

3. Measure the rotation of the input and output gears and show that the machine behaves as you expect.

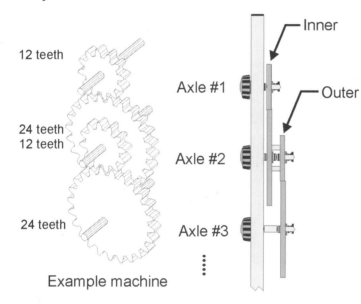

Example machine

Table 2: Gear machine #1

axle	Inner Position X or number of teeth	Outer Position X or number of teeth
1		
2		
3		
4		
5		

4 ## Design your own machine

The gears make ratios containing the numbers 1, 2, and 3 only. These ratios can be combined to make other ratios as long as no factors other than 1, 2, or 3 are used. It would be impossible to build a ratio of 21 with these gears because 21 factors into 7×3. You do not have any gears that can make a ratio of 7.

1. Design and construct a machine that has a ratio of 9:1. Make a table like the one above to record the design and show that the ratio works out mathematically.

2. Design and construct a machine that has a ratio of 4:1. Make a table like the one above to record the design and show that the ratio works out mathematically.

3. Design and construct a machine that has a ratio of 18:1. Make a table like the one above to record the design and show that the ratio works out mathematically. This ratio may require sharing with other groups since it uses at least 6 gears.

5 ## What did you learn?

a. Suppose you needed to make a ratio of 100:1 using gears. Suggest 3 different designs using 3 different combinations of gears. Which design is the smallest? Which has the least gears?

b. Are there reasons you might want to use two pairs of gears instead of 1 pair, even for small ratios? Think about the direction the input and output gears turn.

Work

Question: What happens when you multiply forces in a machine?

In this Investigation, you will:

1. Explore how simple machines are able to multiply forces.
2. Calculate work.

In Investigations 4.1 and 4.2, you learned how two simple machines can be arranged to provide a mechanical advantage. Ropes and pulleys, as do levers, create large output forces from small input forces. In this Investigation you will explore the nature of work and energy and come to an interesting conclusion that is true for all machines.

1 Setting up the experiment

1. Use the force scale to weigh the bottom block. Record this value, in newtons, in column five of the table in Part 2. This value is the *output force* and does not change in the experiment.

2. Using a ropes and pulleys set, clip the end of the yellow string to the bottom block. Pass the string over the middle pulley of the top block.

3. Use the marker stop (cord stop) to mark where the string leaves the top pulley.

4. Lift the bottom block a fixed height (h). The holes in the stand are 5 centimeters apart and you can use the holes as a height reference. Use at least 20 centimeters as your lifting height.

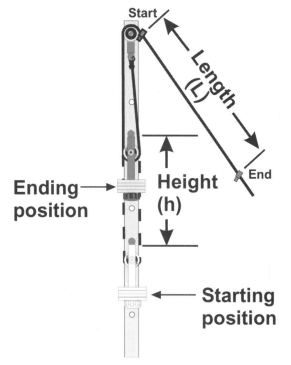

5. Measure how much string length (L) you had to pull to lift the block the chosen distance. You can measure this using the marker stops and a ruler.

6. Using the force scale, measure the force needed to lift the block. This is the *input force*.

7. Record the input force, height difference for the block (h), and string length (L) in the data table on the next page.

8. Leave the last two columns on the table blank for now.

9. Rearrange the yellow strings so that you achieve a mechanical advantage of 2, 3, 4, 5, and 6. For each combination record the height (h), input force, and string length (L) you had to pull to raise the block the required height (h).
   Nature does not give things away for free. You traded something away to get the multiplication of forces.

As the mechanical advantage increases, what happens to the length of the string you have to pull to raise the block?

2   Data table

Mechanical advantage	Height difference for block	String length	Input force	Output force (weight of block)	Work done on block (work output)	Work done by you (work input)
	(meters)	(meters)	(newtons)	(newtons)	(joules)	(joules)

3   What is work?

The last two columns of the data table show the work done on the block and the work done by you. To do work, forces are applied to move objects. Simple machines like the ropes and pulleys have mechanical advantage so that you can do work using less force.

To analyze how work and force are related, a specific definition for work is needed:

Work is the product of force times the distance moved in the direction of the force.

The units of work are newtons × meters (force × distance). The unit newton-meter was given the special name joule after Sir James Joule, who discovered the importance of work in a series of experiments performed between 1843 and 1847.

I joule = I newton × I meter

4 $\frac{a}{b}$ Calculating work done

a.   Calculate the work done on the block. This work is equal to the output force (weight of the block) times the height difference for block. The work done on the block should be the same for all configurations of the strings because the weight of the block and the height it was lifted did not change. You should therefore write the same number in each row of the table under the heading "Work done on block."

b.   Next, calculate the work you did as you pulled on the string to lift the block. In this case, multiply the input force times the string length. For each different mechanical advantage, record the work done on the string under the heading "Work done by you."

The relationship between work and energy

Suppose that you use the ropes and pulleys to lift the block 0.5 meter. If the weight of the block is 10 newtons, the amount of work done on the block is 0.5 m × 10 N = 5 joules. Where does this work go?

When work is done against gravity, it is not necessarily gone, but can be stored for future use. For example, suppose you lift marble A with a pulley as in the picture below.

a.   Marble A can be let back down to lift marble B. The work put into lifting marble A can be recovered and used to lift marble B. Study the picture below carefully. In order for marble A to lift marble B, what must be true about the weights of the two marbles?

b.   Using the arrows in the picture below as a guide, describe the forces in terms of strength and direction on marble A and marble B.

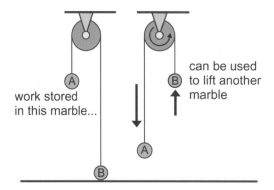

c.   The work that is stored up when the first marble is lifted is a type of **energy**. Do you think the work being used to lift the second marble is the same, or a different type of energy? Explain.

d.   When 10 joules is used to lift the block on the ropes and pulleys set, this work is stored up as energy. If we let the block back down again, we can get the energy back. You can confirm this by noticing that the string is pulling on you as you let the block fall back down. Try this out and explain your results in terms of work and energy.

6   The work-energy theorem

An object that has energy has the ability to do work. The total amount of work that can be done is exactly equal to the energy available. This principle is called the **work-energy theorem** and applies to everything in the universe.

a.   Can you think of one everyday example that demonstrates the work-energy theorem?

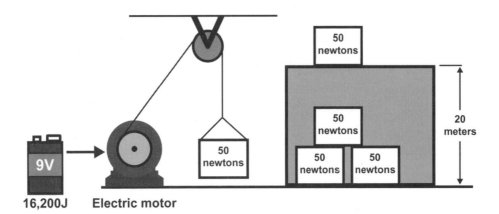

b.   One way to store energy is in a battery. One 9-volt alkaline battery stores approximately 16,200 joules of energy. Suppose you had a perfect electric motor and a pulley with no friction. How many 50-newton boxes can you lift to a height of 20.0 meters using the energy stored in the battery? Solve the problem and show your work.

Energy Conservation

Question: What is energy and how does it behave?

In this Investigation, you will:

1. Discover the relationship between speed and height on a roller coaster.
2. Describe how energy is conserved on a roller coaster.

Think about the last time you went for a bike ride

To pedal your bike up a hill, you have to work hard to keep the bike going. However, when you start down the other side of the hill, you coast! You hardly have to pedal at all. In this Investigation, you will find out what happens to the speed of a marble as it rolls up and down the hills and valleys of the CPO roller coaster.

1 Setting up the roller coaster

Attach the roller coaster to the fifth hole from the bottom of the stand. Use the starting peg to start the marble in the same place each time you roll it down. It sometimes takes a few tries to roll it straight so that it stays on the track. Watch the marble roll along the track. At which place (or places) do you think the marble moves fastest? Why?

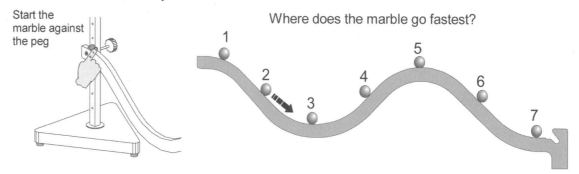

2 Measuring the speed of the marble

To understand what is happening to the marble, you need to measure the speed and the height at different places on the roller coaster.

1. To measure the speed of the marble, attach a photogate so that the marble breaks the light beam as it rolls through.
2. Plug the photogate into input A of the timer and use interval mode.
3. Be sure that the bottom of the photogate is flat against the bottom of the roller coaster. If the photogate is not attached properly, the light beam will not cross the center of the marble and the speed you calculate will not be accurate.

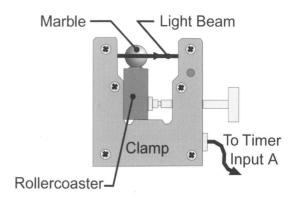

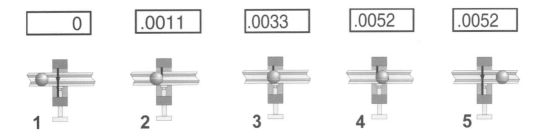

1. The ball has not broken the beam yet. The timer is not counting.
2. The timer starts counting when the front edge of the marble breaks the beam.
3. The timer keeps counting while the beam is blocked by the marble.
4. The timer stops counting when the back edge of the marble goes out of the beam.
5. The display shows the time that the marble blocked the beam.

Speed is the distance traveled divided by time taken to travel that distance. During the time that the timer is counting, the marble moves one diameter. Therefore, the distance traveled is the diameter of the marble, and the time taken is the time from photogate A. **The speed of the marble is its diameter divided by the time from photogate A.**

Use the photogate to test your hypothesis about where the marble would go fastest. Measure and record the speed of the marble at each of the seven places. Positions 2, 4, and 6 should be as close to the same height as you can get. If they are the same height, you can easily compare uphill and downhill motion.

Position number	Time, photogate A (sec)	Distance traveled (cm)	Speed of marble (cm/sec)
1			
2			
3			
4			
5			
6			
7			

a. Did your measurements agree with your hypothesis or did they point to a different hypothesis? If the answer did not agree with your hypothesis, what sort of hypothesis do the observations support about where the marble is fastest?

b. What did you notice about the motion of the marble from the measurements? For example, do you think that going uphill or downhill makes a difference in the speed? Does height affect speed? Which has a larger impact, height or direction (uphill or downhill)?

3 Energy conservation

When the marble speeds up, it is gaining kinetic energy from falling down a hill. The kinetic energy is converted from the potential energy the marble had at the top of the hill. As the marble goes along it trades potential and kinetic energy back and forth.

To measure the kinetic energy, we use the photogate to find the speed of the marble. To get the potential energy, we need to measure the height. The light beam passes through the center of the marble, so you should measure the height from the table to the center of the hole for the light beam.

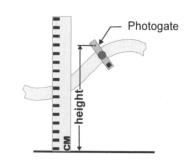

For the positions close to the start, you will have to measure from the base of the stand. Add the height of the base to the height you measure to get the total height.

1. Place the photogate at different places along the roller coaster. Measure the speed and height of the marble at each place.

2. Write your data down in the table below

Position (cm)	Height (cm)	Time from photogate A (sec)	Distance traveled (cm)	Speed of marble (cm/sec)
			1.9	
			1.9	
			1.9	
			1.9	
			1.9	
			1.9	
			1.9	
			1.9	
			1.9	
			1.9	
			1.9	
			1.9	

4   **Graphing height vs. speed**

Take your measurements and make a graph that shows the relationship between height and speed. The graph provided already shows the height of the roller coaster plotted against the position along the track. Plot the speed vs. position on the same graph.

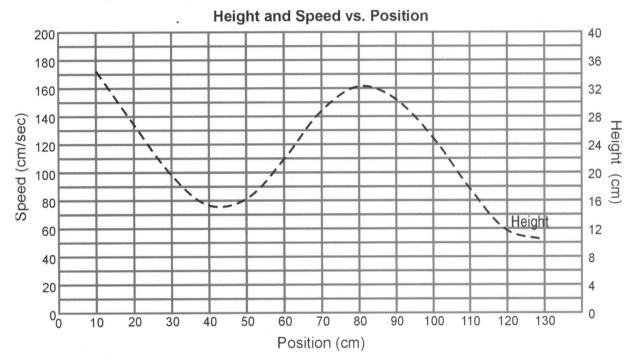

Height and Speed vs. Position

a.   What can you tell from your graph? Describe the relationship you see between the speed of the marble and the height.

b.   Where is the speed of the marble greatest?

c.   Does the uphill or downhill direction matter to the speed of the marble, or is the height the only contributing variable?

d.   Describe the flow of energy between potential and kinetic along the roller coaster. Your answer should indicate where the potential energy is greatest and least, and also where the kinetic energy is greatest and least.

Energy Transformations

Question: Where did the energy go?

In this Investigation, you will:

1. Describe energy transformations in several scenarios.

You have learned that the amount of energy in the universe is constant and that in any situation requiring energy, all of it must be accounted for. This is the basis for the law of conservation of energy. In this Investigation, you will analyze different scenarios in terms of what happens to energy. Based on your experience with the roller coaster, you already know that potential energy can be changed into kinetic energy and vice versa. As you study the scenarios below, identify potential energy to kinetic energy transformations. For each scenario, see if you can also answer the following questions: What other energy transformations are occurring? In each scenario, where did all the energy go?

1 **Kinetic to potential, or potential to kinetic?**

For each scenario, specify whether kinetic energy is being changed to potential energy, or potential is being converted to kinetic. Explain your answers.

a. A roller coaster car travels from point A to point B.

b. A bungee cord begins to exert an upward force on a falling bungee jumper.

c. A football is spiraling downward toward a football player.

d. A solar cell is charging a battery.

2 Energy scenarios

Read each scenario below. Then, working with your group, complete the following for each scenario:

*   Identify which of the following forms of energy are involved in the scenario:
    mechanical, **radiant**, **electrical**, **chemical**, and **nuclear**.

*   Make an *energy flow chart* that shows how the energy changes from one form to another, in the correct order. Use a separate paper (newsprint, if provided) and colored markers to make your flow charts more interesting.

Be prepared to explain to the rest of the class the reasoning behind your group's ideas, and then to discuss them.

1. In Western states, many homes generate electricity from windmills. In a particular home, a young boy is using the electricity to run a toy electric train.

2. A camper is using a wood fire to heat up a pot of water for tea. The pot has a whistle that lets the camper know when the water boils.

3. The state of Illinois generates most of its electricity from nuclear power. A young woman in Chicago is watching a broadcast of a sports game on television.

4. A bicyclist is riding at night. He switches on his bike's generator so that his headlight comes on. The harder he pedals, the brighter his headlight glows.

What Is a Circuit?

Question: What is an electric circuit?

In this Investigation, you will:

1. Construct simple electric circuits using a battery, bulb, switch, and wires.
2. Draw circuit diagrams using electrical symbols.

Electricity is an integral part of our lives. Our homes, stores, and workplaces all use many electrical devices such as electric ovens, TVs, stereos, toasters, motors that turn fans, air conditioners, heaters, light bulbs, etc. In fact, the use of electricity has become so routine that many of us don't stop to think about what happens when we switch on a light or turn on a motor. If we do stop to look, we find that most of what is "happening" is not visible. What exactly is electricity? How does it work?

In this Investigation, you will figure out how to make a bulb light. As you build circuits, you will discover that electricity travels through a specific path, much like water travels through pipes or streams.

Safety Tips: Be careful working with batteries. If they are damaged, return them immediately to your teacher.

If a battery or wire gets hot, disconnect the circuit and ask your teacher for help.

Always have a bulb somewhere in your circuit. Do not connect a wire directly from one terminal of the battery to the other terminal. This is a short circuit, which can start a fire.

1 Building circuits with a battery, a bulb, and a wire

a. Using *only* one battery, one bulb, and one wire, find four different ways you can arrange these three parts that will make the bulb light up. As you work, determine the kinds of connections that are needed to make the circuit work.

b. Record all your circuit attempts. Draw both successful and unsuccessful attempts. The drawing at right shows a simple way to draw the bulb, battery and wire.

c. Make sure your drawings show the difference between the two ends of the battery. Also show exactly where the bulb is touching the wire and the battery.

d. Explain why you think some configurations work and others don't. Record your first thoughts and impressions — don't worry if your answers are right or wrong.

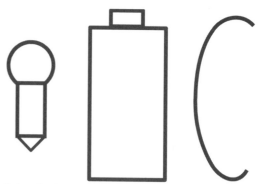

Using simple geometric shapes (circle, rectangle, triangle) and a line, you can draw representations of the light bulb, battery and wire.

2 Using the electric circuits set

In this part of the Investigation, you will build the same circuit you made in part 1, except you will now use the electric circuits set. The set includes a small table, battery holders, and light bulb holders, which makes building circuits a lot easier. Your completed circuit should include one battery and battery holder, one bulb and bulb holder, and two wire connectors. The bulb should light up in the completed circuit.

3 Drawing circuit diagrams

It was pretty difficult drawing the battery and bulb and wire in part 1! People who work with electricity have short-cut methods for drawing electrical parts and circuits. All the electrical parts in a circuit are represented by standard pictures, called *electrical symbols*. Some electrical parts and their corresponding symbols are shown in the picture to the right. Study the symbols and practice drawing them.

 Using these symbols, draw a picture of the circuit you built on the electric circuits table. This type of drawing is called a *circuit diagram*. There is an example of a circuit diagram in section 6.1 of your Integrated Physics and Chemistry book.

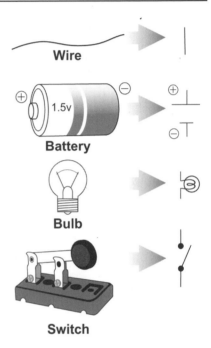

4 Observing how a switch works

1. Add a switch to your circuit. You may need one more wire connector.
2. Check that the switch turns the light bulb on and off.

Examine the switch as it turns the light bulb on and off. Explain how the switch works. Use both words and drawings.

5 What did you learn?

a. Water can travel through air but cannot travel through a solid. Using what you learned in this Investigation, describe some materials that electricity can and cannot travel through.

b. The word "circuit" comes from the same root as the word "circle." Describe the similarities between a circle and the circuits that you built.

c. A circuit that is on and working is sometimes called a "closed circuit." Based on your observations of the switch, explain what "closed" means in a circuit.

d. A circuit that is off or a circuit that is not working is sometimes called an "open circuit." Based on your observations of the switch, explain what "open" means in a circuit.

Charge

Question: What is moving through a circuit?

In this Investigation, you will:

1. Build a simple electroscope.
2. Charge pieces of tape.
3. Observe the electrostatic forces exerted by charged pieces of tape on each other.

To understand electricity, people studied events like lightning and the sparks that occur when certain materials are rubbed together. We now know that the movement of electric charge causes these events. Charge is a concept somewhat difficult to grasp; we see its manifestations around us but we can't "see" charge. In this way, charge is like the wind — we can't see the moving air but we know it exists because it blows against our faces and moves objects around.

Charge comes in two forms, called positive charge and negative charge. In this Investigation you will observe how these two kinds of charge interact with each other.

1 Building a simple electroscope

1. Obtain the following materials: two rectangles of clay about 2 cm by 2 cm by 4 cm, 4 flexible straws, ruler, and Scotch™ brand magic tape.
2. Anchor a flexible straw in each end of each piece of clay. You have 2 clay bases and 4 straws in all.
3. Bend the flexible straws away from each other in each piece of clay. The bent part is called the arm. The arms should be at the same height.
4. Line up the two pieces of clay so that the arms are parallel to each other and about 16 cm apart.

2 Creating static charges - part I

1. Place a piece of tape, about 20 cm long, sticky side down, on your table. This is your "base tape." It will always stay on the table.
2. Tear off a15-cm long piece of tape and turn over about 1/2 cm at the end to make a handle.
3. Place this piece of tape, sticky side down, on the base tape. Smooth the tape down.
4. Quickly tear away the handled tape and wrap the top part of it around one of the electroscope arms. Most of the tape should be dangling.
5. Repeat steps 2 through 3, only this time, place the second piece of tape on an arm on the second piece of clay. (You should still have two free arms on your electroscope.)

3 Observing the interaction between the tapes - part I

1. Line up the two electroscope halves so that the two pieces of tape are parallel to each other. Slowly move the two pieces of clay towards each other.
2. Observe and record what happens to the two pieces of tape.

4   Creating static charges - part II

1. Separate the two pieces of clay so that they are once again about 16 cm apart. Position them so that the two free arms are parallel to each other.

2. Tear off a 15-cm long piece of tape and turn over about 1/2 cm at the end to make a handle.

3. Place this piece of tape, sticky side down, on the base tape.

4. Label the handle A.

5. Tear off another 15-cm long piece of tape and again make a handle.

6. Place this piece of tape, sticky side down, on the A tape, which is still atop the base tape.

7. Label the handle of this second piece of tape B.

8. Remove the A and B tapes keeping them stuck together.

9. While holding them in the air, quickly tear apart the A and B tapes.

10. Place the A tape on one free arm of the electroscope.

11. Place the B tape on the last free arm of the electroscope.

5   Observing the interaction between the tapes - part II

1. Line up the two electroscope halves so that A and B pieces of tape are parallel to each other. Slowly move the two pieces of clay towards each other.

2. Observe and record what happens to the two pieces of tape.

3. Now see how the A and B tapes interact with the first two pieces of tape you prepared. Record what you observe.

6   What did you learn?

a. How many types of interactions did you observe between the pieces of tape?

b. The first tapes you prepared pushed each other away, or *repelled* each other. These two pieces of tape have the same kind of charge. This makes sense since you prepared the tapes in the same way. On the other hand, the A tape has one kind of charge and the B tape has a different kind of charge. Are the first tapes you prepared both A tapes or both B tapes? Explain how you figured this out.

c. Give your hypothesis for how the A and B tapes might have acquired different kinds of charge.

7   ⧗ Extension: Using the electroscope to detect other charged objects

In sixteenth-century England, William Gilbert, the queen's physician, built the first electroscope. He noticed that the electroscope attracted lightweight objects. See if you can reproduce his results.

1. Remove the tape from your electroscope.

2. Prepare and label a fresh set of A and B tapes and place them on two arms anchored in one piece of clay.

3. Take light objects such as thread, small pieces of paper, and hair and slowly bring them close to both the A and B tapes.

4. Record your observations.

7.1

Voltage

Question: Why do charges move through a circuit?

In this Investigation, you will:

1. Measure the voltage of a battery with an electrical meter.
2. Measure the voltage of batteries in and out of circuits.
3. Figure out how batteries must be connected together in order to increase voltage in a circuit.

Have you ever wondered how a battery works? Or what "volts" mean?

You know that batteries have one end marked positive and one end marked negative. A battery supplies energy to create electric current that flows from positive to negative. The energy you supplied by raising and lowering the string with the ropes and pulleys could do work. In a similar way, the electric current that flows through a wire can also do work. *Voltage* describes how much energy is available to make electric current flow and do work. The higher the voltage, the more current will flow and do work for us. The work includes lighting bulbs, heating toast, and turning electric motors.

◆ **Safety Tips: Be careful working with batteries. If they are damaged, return them immediately to your teacher.**

If a battery or wire gets hot, disconnect the circuit and ask your teacher for help.

Always have a bulb somewhere in your circuit. Do not connect a wire directly from one terminal of the battery to the other terminal. This is a short circuit, which can start a fire.

1 | **Measuring voltage across a battery**

1. Gather the following materials: electrical meter and its two test leads, and a battery.
2. Connect the two meter leads to the meter as shown in the bottom of the picture at right.
3. Set the meter to measure DC volts.
4. Place the red positive lead of the meter on the positive terminal of the battery.
5. Place the black negative lead of the meter on the negative terminal of the battery.
6. Look at the voltage reading. If the number is not close to 1.5 volts or if the range needs to be adjusted, ask your teacher for help.
7. Record the voltage of the battery.

2   ## Measure voltage across a battery in a circuit

1. Gather the following additional materials: a battery holder, a bulb, a bulb holder, and two connectors.

2. Build a circuit with the battery you just tested, a battery holder, a bulb, a bulb holder, and two connectors.

3. Predict what the voltage of the battery will be while it is lighting the bulb. Also explain the reasoning behind your prediction.

4. Measure the voltage across the battery exactly as you did in part 1. DO NOT DISCONNECT THE CIRCUIT.

5. Record the voltage of the battery while it is lighting the bulb.

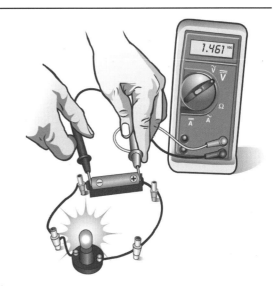

3   ## What did you learn?

a. Was your prediction correct?

b. Was there much difference in the battery voltage when it was not lighting the bulb and when it was lighting the bulb?

c. A battery has chemicals inside that react with each other and release energy. This energy separates and moves the charges to each terminal of the battery. Draw a picture that shows how the charges separate and to which terminals they migrate.

4   ## Building circuits with two batteries

How many batteries does a small flashlight use? How about a large radio? What happens when you wire batteries together?

Build circuits with two batteries and two holders, one bulb and holder, and three wires. Connect the two batteries in four different configurations as shown. For each configuration, do the following:

1. Measure voltage across both batteries before adding the bulb.

2. Predict if the bulb will light, then connect the bulb and check.

3. Measure voltage across the bulb. Do this by placing one meter lead on one side of the bulb holder and the other meter lead on the other side of the bulb holder.

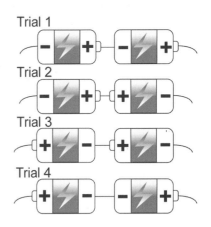

Examine your data carefully. Then, discuss the following questions with your group and record your answers.

a. Describe in words how you should wire batteries together to light the bulb.

b. Each battery is 1.5 volts. Explain how to calculate voltage when two batteries are connected.

c. Compare the brightness of a bulb in a one-battery circuit to a bulb in a two-battery circuit. How is the bulb's brightness related to energy transfer in each circuit?

d. Explain the meaning of the voltage reading across the bulb.

Current

Question: How does current move through a circuit?

In this Investigation, you will:

1. Measure and compare current at different points in a circuit.
2. Compare current in circuits with one and two bulbs.

Why does a bulb light? When you put a battery in a circuit, electric current flows through the wires and makes things happen. The current carries energy from the battery to a bulb or motor. You can increase the amount of energy in two ways. The higher the flow of current, the more the energy can be carried. The higher the voltage, the more energy can be carried by the same amount of current.

Safety Tips: Be careful working with batteries. If they are damaged, return them immediately to your teacher.

If a battery or wire gets hot, disconnect the circuit and ask your teacher for help.

1 Building test circuit #1

1. Gather the following materials: electrical meter and its two test leads, a battery and battery holder, a bulb and bulb holder, and two connectors.
2. Build test circuit 1 with one battery and battery holder, one bulb and bulb holder, and two connectors, as shown in the schematic at right. There are two points marked on the schematic, A and B, which is where the connectors are attached to the bulb holder. Make sure that you can easily identify these points in your circuit.

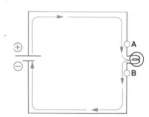

2 Measuring current through test circuit #1

To measure current, the meter must be placed *in* the circuit so the current has to flow through the meter. Follow the instructions below carefully.

1. Connect the two meter leads to the meter as shown right.
2. Set the meter to measure DC current at the highest range.
3. Remove the connector between the positive terminal of the battery and the bulb holder.
4. Place the red positive lead of the meter on the post attached to the positive terminal of the battery.
5. Place the black negative lead of the meter on the free post attached to the bulb holder. You should now have a complete circuit. The bulb should light and you should get a reading on the meter.
6. Record the current at point A.

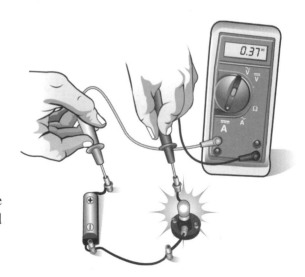

7. Predict what the current at point B will be. Record your prediction.

8. Following the same procedure you did for point A, use your meter to measure current at point B. The positive lead of the meter should be closest to the positive battery terminal, and the negative lead of the meter should be closest to the negative battery terminal.

9. Record the current at point B.

10. Remove the meter and reconnect the circuit. Leave it connected while you complete part 3.

3 ## Building test circuit #2

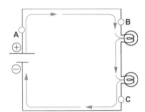

1. Gather the following additional materials: one battery and battery holder, two bulbs and bulb holders, and three connectors.

2. Build the circuit in the diagram on the left. Make sure that you can easily identify points A, B, and C where the connectors are attached.

4 ## Comparing test circuits #1 and #2

Compare the brightness of the bulbs in test circuits 1 and 2. Record your observations and disconnect test circuit 1.

5 ## Measuring current through test circuit #2

1. Using the same procedure you followed in part 2, measure and record current at point A.

2. Predict what the current will be at points B and C.

3. Using the same procedure you followed in part 2, measure and record current at points B and C.

6 ## What did you learn?

a. Review the two current readings for circuit 1. What conclusions can you draw from these results?

b. Review the three current readings for circuit 2. What conclusions can you draw from these results?

c. Transfer all your results for circuit 1 and circuit 2 into the table below. Compare the current readings in the two circuits. What happened to current when you added a bulb to the circuit?

	Current in circuit 1 (amps)		Current in circuit 2 (amps)
point A		point A	
point B		point B	
		point C	

d. You probably determined that adding a bulb to the circuit reduced the current. With the rest of your group propose an explanation. Be prepared to present and defend your explanation.

7.3

Resistance

Question: How well does current travel through different materials and objects?

In this Investigation, you will:

1. Determine how objects differ in their ability to resist current.
2. Classify materials as conductors, insulators, or semiconductors.
3. Compare the resistance of identical pieces of copper and aluminum wires.
4. Determine how electrical resistance varies with length.

Materials differ in their ability to allow current to flow through them. This is a good thing! It means that we can build circuits out of metals that easily carry current. We can block the flow of current using air, glass, or plastic. *Resistance* is the quantity that describes how much an object will prevent (resist) the flow of current. Resistance is measured in units called ohms.

1 **Measuring resistance of everyday objects**

1. Gather the following materials: electrical meter and its two test leads, and resistance test objects.

1 Examine the objects and try to determine what material each is made out of. Include air as one of your test objects. You can ask your teacher for assistance. Record your answers in Table 1.

2. Connect the two meter leads to the meter as shown at right.

3. Set the meter to measure resistance.

4. Measure the resistance of each object. To do this, attach the black negative meter lead to one end of the test object and then attach the red positive meter lead to the other end of the test object. (Use your ruler to measure the resistance of 1 centimeter of air.)

5. Some materials may have a high resistance and the meter will read OL. Record these readings as "very high." Record all resistances in Table 1.

Table 1: Resistance of common objects

Object	Material, if known	Resistance in ohms	Object	Material, if known	Resistance in ohms

2   Identifying conductors and insulators

To roughly describe the ability of different kinds of materials to conduct current, we say that a material is a conductor (conducts easily), an insulator (conducts poorly), or a semiconductor (in-between). All of these materials are useful when we construct circuits.

Table 2: Classifying materials as conductors, insulators, or semiconductors

Object / material listed from low to high resistance	Resistance in ohms (from Table 1)	Conductor, insulator, or semiconductor	Was your classification correct?

1. Rearrange the list of objects you tested (in Table 1) so that the readings of resistance go from lowest to highest. Copy your rearranged list of objects and their resistance into Table 2.

2. Look at your results and try to classify the objects you tested under one of these three categories: conductors, insulators, and semiconductors. As a guideline, remember that bulbs and wires are conductors and air is an insulator. (Hint: It is likely that only one item on your list is a semiconductor.) Write down your classifications in column 3.

3. Check your results against the table on page 118 of your book. How well did you do? Record whether or not your classification was correct in column 4.

3   Measuring and comparing resistance of copper and aluminum

a. Your teacher will give you two identical wires of aluminum and copper. Which metal do you think will have more resistance? Why?

b. Measure the resistance of both pieces of metal. You can bend the wire so that the meter leads can reach the ends. Record your results.

c. Which metal has the lowest resistance? Do you know if this metal is commonly used in electric circuits?

d. Fold each piece of wire neatly in half and mark the halfway point. Unfold the wire and measure resistance from the halfway point to one end of the wire. Record your results for copper and aluminum.

e. Compare the resistance for the whole piece of each metal with the half piece. How does resistance vary with length?

f. How do you think resistance of a wide wire will compare with that of a thin wire of the same length? Discuss this question with your group and record your answer. Think about the flow of water through narrow and wide pipes.

Ohm's Law

Question: How are voltage, current, and resistance related?

In this Investigation, you will:

1. Build circuits using variable and fixed resistors.
2. Measure change in current when resistance is changed.
3. Measure and graph change in voltage when current is changed.
4. Use your data and graph to determine the relationship between voltage, current, and resistance.

When working with circuits, you may need to know how much voltage will light a particular light bulb, or how much current will be in a circuit so you can choose the correct size wire to use. German physicist Georg S. Ohm (1787-1854) experimented with circuits to find out how voltage, current, and resistance are related mathematically. The relationship he discovered is called **Ohm's law**.

1 | **How does changing resistance affect current?**

A *resistor* is used in a circuit to provide resistance. In this part of the Investigation you will use a *variable resistor*. As you turn the dial of the variable resistor, its resistance goes up. A variable resistor is also called a *potentiometer*. Many dials you use everyday, like dimmer switches, are potentiometers.

1. Gather the following materials: Electrical meter and test leads, two batteries and holders, one bulb and holder, a switch, a potentiometer, and four wire connectors.
2. Build a circuit with two batteries, one bulb, the switch and your potentiometer. Record what happens when you turn the dial.
3. Turn the potentiometer until the bulb is very dim.
4. Measure current and record the value in Table 1.
5. Turn the circuit off and measure resistance across the potentiometer (be careful not to touch the dial as you do this). Record the value in Table 1.
6. Make the bulb a little bit brighter and repeat steps 4 and 5. Continue until you have completed Table 1 for five settings of the potentiometer.

Table 1: Change in current vs. change in resistance for a potentiometer

potentiometer setting	current (amps)	resistance (ohms)
First potentiometer setting		
Second potentiometer setting		
Third potentiometer setting		
Fourth potentiometer setting		
Fifth potentiometer setting		

Examine your data. Describe in words what happens to current as resistance is increased.

2   How does changing voltage affect current?

In this part of the Investigation your teacher will give you a *fixed resistor*. This component adds resistance to a circuit, but its resistance does not change.

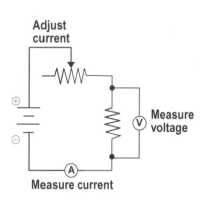

Adjust current

Measure voltage

Measure current

1. Use the electrical meter to measure the resistance of your resistor. Record the value in the second column, all five rows, of Table 2.

2. Build a circuit with two batteries, your resistor, and the potentiometer as shown in the diagram at right.

3. Measure the current through the circuit, and the voltage across the resistor. Record the values in Table 2.

4. Change the setting of the potentiometer and measure current and voltage again (you do not need to measure resistance across the potentiometer).

5. Repeat for at least five settings of the potentiometer. Record all values of current and voltage in the table.

Table 2: Change in voltage vs. change in current for a resistor

potentiometer setting	resistance (ohms)	current (amps)	voltage (volts)
First potentiometer setting			
Second potentiometer setting			
Third potentiometer setting			
Fourth potentiometer setting			
Fifth potentiometer setting			

Examine the data in your table. Describe in words what happens to the voltage across the resistor as the current increases.

3   Finding the relationship between voltage, current, and resistance

a. Graph the data from part 2. Put voltage on the *y*-axis and current on the *x*-axis. Label your *x*- and *y*-axes and title your graph.

b. The slope of a line is rise over run. For the graph of voltage vs. current, slope is change in voltage (rise) over change in current (run). Calculate the slope of the graph. What other electrical quantity in the circuit does the slope approximately equal?

c. You just found out that the slope of the voltage vs. current graph is the resistance. This is the equation for Ohm's law. Write the mathematical equation for Ohm's law using the following: V stands for voltage, I stands for current, and R stands for resistance.

d. Most circuits use fixed voltage sources. Different values of current are needed to run different devices and appliances. With this information, explain the importance of resistors in a circuit.

Work, Energy, and Power

Question: How much does it cost to use the electrical appliances in your home?

In this Investigation, you will:

1. Read appliance labels to determine their power rating.
2. Calculate the approximate number of kilowatt-hours each appliance uses in a month.
3. Calculate the approximate cost of running each appliance using electric company rates.

You have learned how to measure three electrical quantities: voltage, current, and resistance. In this Investigation, you will learn about a fourth quantity, power, which you have already studied in the context of mechanics. You will find the power ratings of electrical appliances and use this information to estimate electrical costs.

1   Find the power rating of home appliances

You will need to complete the first part of this Investigation at home. Your assignment is to find five electrical appliances that have a label with the device's power rating in watts or kilowatts. Some appliances you might investigate are a blender, coffee maker, toaster oven, microwave, television, hair dryer, space heater, room air conditioner, or an electric drill. The rating is often stamped on the back or the bottom of the appliance.

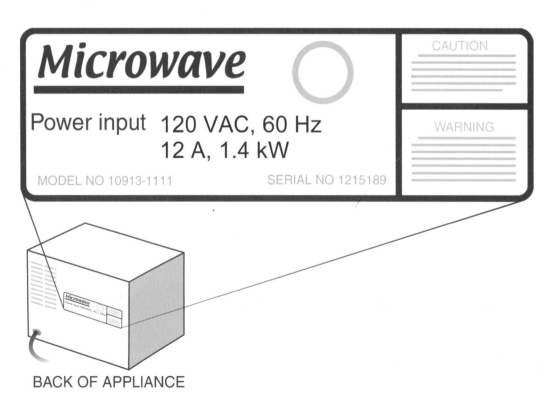

In the above example the power rating is 1.35 kW.

1. Fill out the first two columns of Table 1 as you find the power rating of each appliance. The second column should be in kilowatts.

2. Convert any power ratings listed in watts to kilowatts. To convert to kilowatts, divide the number of watts by 1,000. For example, 1500 watts is equal to $1500 \div 1000$, or 1.5 kilowatts. Fill in the kilowatt column for each device.

3. Finally, estimate the number of hours the device is used each month. Assume that one month equals 30 days. If your coffee maker is used for a half hour each morning, you would calculate one-half hour times 30 days equals 15 hours per month. You may need to talk to other people in your home to get the most accurate estimate possible.

4. After you have filled in the estimated monthly use column, you are ready to complete the rest of the Investigation in class.

Table 1: Power rating, usage, and cost of household appliances

Appliance	Power rating in kilowatts	Estimated hours per month in use	Number kWh per month	Price per kWh	Total cost per month

2   Estimate the number of kilowatt-hours each appliance uses in a month

In order to determine how much your household spends each month to use some of your appliances, you must first calculate the number of kilowatt-hours expended per month.

To do so, simply multiply the power rating in kilowatts (from the second column) by the number of hours the appliance is used each month. If you use a 1-kilowatt toaster for five hours a month, you would multiply 1 times 5.

Write your answers in column 4 of Table 1, as shown in the sample below.

Appliance	Power rating in kilowatts	Estimated hours per month in use	Number kWh per month	Price per kWh	Total cost per month
Microwave	1.35 kW	22 hours	29.7		

3   Determine the monthly cost of using your appliances

Utility companies charge consumers for the number of kilowatt-hours of electricity they use each month. Many houses and apartments have a meter attached to the outside of the building. The meter uses a system of spinning disks to record how much electricity you use. Someone from the electric company reads the meters once each month.

Find out how much you pay per kilowatt-hour (or kWh). In some areas, one utility company provides all the electricity to an entire region, while in another places, several electric companies compete for customers.

a. Research your area and write the price per kilowatt-hour in column 5 of Table 1.

b. Calculate the amount of money your household spends to operate each appliance during one month. Multiply the kilowatt-hours per month by the price per kilowatt-hour in order to determine your cost.

4   Analyze your data

a. Compare your results with those of the other members of your group. List the three appliances from your group that had the highest power ratings in Table 2.

b. Think about the function of each appliance listed above. What kind of work is being done? In other words, electrical energy is converted into what other type(s) of energy?

c. Do you see any similarities in the kinds of work being done by the three appliances in Table 2? If so, what are they?

d. Suggest one practical way you or another group member could reduce your electricity bills.

e. Discuss the effect of climate on electricity use. What climate factors might influence which month has the peak electrical use in your area?

f. Name one other factor (not related to climate) that may influence which month has the highest electricity use in your area.

Table 2: Appliances with the highest power ratings

Appliance	Power rating in kilowatts

5   ## What do you buy from the electric utility company?

People often use the phrase "power plant" to refer to their local electric company. You may have heard people say that electric companies "sell power" to their customers, or that there was a "power shortage" in a particular area. Let's take a look at these phrases from a scientific perspective. What, exactly, do electric companies sell?

We know that electricity bills charge for the number of kilowatt-hours (or kWh) used per month.

Let's first change kilowatt-hours to the units of watts and seconds:

$$1 \text{ kilowatt} \cdot \text{hour} \times \frac{1000 \text{ watts}}{\text{kilowatt}} = 1000 \text{ watt} \cdot \text{hours}$$

$$1000 \text{ watt} \cdot \text{hour} \times \frac{3600 \text{ seconds}}{\text{hour}} = 3,600,000 \text{ watt} \cdot \text{seconds}$$

(You may remember from previous study of fractions that a term appearing in both the numerator and denominator will cancel when the fractions are multiplied.)

Power is equal to the amount of work done per unit of time, or the amount of energy transferred in a circuit per unit of time. In specific units, a watt is equal to joules per second. We substitute the fundamental units of joules per second for watts.

$$3,600,000 \left(\frac{\text{joules}}{\text{second}} \right) \cdot \text{seconds} = ?$$

a.   Which terms in the last equation will cancel?

b.   After canceling the terms that appear in both the numerator and denominator, what is the fundamental unit that remains?

c.   Is the remaining unit a measure of energy, work, or power?

d.   Do electric companies sell energy, work, or power?

9.1 **More Electric Circuits**

Question: What kinds of electric circuits can you build?

In this Investigation, you will:

1. Build and compare series and parallel circuits.
2. Apply your knowledge of circuits to a real situation.

There are two different types of circuits, called series and parallel circuits. *Series circuits* have only one path for the flow of current. *Parallel circuits* have two or more paths for the flow of current. What does a simple circuit that rings a warning bell in your car have in common with the complex circuits that run computers? All circuits use series and parallel circuits, by themselves or combined with each other. In this Investigation, you will build these circuits and explore a common application of them.

◆**Safety Tips: Be careful working with batteries. If they are damaged, return them immediately to your teacher.**

If a battery or wire gets hot, disconnect the circuit and ask your teacher for help.

Always have a bulb somewhere in your circuit. Do not connect a wire directly from one terminal of the battery to the other terminal or you will make a short circuit.

1 **Building two kinds of circuits**

1. Gather the following materials: two batteries and battery holders, two bulbs and bulb holders, and six connectors.
2. Build Circuit 1 pictured at right.
3. Trace the circuit path with a pencil from positive terminal to negative terminal. Does the current have any choice about where to go?

a.) Describe the brightness of the two bulbs.

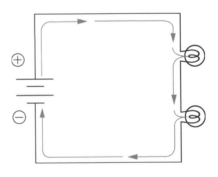

Circuit 1 (series circuit)

1. Build Circuit 2 pictured at right. The circuit "branches" at the square dots. If you are not sure how to build this configuration, ask your teacher for help.
2. Trace the circuit path with a pencil from positive terminal to negative terminal. Does the current have any choice about where to go?

b.) Describe the brightness of the two bulbs.

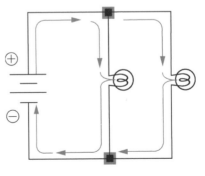

Circuit 2 (parallel circuit)

2 Analyzing your results

a. Compare the brightness of the bulbs in each kind of circuit. Which circuit has a greater transfer of energy?

b. Your household wiring is a parallel circuit, with each appliance or device on a separate branch of the circuit. With your group, discuss the possible advantages of using parallel circuits for a home. You can experiment with your parallel circuit to help you answer this question.

c. Write two paragraphs summarizing the points you discussed with your group, about the advantages of parallel circuits in the home.

3 An application of series and parallel circuits

Many circuits include multiple switches that are arranged in both series and parallel combinations. What is the purpose of these combinations?

If two switches are arranged in series, then both switches must be on for the circuit to work. This type of arrangement is called an **AND circuit**. If two switches are arranged in parallel, then only one switch needs to be on for the circuit to work. This type of arrangement is called an **OR circuit**.

Building an AND circuit

1. Gather the following additional materials: two switches and one connector. Build Circuit 3 pictured to the right.

2. Is this a series or parallel circuit?

3. Place a label next to each switch. Label one of the switches 1 and the other switch 2.

4. Try all combinations of switches: both on, both off, #1 on and #2 off, and #2 on and #1 off.

5. Record what happens to the bulb in each case.

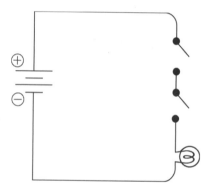

Circuit 3 (AND circuit)

Building an OR circuit

1. Build Circuit 4 pictured to the right.

2. Is this a series or parallel circuit?

3. Place a label next to each switch. Label one of the switches 1 and the other switch 2.

4. Try all combinations of switches: both on, both off, #1 on and #2 off, and #2 on and #1 off.

5. Record what happens to the bulb in each case.

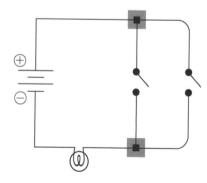

Circuit 4 (OR circuit)

A car will sound a warning bell if you open the door while the lights are on. Is this circuit an AND circuit or an OR circuit? Explain your reasoning.

9.2 Series Circuits

Question: How do you use Ohm's law in series circuits?

In this Investigation, you will:

1. Determine how to calculate total resistance in a series circuit.
2. Build a circuit with a dimmer switch.

⬥**Safety Tips: Be careful working with batteries. If they are damaged, return them immediately to your teacher.**

If a battery, resistor, or wire gets hot, disconnect the circuit and ask your teacher for help.

Always have a bulb or resistor somewhere in your circuit. Do not connect a wire directly from one terminal of the battery to the other terminal. This is a short circuit, which can start a fire.

1 Adding resistors in series circuits

1. Gather the following materials: Electrical meter and test leads, two batteries and battery holders, two 5-ohm resistors, one 10-ohm resistor, and five wire connectors.
2. Label the three resistors R1, R2, and R3. Measure the resistance of each and record the values in Table 1.

Table 1: Voltage and resistance values of your parts

R1 Resistance (ohms)	R2 Resistance (ohms)	R3 Resistance (ohms)	Battery voltage (volts)

3. Build circuit 1 as shown right. Use the R1 resistor.
4. Use the electrical meter to measure the voltage across both batteries. Record the value in Table 1.
5. Use the electrical meter to measure current through the circuit. Record the value in Table 2 on the next page.
6. Add the R2 resistor to the circuit. Your circuit has two resistors in total.
7. Measure current through the circuit. Record the value in Table 2.
8. Add the R3 resistor to the circuit. Your circuit has three resistors in total.
9. Measure current through the circuit. Record the value in Table 2.
10. Using Ohm's law (in the form R = V/I), calculate total resistance in each circuit, using the battery voltage (from Table 1) and the current for each circuit (from Table 2).
11. Record your results in Table 2.

Study your calculated resistances in Table 2. What is the rule for calculating total resistance in a series circuit, from individual resistances?

Table 2: Measurements of current when resistors are added in a circuit

	Circuit with R1	Circuit with R1 and R2	Circuit with R1, R2, and R3
Current in amps			
Resistance in ohms			

2   Building a circuit with a dimmer switch

Resistors are commonly used in series circuits. When a resistor is connected in series with a device, the energy of the charges moving through the circuit is divided up between the two components. Build a circuit with one battery, one bulb, and the potentiometer. In this circuit, the potentiometer and the bulb are connected in series. Observe what happens to the bulb when you turn the dial.

Can you think of other dials that turn that might have a potentiometer inside? With your group, list possible potentiometers. For each example in your list, explain why changing resistance is useful.

3   Finding the resistance of a bulb

If you measure the resistance of a bulb your value will not be very useful. This is because the resistance of a bulb changes depending on the amount of current through it. It *is* useful to know the resistance of your bulb at different values of current! You will find this information using the following procedure:

1. Using the dimmer switch circuit, turn the potentiometer until the bulb is very dim.
2. Record approximate bulb brightness in Table 3.
3. Measure voltage across the bulb. Record the value in Table 3.
4. Measure current through the circuit. Record the value in Table 3.
5. Make the bulb a little bit brighter and repeat steps 2, 3 and 4. Continue until you have completed Table 3 for five settings of the potentiometer.
6. Use Ohm's law to calculate bulb resistance and fill in the last column of Table 3.

Table 3: Resistance of a bulb at different levels of current

Potentiometer setting	How bright is the bulb?	Bulb voltage (volts)	Current (amps)	Bulb resistance (ohms)
First setting				
Second setting				
Third setting				
Fourth setting				
Fifth setting				

a.   Graph bulb resistance vs. current for each potentiometer setting. Label your axes and title your graph. (Keep this graph for use in your next Investigation.)

b.   What happens to bulb resistance when current is higher?

c.   At higher temperatures, the tungsten atoms in the light bulb filament move around more. With your group, propose an explanation for why resistance of tungsten increases with temperature.

9.3 Parallel Circuits

Question: How do parallel circuits work?

In this Investigation, you will:

1. Build and analyze parallel circuits.
2. Determine how total current and branch currents are related in parallel circuits.
3. Apply your understanding of parallel circuits by building a test voltage circuit.

In the last Investigation, you learned how to use Ohm's law in series circuits. In this Investigation, you will build parallel circuits and measure their electrical quantities. Parallel circuits are complex and are not intuitive, so you will need to examine your data carefully to understand how these circuits work.

◆ **Safety Tips: Be careful working with batteries. If they are damaged or broken, return them immediately to your teacher.**

1 ## Measuring current and voltage in a parallel circuit

Series Circuit

1. Gather the following materials: Electrical meter and its test leads, two batteries and battery holders, two bulbs and bulb holders, and six wire connectors.
2. Using both batteries, build the series circuit shown right.
3. Measure current through the circuit and record it in the table below.
4. Measure and record the voltage drop across the bulb. Record the value in the table.
5. Calculate resistance using Ohm's law. Record it in the table.

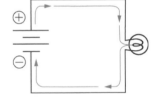

Parallel Circuit

1. Using both batteries, build the parallel circuit shown at right. Measure current through branch 1 and branch 2. Record the values in the table below.
2. Measure and record the voltage drop across each bulb.
3. Using Ohm's law, calculate the resistance in each branch. Record the values in the table below.

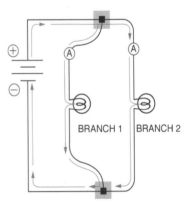

Series circuit		Parallel circuit	branch 1	branch 2
Current		**Current**		
Voltage drop		**Voltage drop**		
Resistance		**Resistance**		

2   **What did you learn?**

a.   Compare the current, voltage drops, and resistance in the series circuit with the parallel circuit.

b.   Your results should indicate that each branch of the parallel circuit is like another series circuit attached to the battery. As a result, the voltage drop is the same in all branches of a parallel circuit, and is equal to the voltage provided by the battery. What is happening in the battery as more parallel branches are added?

3   **What is important about current values in parallel circuits?**

a.   In parallel circuits, there is one part of the circuit path where all the charges flow through. This is where the current leaves and enters the battery terminals. In your parallel circuit, measure the total current at one of the battery terminals. Record your results.

b.   Compare the total current you just measured with the branch currents in the table above. What is the relationship between branch currents and total current in a parallel circuit?

4   **Building a test voltage circuit**

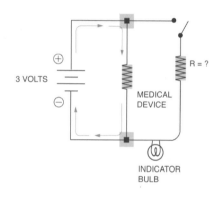

3 VOLTS

R = ?

MEDICAL
DEVICE

INDICATOR
BULB

Portable electrical devices like radios and cell phones run on batteries. Usually, you only discover that the batteries are drained in these devices when they stop working. However, for some portable medical or industrial equipment, it is important to be able to anticipate when batteries need to be replaced. In this part of the Investigation, your challenge is to build a voltage test circuit that alerts you when battery voltage has dropped! A sample test voltage circuit is shown at left. Your goal is to determine the resistance that will cause the bulb to go out at 80 percent of the battery voltage. Follow the steps below; or, for a more difficult challenge, determine the resistance on your own.

a.   Use one battery, one bulb, and your potentiometer to build a dimmer light circuit. Slowly decrease resistance until the light bulb goes out. Measure and record current.

b.   Study the test voltage circuit diagram above. What is the voltage drop across each branch?

c.   What will be the voltage drop if the total battery voltage drops to 80 percent of its original value?

d.   Use Ohm's law to calculate the *total* resistance needed in the second branch of the test voltage circuit. This is the resistance that will cause the bulb to go out at 80 percent of the battery voltage! Use the voltage from step 4(c) and the current from step 4(a) to calculate total resistance.

e.   Use the graph of bulb resistance vs. current from the last Investigation to figure out the bulb resistance at the current you measured in step 4(a).

f.   Calculate the unknown resistance shown in the test voltage circuit. You know the total resistance from step 4(d) and the bulb resistance from step 4(e).

g.   Build the test voltage circuit. Use a 10-ohm resistor to represent the medical device. Before adding the potentiometer to the circuit, set it to the resistance you calculated in step 4(f). If your batteries are fully charged, the bulb should light when you turn on the switch!

h.   Your teacher will give you some used batteries. Label them and place them in your circuit. See if the light is off when you turn the switch!

10.1   Permanent Magnets

Question: What effects do magnets have?

In this Investigation, you will:

1. See how two magnets affect each other.
2. Measure the strength of the magnetic force.
3. Determine what kinds of materials are affected by magnets.
4. Determine if the magnetic force can be blocked by nonmagnetic materials.

In this Investigation, you will experiment with magnets in order to learn more about magnets and magnetic forces. The magnets you will use may not look like other magnets you've seen. The poles are on the opposite faces, as shown in the picture.

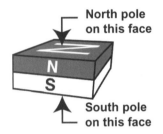

North pole on this face

South pole on this face

1   Describing the forces that two magnets exert on each other

a.   Try holding two magnets with their south poles facing each other. What happens?

b.   Try holding two magnets with their north poles facing each other. What happens?

c.   Try holding two magnets with north and south poles facing each other. What happens?

d.   Write down a rule that describes how magnets exert forces on each other. Your rule should take into account your observations from steps a-c, and should use at least two of the following words: attract, repel, north, south, and pole.

2   # Determining how far the magnetic force reaches

How far does the magnetic force of a magnet reach? This is an important question for machines that use magnets.

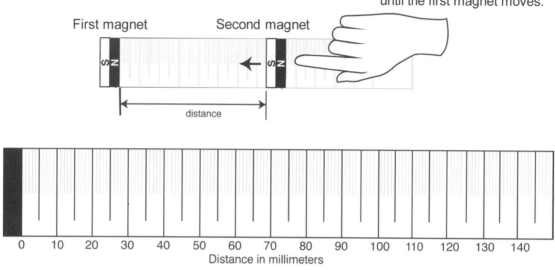

1. Place one magnet on the solid rectangle on the ruler above and slide a second magnet closer and closer until the first magnet moves. Practice the technique several times before recording data.

2. In Table 1 below, record the distance between the magnets when you first see movement. Measurements that are **precise** are very exactly stated. For example, a single measurement of 32.25 millimeters is more *precise* than a measurement of 32 millimeters. Move the magnet slowly enough to make your distance measurements precise to 0.5 millimeters. Try each of the combinations of poles, north-north, south-south, and north-south.

3. For each combination do three tries, and average your three distances. (To get the average, add the three distances together and divide the total by 3.) Record the average in Table 1.

4. When referring to many measurements of the same quantity, **precision** describes how close the measurements are to each other. Estimate the precision (in millimeters) of your measured magnet interaction distance using the largest difference between any one measurement and the average.

5. Look at your results and compare the average distances for the three combinations of poles. Are the attract and repel distances *significantly* different? In science, "significantly" means the differences are larger than the precision of your measurement.

Table 1: Magnetic forces between two magnets

	N-S	S-S	N-N
Distance 1			
Distance 2			
Distance 3			
Average distance			

3 | **Testing materials to see if they are affected by magnets**

Not all materials are affected by magnetic forces. In this part of the Investigation you will see which materials respond to a magnet.

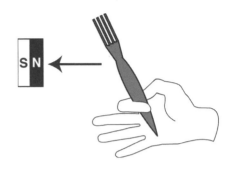

Use one of your magnets to try the set of materials your teacher will give you. You can try other materials in the classroom as well. See if each object is affected by the magnet. If it is, determine whether it is attracted to or repelled by the magnet. Record your data in Table 2 below.

Table 2: How different objects are affected by magnets

Object	Material composition	Attract	Repel	No effect

The word "magnetic" is used to describe things that are affected strongly by magnets. Look at your data table. How would you describe the things that are magnetic and the things that are not? Use the following words in your answer: magnetic and nonmagnetic.

4   Do nonmagnetic materials affect the magnetic force?

You may have experimented with making a magnet move on top of a table by moving a second magnet underneath the table. Does the table affect the strength of the magnetic force? In this part of the Investigation, you will find out if magnetic forces get weaker or stronger passing through nonmagnetic materials.

1. From Table 2 above, choose several nonmagnetic materials.
2. Place one magnet on the black rectangle on the ruler below and slide a second magnet closer and closer until the first magnet moves.
3. Record the distance in table 3 when you first see movement.
4. Put each nonmagnetic material between the two magnets and repeat the experiment.

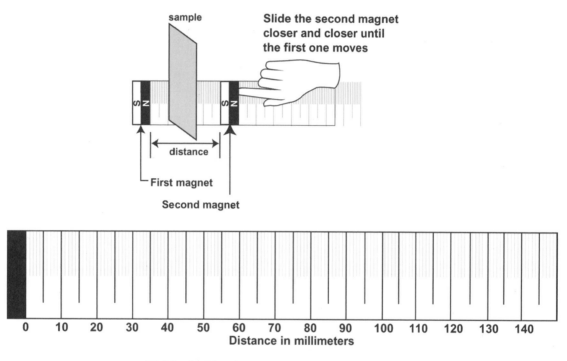

Table 3: Testing nonmagnetic materials

	N-S	S-S	N-N
Distance 1			
Distance 2			
Distance 3			
Average distance			

What did you find out about how magnetism is affected by nonmagnetic materials? Use the words *force* and *distance* in your answer.

10.2 Electromagnets

Question: Can electric current create a magnet?

In this Investigation, you will:

1. Build an electromagnet.
2. Measure the electromagnet's strength as the current is varied.

Electromagnets are magnets that are created when there is electric current through a wire. The simplest electromagnet uses a coil of wire, often wrapped around some iron or steel. The iron or steel concentrates the magnetic field created by the current in the coil.

By controlling current, you can easily change the strength of an electromagnet or even turn its magnetism on and off. Electromagnets can also be much stronger than permanent magnets because the electric current can be great. For these reasons, electromagnets are widely used. Stereo speakers, toasters, doorbells, car alternators, and power plant electrical generators are just a few of the many devices that use electromagnets.

Safety Tip: Disconnect your electromagnet when not in use, as the batteries can get hot.

1 Build an electromagnet

1. Collect the following materials: three batteries and holders, magnet wire, two nails, a permanent magnet, 10 paper clips, and sandpaper.

2. Wrap one nail tightly with magnetic wire as shown at right. Make sure your wire turns are neat, tight, and evenly spaced or the electromagnet may not work. Use all of the magnet wire except for about 30 cm of wire straight on each end. This is your electromagnet coil.

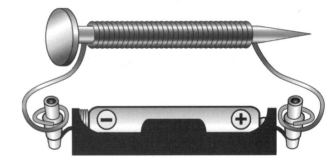

3. Sand the two ends of the wire, as they have a coating on them.

4. Attach the ends of the coil to one battery on the electricity grid. Wrap each end of the electromagnet wire tightly around the posts connected to the battery.

2 Compare electromagnets and permanent magnets

a. This coil certainly doesn't look much like the permanent magnets we are more familiar with. Using what you know about magnets from the last Investigation, think of at least two tests to show that your electromagnet acts like the permanent magnets you used in that Investigation. Record your two proposed tests.

b. Perform the two tests. Record your observations.

c. Does the electromagnet act like a permanent magnet? Write down your conclusion, and how you arrived at it.

3   ## The right hand rule

In an electromagnet, the magnetic poles are located at each end of the coil. Which end is the north pole depends on the direction of the electric current. When your fingers curl in the direction of current, your thumb points toward the magnet's north pole. This method of finding the magnetic poles is called the *right hand rule*.

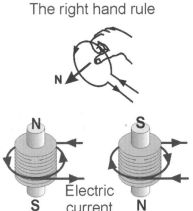

The right hand rule

a. Determine the direction of current through the electromagnet. (The current flows from the positive terminal to the negative terminal.)

b. Use the right hand rule to determine the north and south poles of your electromagnet. Record your answer with a drawing.

4   ## What happens to the strength of an electromagnet when you increase the current?

1. Measure the current through your electromagnet and test how many paper clips it can pick up.

2. Increase the current through the electromagnet by connecting it to two batteries. Again measure the current and test how many paper clips it can pick up.

3. Repeat step 2 using three batteries.

4. Record all your results in the table below.

Number of batteries	Current (in amps)	Number of paper clips picked up
1		
2		
3		

5   ## What did you learn?

a. Draw a graph showing how the number of paper clips picked up by the magnet varies as the current is increased. Answer the following questions first: Which variable goes on the *x*-axis? Which variable goes on the *y*-axis?

b. Label your axes and title your graph.

c. What is your conclusion about the relationship between current and strength of the electromagnet?

d. Prepare a poster summarizing the results of this experiment. Include your data table and graph on the poster. Display your electromagnet with your poster.

e. Look at other groups' electromagnets, data tables, and graphs. Did some electromagnets work better than others? Write down anything you notice that might explain differences in performance.

10.3 **Electric Motors and Generators**

Question: How does an electric motor or generator work?

In this Investigation, you will:

1. Build an electric motor and measure its speed.
2. Design different electric motors and evaluate them for speed and electric power.
3. Build and test several designs of electric generator.

Electric motors are everywhere. You find them in locomotives, washing machines, cars, tools, spacecraft, and anywhere else that we use powered machines. All electric motors use one or both of the two kinds of magnets we just explored, permanent magnets and electromagnets. Permanent magnets are useful because they create the magnetic field without needing any electricity. We will discover that electromagnets are necessary because the north and south poles can be reversed.

1   **Getting the rotor to spin**

Electric motors spin because of the action of magnetism. Try to get the rotor to spin by manipulating magnets.

1. Take the motor apart, and put 6 magnets in the rotor so they are evenly spaced and alternate North - South facing outwards.
2. Bring a stack of two or three magnets close and try to repel one of the magnets in the rotor. The rotor should spin a little.
3. As soon as you move one magnet, reverse the magnet in your fingers and try to get attract, then repel the next magnet on the rotor.
4. By sequentially reversing the magnet in your fingers, try to push and pull on the magnets in the rotor to get the motor to spin.

The reversing of the magnet in your fingers is the key to making the rotor spin.

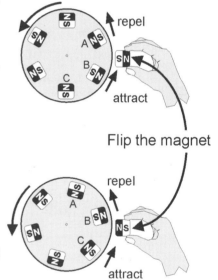

a. When is the right time to reverse the magnet in your fingers? Think about where the magnets in the rotor are.

b. How could you make the rotor spin the other way?

2   **Making a 4-pole electric motor**

The key to understanding how electric motors work is learning how electromagnets are used to alternately attract and repel other magnets. If we arrange the electromagnets and permanent magnets just right, the rotor will turn when electricity is connected. The first motor to build is called a 4-pole motor because you are going to use 4 magnets to make 2 north poles and 2 south poles in the rotor.

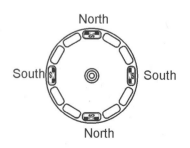

All electric motors use some kind of switch to change the electromagnets from north to south at the right time. The device which makes the electromagnets change form north to south is called the **commutator**. The commutator in the Electric Motor you are building is a plastic disk and it switches the electromagnets using light.

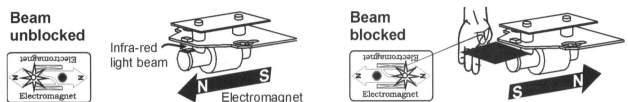

When the light is not blocked (see diagram above) the current flows in a direction to make the north pole at the front of the electromagnet. Blocking the beam causes the current to reverse, making a north pole at the back, and a south pole at the front. There are two green LED's that indicate where the north pole is.

The commutator disks have alternating black and clear sections around the edge that switch the electromagnets by blocking the light beam. Aligning the clear/black edges with the centers of the magnets ensures that the switching happens in the right place.

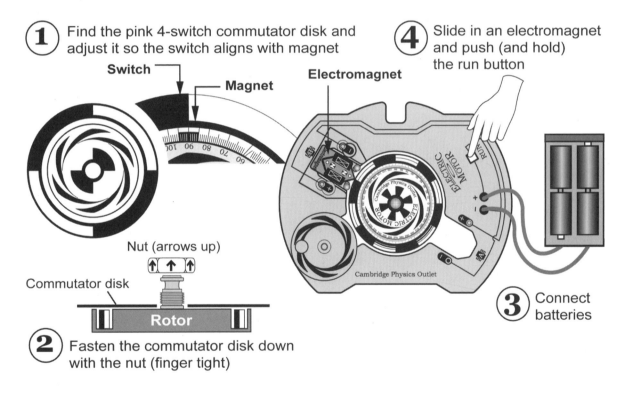

1. Find the red four-pole commutator disk shown in the picture.
2. Arrange 4 magnets so the north or south poles alternate as shown.
3. Be sure the disk is aligned so the border between clear and black is centered on each of the four magnets. The border is where the electromagnet will switch from north to south and back.
4. Finger tighten the big nut to secure the switch plate once you have it aligned with the magnets.
5. Attach one electromagnet to any position. To make the electrical connections the electromagnet should be pushed forward and the thumb-nuts gently tightened. Don't over-tighten the thumb nuts.
6. Push and hold the RUN button. You usually need to give the motor a push to get it started spinning.

3 Designing and testing different electric motors

Design and test a working electric motor for each of the commutator disks. Use the design charts to record your design, including the direction (north and south) and position of all magnets. Put an X where you placed the electromagnet. Record only designs that work. Keep changing things until you get a design that works for each commutator disk.

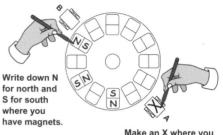

Write down N for north and S for south where you have magnets.

Make an X where you have an electromagnet.

Pink Disk

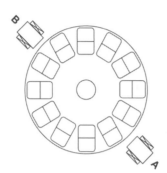

Orange Disk

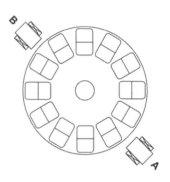

Blue Disk

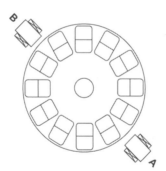

Yellow Disk

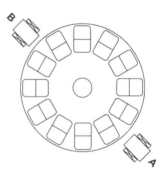

Green Disk: Version 1

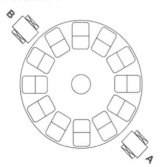

Green Disk: Version 2

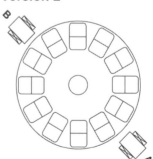

4   Testing for Performance

Engineers usually want to build the best possible machine. Somewhere along the process of design we must define exactly what 'best' means. The word 'best' might mean fastest, least expensive, lightest, strongest, most shock resistant, or most attractive. It is usually impossible to be best in all categories. The engineer has to choose which categories to be best in depending on what the machine will be used for. One convenient measure for an electric motor is the top speed of the rotor. We can choose the best design as the one that goes fastest.

1. Set up the photogate timer with one photogate attached to the motor as shown. When the photogate is all the way in the slot, the black and clear segments of the disk break the beam as the motor spins.

2. Set the timer to measure FREQUENCY. When measuring frequency, the timer counts the number of times the beam is broken in one second. As the motor speeds up, the light beam gets broken more times per second.

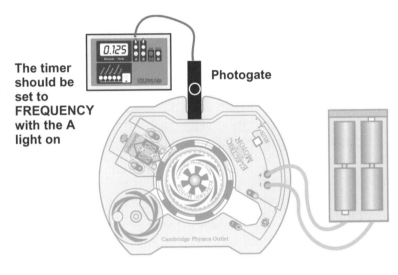

$$\text{Rotation speed (rpm)} = \frac{\text{frequency}}{\text{Number of black segments}} \times 60 \, \tfrac{\text{sec}}{\text{min}}$$

We want to calculate the speed in revolutions per minute (rpm). The formula above shows you how to calculate the speed if you know how many times the light beam gets broken for each turn of the disk.

You can adjust things to make the motor go faster. Adjust your design until you have reached what you think is the highest speed you can get.

a. Which motor design gave you the highest speed and why do you think it was higher than the others? Your answer should identify the commutator disk and number of magnets you used.

b. What variables did you adjust that had an effect on the speed? Can you give any explanation for why you think the variables you adjusted made a difference to the speed?

c. What would happen to your speed comparisons if the batteries were fully charged for the first trial but slowly lost their power later in the experiment?

d. Can you think of a way to be sure the experimental results were not affected by the draining of the batteries? Write down a procedure that would give you a way to check whether the batteries were still the same all through the experiment.

5   How much electricity does a motor use?

It takes electrical current to make the electromagnet work, and voltage to provide the energy to make the current flow.

1. Build a motor design that you know works well.

2. Check the voltage of the battery pack with the motor off. It should be at least 6 volts.

3. To measure voltage, connect the meter to two (+ and -) thumb-nuts anywhere on the motor. Measure the voltage with the motor on, but stopped. Use your finger to stop the motor from turning. Also measure the voltage with the motor spinning. Record the measurements in the table below.

4. Connect the meter in series with the battery pack so you can measure the current used by the motor. Measure the current with the motor on but stopped, and with the motor on and running.

Table 1: Electrical measurements

	Motor on & stopped		Motor on and running
Voltage (volts)		Voltage (volts)	
Current (amps)		Current (amps)	

a. Is there a difference in the voltage with the motor stopped compared to when it is running?

b. Is there a difference in the current with the motor stopped compared to when it is running?

c. Power is equal to voltage times current. Calculate the power used by the motor when it is on but stopped, and also when it is on and running.

Table 2: Power calculations

	Motor on & stopped		Motor on and running
Power (watts)		Power (watts)	

d. Does the motor use more power when it is running or when it is stopped but still on? Use your observations to explain why electric motors in machines often burn out if the machine jams and the motor is prevented from turning even though the electricity is still on.

e. When the motor is running, the energy goes to overcoming friction and adding kinetic energy to the rotor by making it go faster. Where does the energy go when you stop the motor from turning but the electricity is still flowing?

f. How much power does your motor use compared to a 100 watt light bulb? Your answer should show a calculation of how many motors you could run using the electricity used by the 100 watt bulb.

g. The horsepower is the average power that could be produced by a working horse. One horsepower is equal to 746 watts. Electric motors are usually rated in horsepower. For example, a table saw might have a 1.5 horsepower electric motor. Calculate how many horsepower your motor makes.

6   Electric generators

Moving current in a wire makes magnetism. That is how electromagnets work. The opposite process also works. Moving a magnet near a coil of wire makes current flow in the wire.

The generator coil does not have the light sensor. The coil of wire is connected directly to the positive and negative terminals.

Connect the meter to the coil terminals and set the meter to measure AC volts.

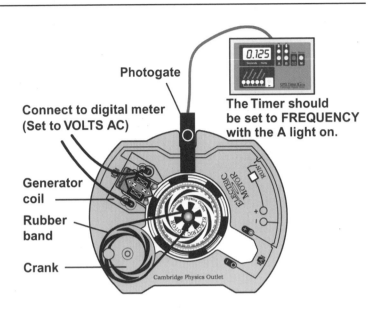

Photogate

Connect to digital meter (Set to VOLTS AC)

The Timer should be set to FREQUENCY with the A light on.

Generator coil

Rubber band

Crank

1. Put two magnets in the rotor on opposite sides of the rotor, with north and south alternating facing out.

2. Put the blue disk on the rotor and fasten it with the nut. It does not matter how you rotate the disk since it is only being used to break the light beam to measure the speed of the rotor.

3. Attach a photogate as you did before and set the timer to measure frequency. The higher the frequency, the faster the rotor is turning.

4. Stretch a rubber band around the crank and the spindle of the motor. You can spin the rotor by turning the crank. The timer will measure the speed and the meter will measure the amount of electricity you generate.

5. With two magnets in the rotor, spin the motor at frequencies of 20, 40, and 80 on the timer. Measure and record the voltage you generate in the table.

6. Repeat the last step with 4 magnets in the rotor, 6 magnets, and 12 magnets. The magnets should always alternate north and south. For each change of magnets, run the same frequencies (20, 40, 80). Record all the data in the table below.

Table 3: Electric generator data (AC volts)

Rotation frequency	Voltage with 2 magnets	Voltage with 4 magnets	Voltage with 6 magnets	Voltage with 12 magnets
20 Hz				
40 Hz				
80 Hz				

Look at your measurements and compare the voltages you got with different numbers of magnets and different speeds.

a. How does increasing the speed affect the voltage generated? If you double the speed, how much does the voltage change?

b. How does changing the number of magnets affect the voltage generated? If you double the number of magnets, how much does the voltage change?

Harmonic Motion

Question: How do we describe the back-and-forth motion of a pendulum?

In this Investigation, you will:

1. Measure the amplitude and period of a pendulum.
2. Determine how to change the properties of a pendulum.
3. Design and build a pendulum clock that accurately measures 30 seconds.

 Harmonic motion is the term used to describe motion that repeats itself over and over. An oscillator is something that makes harmonic motion. A pendulum is a good example of an oscillator. In this Investigation you will measure and explain the properties of a pendulum. You will need to apply the concepts of cycle, period, and amplitude to accurately describe the harmonic motion of your pendulum.

1   Setting up the pendulum

Attach the pendulum to one of the top holes in the stand.

Attach a photogate so the pendulum bob swings through the light beam. Adjust the position of the string in the slot so the pendulum bob swings through the photogate without hitting the sides. You may also have to adjust the leveling feet at the bottom of the stand.

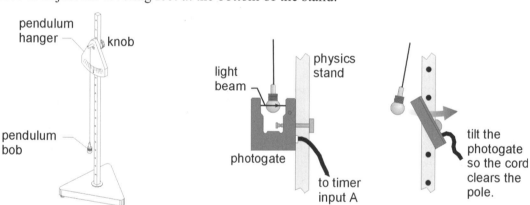

Put the Timer in period mode and attach a single photogate to input A. Use the "A" button and the reset button to make measurements.

1. When the **A** light is **on**, the display shows the period defined by successive breaks in the light beam.
2. The red (**O**) button resets the timer to zero.

When the pendulum swings through the photogate, the timer will measure the period of time between two light beam breaks. It takes a few swings for the timer to make the measurement.

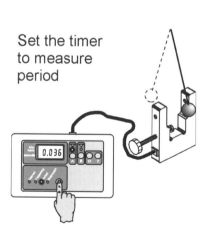

Set the timer to measure period

NOTE: The picture to the right shows a pendulum completing one cycle. The length of time for the pendulum to complete one cycle is called the period.

The timer in period mode measures time between the first break and the second break of the light beam on the photogate. This length of time is only half of the actual period because the pendulum swing time before the first break and after the second break is not measured. To get the correct length of time for the complete period, multiply the timer reading by two.

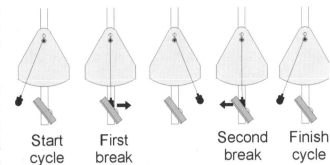

| Start cycle | First break | | Second break | Finish cycle |

2   Testing the three variables

In this experiment, the period of the pendulum is the only dependent variable. There are three independent variables: the mass of the bob, the amplitude of the swing, and the length of the string.

Measuring the length of the string

1. The length of the string can be changed by sliding it through the slot in the peg. Measure the length of the string from the bottom of the string peg to the bottom of the washers.

2. There are washers that you can use to change the mass of the bob.

3. The amplitude can be changed by varying the angle that the pendulum swings.

Design an experiment to determine which of the three variables has the largest effect on the period of the pendulum. Your experiment should provide enough data to show that one of the three variables has much more of an effect that the other two. Be sure to use a consistent technique that gives you consistent results.

Table 1: Period, Amplitude, Mass, and Length Data

Number of washers	Amplitude (degrees)	String length (cm)	Time from timer (seconds)	Period of pendulum (seconds)

3   Analyzing the data

a.   Of the three things you can change (length, mass, and angle), which one has the biggest effect on the pendulum, and why? In your answer you should consider how gravity accelerates objects of different mass.

b.   Split up your data so that you can look at the effect of each of the three variables by making a separate graph showing how each one affects the period. To make comparison easier, make sure all the graphs have the same scale on the *y*-axis (period). The graphs should be labeled like the example below.

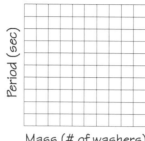
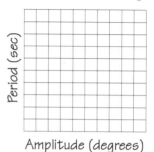

4   Applying what you know

Pendulum clocks were once among the most common ways to keep time. It is still possible to find beautifully made pendulum clocks for sale today. To make a pendulum clock accurate, the period must be set so a certain number of periods equals a convenient measure of time. For example, you could design a clock with a pendulum that has a period of 1 second. The gears in the clock mechanism would then have to turn the second hand 1/60th of a turn per swing of the pendulum.

a.   Using your data, design and construct a pendulum that you can use to accurately measure a time interval of 30 seconds. Test your pendulum clock against the electronic stopwatch.

b.   Mark on your graph the period you chose for your pendulum.

c.   How many cycles did your pendulum complete in 30 seconds?

d.   If mass does not affect the period, why is it important that the pendulum in a clock is heavy?

e.   Calculate the percent error in your prediction of time from your pendulum clock. The percent error is 100 times the difference between your prediction and 30 seconds, divided by 30 seconds.

f.   You notice in a magazine that a watch manufacturer advertises that its quartz watch loses no more than 5 seconds per month. Assume that the watch loses the maximum amount (5 seconds) in 31 days. Calculate the percent error of the quartz watch by comparing 5 seconds to the number of seconds in a month.

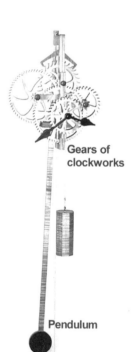

Gears of clockworks

Pendulum

5   Damping and energy loss

Like all moving systems, oscillators lose energy due to friction. That means any machine that uses an oscillator has to have a way to put energy back in to keep things swinging! Grandfather clocks have heavy weights that slowly fall down and give up their energy to keep the pendulum swinging at a constant amplitude. The weights have to be lifted every few days or the clock runs out of energy and stops.

Set up an experiment to investigate how fast the pendulum loses energy.

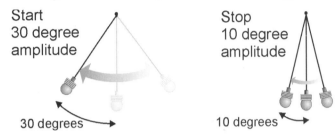

1. To measure the energy-loss record the time it takes the pendulum amplitude to decrease from 30 degrees to 10 degrees.
2. Change the mass four times, keeping string length constant.
3. Change the string length four times, keeping mass constant.

Table 2: Damping Data

Mass (washers)	String length (cm)	Time to decay from 30 degrees to 10 degrees (sec)

a.   Plot two graphs that show how the damping time changes with mass and string length.

b.   Suppose you had to design a real pendulum clock that would keep swinging for many days. From the results of your experiment, how would you choose string length and mass? Explain how your choices are based on your observations.

11.2 **Graphs of Harmonic Motion**

Question: How do we make graphs of harmonic motion?

In this Investigation, you will:

1. Create graphs showing harmonic motion.
2. Use graphs of harmonic motion to determine period and amplitude.

1 Simple harmonic motion graph

 Make a graph from the data table below. Draw a smooth curve that most closely shows the pattern in the data. Answer the questions about the graph.

time (sec)	0.5	1.0	1.5	2.0	2.5	3.0	3.5	4.0	4.5	5.0	5.5	6.0	6.5	7.0	7.5	8.0	8.5	9.0
position (cm)	0.9	0.9	0.0	-0.9	-0.9	0.0	0.9	0.9	0.0	-0.9	-0.9	0.0	0.9	0.9	0.0	-0.9	-0.9	0.0

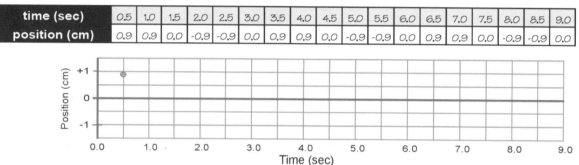

a. What is the amplitude of the graph in centimeters?

b. What is the period of the graph in seconds?

2 Comparing harmonic motion graphs

 Two different groups of students are doing experiments on giant pendulums with very long periods. Both groups use the same clock to record time. Below are two sets of position vs. time data, one from each group. Graph the data and answer the questions.

time (sec)	0.5	1.0	1.5	2.0	2.5	3.0	3.5	4.0	4.5	5.0	5.5	6.0	6.5	7.0	7.5	8.0	8.5	9.0
position #1 (cm)	0.7	1.0	0.7	0.0	-0.7	-1.0	-0.7	0.0	0.7	1.0	0.7	0.0	-0.7	-1.0	-0.7	0.0	0.7	1.0
position #2 (cm)	0.0	0.7	1.0	0.7	0.0	-0.7	-1.0	-0.7	0.0	0.7	1.0	0.7	0.0	-0.7	-1.0	-0.7	0.0	0.7

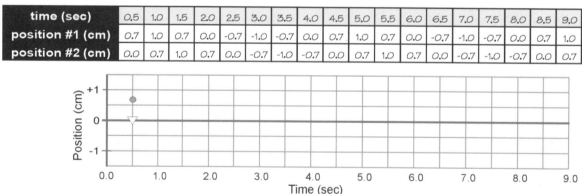

a. Which pendulum was most probably released first? In your answer you must use the word "phase" to explain how you chose which pendulum started first.

b. How much time was there between the start of the lead pendulum and the start of the other pendulum?

3 A complex harmonic motion graph

A clever inventor is trying to build a pendulum that can have two periods at the same time. The pendulum is actually two pendulums, with a very light, short pendulum swinging from a much heavier long pendulum, as shown in the diagram. The position vs. time graph for the combined pendulum was measured. The combined position is the position of the small pendulum while it is swinging from the long pendulum. The graph below shows the motion of the combined pendulum. Answer the three questions from this graph.

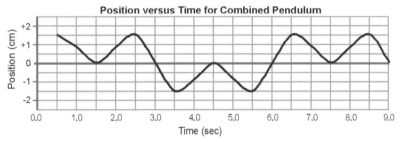

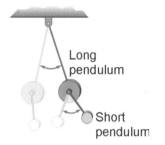

a.   What is the amplitude of the combined pendulum in centimeters?

b.   What is the period of the combined pendulum in seconds?

c.   In one or two sentences, describe the difference between the graphs of the single pendulums and the graph of the combined pendulum.

4 How to get a complex graph

The inventor has a theory that the combined motion is the sum of the separate motions of the short and long pendulum. The inventor measured the position vs. time for the short pendulum and the long pendulum separately. To test this theory, add up the positions for the short and long pendulums that were measured separately. For each point in time, write the sum on the line in the table below labeled "Long plus short." Graph the position vs. time for the combined pendulum.

a.   Does the graph confirm or disprove the inventor's theory? Explain your answer in a few sentences.

time (sec)	0.5	1.0	1.5	2.0	2.5	3.0	3.5	4.0	4.5	5.0	5.5	6.0	6.5	7.0	7.5	8.0	8.5	9.0
Long Pendulum (cm)	0.5	0.9	1.0	0.9	0.5	0.0	-0.5	-0.9	-1.0	-0.9	-0.5	0.0	0.5	0.9	1.0	0.9	0.5	0.0
Short Pendulum (cm)	1.0	0.0	-1.0	0.0	1.0	0.0	-1.0	0.0	1.0	0.0	-1.0	0.0	1.0	0.0	-1.0	0.0	1.0	0.0
Long plus Short (cm)																		

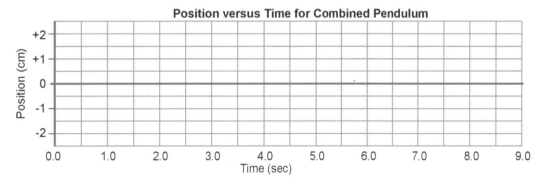

11.3 Simple Mechanical Oscillators

Question: What kinds of systems oscillate?

In this Investigation, you will:

1. Create an oscillator and measure its period.
2. Apply the concepts of restoring force and inertia to change the period of your oscillator.

When we disturb a system in equilibrium we often get motion. In addition, we *sometimes* get harmonic motion. A marble on the curved track of the roller coaster is a good example. There is an equilibrium for the marble at the bottom of the valley. If we move the marble partly up the hill and release it, we get harmonic motion. The marble oscillates back and forth around its equilibrium point.

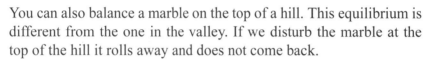

You can also balance a marble on the top of a hill. This equilibrium is different from the one in the valley. If we disturb the marble at the top of the hill it rolls away and does not come back.

The top of a hill is an example of *unstable* equilibrium. In unstable systems there are forces that act to pull the system *away* from equilibrium when disturbed. The bottom of a valley is an example of *stable* equilibrium. In a stable system there are forces always acting to restore the system to equilibrium when it is disturbed. We find harmonic motion in stable systems.

1 Find an example of a stable system and an unstable system

a. Describe your example of a stable system in one or two sentences. What happens when you push it a little away from equilibrium? Write one sentence that describes the motion.

b. Describe your example of an unstable system in one or two sentences. What happens when you push the unstable system a little away from equilibrium? Write one sentence that describes the motion.

2 Making a mechanical oscillator

With mechanical systems like a pendulum, harmonic motion comes from the action of forces and inertia. A *restoring force* is any force that always tries to pull a system back to equilibrium. The restoring force (or gravity) always pulls the pendulum toward center no matter which side it is on. Because it has inertia, the pendulum overshoots, passes right through the middle, and keeps going. The restoring force then slows it and accelerates it back toward equilibrium. But, the pendulum overshoots again and goes too far the other direction. The cycle (below) repeats over and over to create harmonic motion.

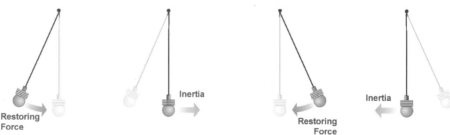

✐ To make a mechanical oscillator, you need to provide some kind of restoring force connected to a mass that can supply the inertia. A rubber band with a steel bolt tied to the middle makes a perfect oscillator. So does a wok and a tennis ball. See if you can find a creative way to make your own oscillator.

a. Create a system that oscillates. You may use anything you can find, including springs, rubber bands, rulers, balloons, blocks of wood, or anything else that may be safely assembled.

b. Draw a sketch of your system and identify what makes the restoring force.

c. On your sketch, also identify where the mass that creates the inertia is located.

3 Measuring and changing the period of your oscillator

Rubber bands, strings, elastic bands, and curved tracks can all provide restoring forces. Steel marbles, wood blocks, or even the rubber band itself, have mass to supply inertia. To change the period of your oscillator, you need to change the balance between force and inertia.

Period is proportional to the ratio of $\dfrac{\text{Mass (Inertia)}}{\text{Restoring Force}}$

To INCREASE the period ...	To DECREASE the period ...
increase the mass, or	decrease the mass, or
decrease the restoring force	increase the restoring force

a. Estimate or measure the period of your oscillator in seconds. You may use photogates or stopwatches to make your measurements. Describe how you made your measurement and write down some representative periods for your oscillator.

b. Describe and test a way to increase the period of your oscillator. Increasing the period makes the oscillator slow down.

c. Describe and test a way to decrease the period of your oscillator. Decreasing the period makes the oscillator get faster.

4 Applying what you learned

Trees are oscillators when they sway in the wind, or in an earthquake. A large tree, like an oak, has a very strong trunk and it takes a large force to bend it. A slender tree, like a willow, has a more flexible trunk that can be bent with much less force. Which tree do you think has a longer period of oscillation, a big oak tree or a slender willow tree?

5 Oscillating buildings

If the period is very short, the oscillator cannot move very far in one cycle and the amplitude is small. If the period is long, there is more time for movement and the amplitude can be much larger.

Tall buildings also sway in the wind, and in earthquakes. The same principle applies to buildings as to trees and pendulums. If a building is strong or short it is stiffer. Stiff buildings require more force to bend. A tall thin building, like a tower, bends under less force. Suppose you have a short, stiff building and a tall slender building. In one paragraph, explain which one is likely to sway more in the wind using the comparison of the period and amplitude of each building.

12.1   Waves

Question: How do we make and describe waves?

In this Investigation, you will:

1. Create wave pulses on an elastic cord.
2. Measure the speed at which wave pulses travel.
3. Observe how changing conditions can speed up or slow down a wave.

A wave pulse is a short burst of a wave. The wave pulse is launched and can move and reflect from objects it encounters. Radar uses wave pulses to detect incoming aircraft or speeding cars. An elastic string is a good tool for making wave pulses and learning how they move.

1   Setting up the experiment

You will need about 3 meters of space to make your wave pulses. Two tables or desks spaced apart work well. You will also need one person to hold a spring scale at the end of the elastic string, and one person to pull the string to make a wave pulse.

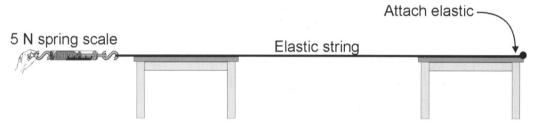

1. Use strong tape (or a knot) to fasten one end of your elastic string to one table.
2. Take the other end of the string and make a small knot to attach a spring scale that can measure 5 newtons of force. The string should be stretched so that the string measures one newton of force.
3. While the very end of the string is being held with a force scale, another person holds the string with their left hand about 10 centimeters away from the edge (between the table and the force scale), as shown in the diagram. The string should be held so that the string is pressed against the table top. With their right hand, this person pulls the string down about 5-8 centimeters and release it as shown in the diagram to the right.

   10 cm

   Making a wave pulse

4. Observe the wave pulse as it moves down the string toward the attached end.

   Would you describe the speed of the wave pulse as fast or slow?

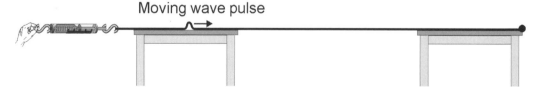

2   Measuring the speed of a wave

Because the pulse moves so fast, you will need photogates to measure its speed.

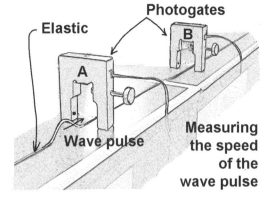

1. Set up two photogates about 20 centimeters apart on the table nearest to where you launch the pulse. The photogates should be upside down and centered on the elastic string as shown in the diagram.

2. Connect the electronic timer in interval mode with both A and B lights on to measure the time interval between photogate A and photogate B.

3. When you snap the pulse it will break the beam first in A then in B. You can calculate the speed of the pulse by dividing the distance from A to B by the time it takes to get from A to B.

4. Not every pulse will give you an accurate reading. The string bounces a lot and each bounce breaks the beam. You only want to record times when you are sure the movement of the pulse is what triggered the photogates at both A and B. For tensions greater than 1/2 newton, the times will should fall between 0.0100 seconds and 0.0200 seconds. Measurements longer than 0.04 seconds are probably due to extra bounces of the string, so they should not be kept.

Make a few trials and calculate the speed of the wave pulse. If you are careful to keep the string stretched the same amount, your timing data should be repeatable to about 0.001 seconds or better.

Table 1: Initial data on the speed of the wave pulse

Trial #	Distance between photogates (m)	Time from A to B (seconds)	Speed of pulse (m/sec)

3   Changing the string tension

Try measuring the speed of the wave pulse with the string stretched tighter. Tensions between 1 newton and about 3 newtons will give you good results.

a. What effect does changing the tension have on the speed of the wave pulses?

b. From what you know about forces, explain why the higher tension makes the waves move faster.

Table 2: String tension data

String tension (N)	Distance between photogates (m)	Time from A to B (seconds)	Speed of pulse (m/sec)

12.2

Waves in Motion

Question: How do waves move and interact with things?

In this Investigation, you will:

1. Create waves in water.
2. Observe how waves can pass through holes and bend around corners.
3. Observe how waves reflect from boundaries.

Waves are oscillations that spread out from where they start. A ball floating on the water is a good example of the difference between a wave and ordinary harmonic motion. If you poke the ball, it moves up and down (A). The oscillating ball creates a wave on the surface of the water that spreads outward, carrying the oscillation to other places (B). A second ball floating farther away also starts oscillating as soon as the wave reaches it (C). The wave started by an earthquake can travel all around the world and reach places far away from where it began.

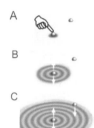

1 ## Making waves in a ripple tank

Take your flat pan and fill it with about 1/2 centimeter of colored water. The color will help you see the waves.

Find a ruler or other straight object that fits in the tray. If you make a single, gentle back and forth motion with the ruler you can launch a wave that goes across the tray. The ruler makes nearly straight plane waves.

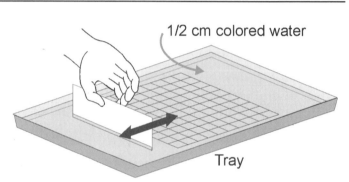

1/2 cm colored water

Tray

a.   Draw a sketch that shows the wave front of your plane wave. Also on your sketch, draw an arrow that shows the direction the wave moves.

b.   Is the wave front parallel or perpendicular to the direction the wave moves?

c.   Would you consider your water wave a transverse wave or a longitudinal wave?

2 ## Circular waves

Next, take your finger tip and poke the surface of the water. Disturbing the surface in a point makes a circular wave that moves outward from where you touched the water.

a.   Draw another sketch that shows the circular wave fronts and include at least 4 arrows that show the direction each part of the wave moves.

b.   At every point along the wave, are the wave fronts more parallel or perpendicular to the direction the wave moves?

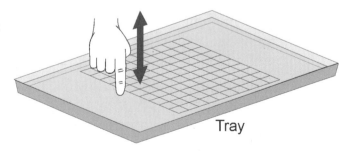

Tray

3 Passing through cracks

1. Take some blocks of wood or other objects and put them in your tray so they block the whole width except for a small opening near the center. The opening should be about a centimeter wide.

2. Make a plane wave that moves toward the center and observe what happens to the part of the wave that goes through the opening.

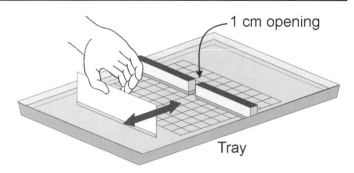

Diffraction is a process that reshapes waves as they move through and around openings or corners. Because of diffraction, waves spread out after passing through openings or around corners.

a. Sketch the shape of the wave fronts before and after the opening.

b. Does the wave change shape when it passes through the opening? If you see any change, your answer should say what kind of shape the wave changes into.

4 Bouncing off walls

1. Take the straight wave maker and make a plane wave that moves at an angle toward the edge of the tray.

2. Observe what happens to the wave as it hits the edge.

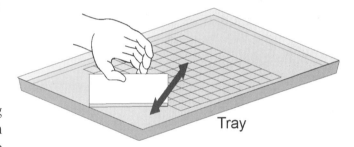

Reflection is the process of waves bouncing off obstacles, like the side of the tray. When a wave reflects, it changes its direction. The wave may also change its shape.

a. Draw a sketch that shows what happens to the wave front when it hits the side of the tray.

b. Draw an arrow showing the direction of the wave approaching the side.

c. Draw another arrow showing the direction of the wave after it reflects from the side.

d. Do you see any relationship between the incoming and outgoing arrows?

5 Applying your knowledge

a. You can easily hear a person talking through a crack in the door, even though you cannot see them. Do any of your observations provide a clue to why sound can get through tiny cracks?

b. Ocean waves can get many meters high. Big waves on the ocean tend to occur on very windy days. Explain how wind might contribute to making big waves. Use a sketch in your explanation.

12.3   Natural Frequency and Resonance

Question: What is resonance and why is it important?

In this Investigation, you will:

1. Create standing waves on a vibrating string.
2. Learn about resonance.
3. Learn how musical instruments create only the frequencies we want.

You discovered that the pendulum oscillated at only one frequency for each string length. The frequency at which objects vibrate is called the natural frequency. Almost everything has a natural frequency, and most things have more than one. We use natural frequency to create all kinds of waves, from microwaves to the musical sounds from a guitar. In this Investigation you will explore the connection between frequency of a wave and its wavelength.

1   Setting up the experiment

Connect the timer to the sound and waves generator as shown in the diagram. The telephone cord connects the timer and wave generator. The black wire goes between the wave generator and the wiggler.

1. Attach the fiddle head to the top of the stand, as high as it goes.
2. Attach the wiggler to the bottom of the stand, as low as it goes.
3. Stretch the elastic string a little (5-10 cm) and attach the free end to the fiddle head. Loosen the knob until you can slide the string between any two of the washers. GENTLY tighten the knob just enough to hold the string.
4. Turn on the timer using the AC adapter.
5. Set the wave generator to WAVES using the button. The wiggler should start to wiggle back and forth, shaking the string.
6. Set the timer to measure FREQUENCY. You should get a reading of about 10 Hz. 10 Hz means the wiggler is oscillating back and forth 10 times per second.
7. Try adjusting the frequency of the wiggler with the frequency control on the wave generator. If you watch the string, you will find that interesting patterns form at certain frequencies.

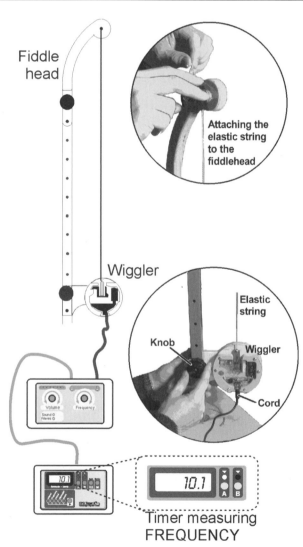

Fiddle head

Attaching the elastic string to the fiddlehead

Wiggler

Elastic string

Knob

Wiggler

Cord

Timer measuring FREQUENCY

2 Resonances of a vibrating string

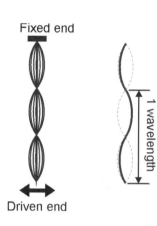

Fixed end

1 wavelength

Driven end

At certain frequencies the vibrating string will form wave patterns like those shown in the picture. Each of the patterns occurs at a *resonance* of the string. The resonances are called harmonics and they are described by the number of 'bumps' seen on the vibrating string.

The wavelength of each harmonic is the length of one complete wave. One complete wave is two "bumps." Therefore, the wavelength is the length of two bumps. The string is 1 meter long. If you have a pattern of three bumps, the wavelength is 2/3 meter, since three bumps equal 1 meter and a whole wave is two of the three bumps.

Harmonics 1 - 4 for the string

1st   2nd   3rd   4th

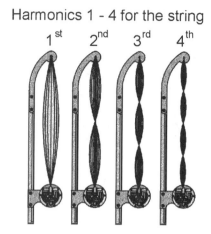

Adjust the frequency to obtain the first harmonics of the string and record the frequency and wavelength for each one. You should fine-tune the frequency to obtain the largest amplitude before recording the data for each harmonic resonance. Look for number 2-6 before looking for the first one. The first harmonic, also called the *fundamental*, is hard to find exactly. Once you have the frequencies for the others, they will provide a clue for finding the frequency of the first harmonic.

Table 1: Frequency, harmonic and wavelength data

Harmonic #	Frequency (Hz)	Wavelength (m)	Frequency times wavelength (m/sec)
1			
2			
3			
4			
5			
6			
7			
8			
9			
10			

The harmonics greater than 10 are hard to see. You may have to look for patterns of fuzzy-still-fuzzy-still to detect the small movements of the string.

3 Analyzing the data

a. In one or two sentences describe how the frequencies of the different harmonic patterns are related to each other.

b. Why is the word *fundamental* chosen as another name for the first harmonic?

c. In one or two sentences, describe how the product of frequency times wavelength changes compared to the changes in frequency or wavelength separately.

d. If the frequency increases, what happens to the wavelength? Your answer should say if the wavelength changes and by how much it changes compared to the change in frequency.

4 Frequency and energy

Do a few more experiments to measure the amplitude of the wave patterns for each harmonic. The amplitude is 1/2 the width of the wave at the widest point. You should measure at least five different harmonics, including the sixth or higher.

If the amplitude of the wave is larger, the wave has more energy, because it takes more force to stretch the string a greater distance. The wiggler applies electrical energy to vibrate the string. The wiggler supplies about the same amount of energy to each harmonic.

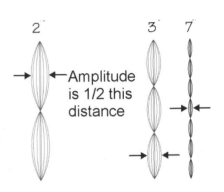

Table 2: Frequency vs. amplitude data

Harmonic #	Frequency (Hz)	Amplitude (cm)

Use your data to answer the questions.

a. Make a graph showing how the amplitude changes with frequency.

b. Suppose you had a wave maker which allowed you to adjust the input energy so all the waves could have the same amplitude. You then used this wave maker to create two waves with equal amplitude, but one had a higher frequency than the other. If the amplitude is the same, which wave has more energy, the higher frequency wave or the lower frequency wave? Use your results to explain your answer.

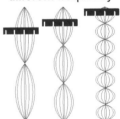

Equal amplitude but different frequency

Which has the most energy?

5   **Force and natural frequency**

As you saw with the vibrating string, when you vibrate something at its natural frequency you can get very large amplitude waves. Sometimes you want large amplitude waves, like in a vibrating guitar string that is making sound.

Sometimes you don't want large amplitudes, like in the motion of large buildings. For this reason, people make sure that the natural frequency of a building is different from any frequency likely to occur in an earthquake. One way to change the natural frequency is to change the amount of force it takes to move the system.

1. Loosen the knob on the fiddle head and attach a spring scale to the end of the elastic string.

2. While the knob is loose, stretch the string until the spring scale indicates the force that you want for the string tension.

3. Gently tighten the knob to hold the string without changing the tension.

4. Adjust the frequency of the wave generator until you have the third harmonic wave. Remember to fine-tune the frequency until the amplitude of the wave is as big as it can get.

5. Record the frequency in the data table.

Repeat steps 2-5 for each different string tension.

Table 3: Frequency vs. string tension data

Harmonic #	Tension (N)	Frequency (hz)
3	0.5	
3	1.0	
3	1.5	
3	2.0	
3	2.5	
3	3.0	

6   **Applying what you learned**

a. What happens to the natural frequency as you increase the tension of the string? In your answer discuss why this is useful in tuning a musical instrument such as a guitar or piano. You may need to do some research to investigate how guitars and pianos are tuned.

b. As the tension is increased, making the string stiffer, what happens to the amplitude of the wave? An earthquake is like the wiggler in that it makes the ground shake back and forth with a certain frequency. How do your results relate to making tall buildings sway less in an earthquake? You should consider what happened to the amplitude of the wave when you increased the tension in the string to answer the question.

13.1

Sound

Question: What is sound and how do we hear it?

In this Investigation, you will:

1. Learn about the range of human perception of sound.
2. Learn how to design double-blind experiments.

The ear is a very remarkable sensor. Sound waves that we can hear change the air pressure by one part in a million! In this Investigation, you will learn about the range of frequencies the ear can detect and also how small a difference in frequency we can perceive. Because sound is about perception, and people are different, we will have to use some very interesting techniques to make experiments reliable.

1   How high can you hear?

The accepted range of frequencies the human ear can hear ranges from a low of 20 Hz to a high of 20,000 Hz. Actually, there is tremendous variation within this range, and people's hearing changes greatly with age and exposure to loud noises.

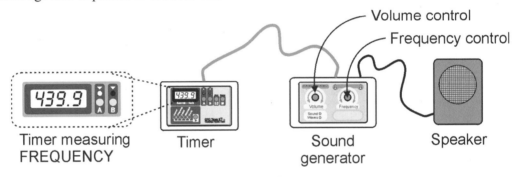

Connect your sound generator to a timer set to measure FREQUENCY. Connect a speaker to the sound generator. When you turn the timer on, you should hear a sound and the timer should measure a frequency near 440 Hz.

There are two knobs for frequency and volume control. Try adjusting the frequency and see how high and low it will go.

See if you and your group can agree on a frequency where you hear the sound as low, medium, high, and very high frequency. Write frequencies of sound that you think sound low, medium, high, and very high. Don't try to be too exact, because the words "low," "medium," and "high" are themselves not well defined. It is difficult to agree exactly on anything that is based completely on individual human perception.

Table 1: How we hear frequencies of sound

Description	Frequency (Hz)
Low	
Medium	
High	
Very high	

2   Testing the upper frequency limit of the ear

To start with a simple experiment, your teacher has a sound generator that can make frequencies up to 20,000 Hz. When the teacher asks, raise your hand if you can hear the sound. Don't raise your hand if you can't hear. Someone will be appointed to count hands and survey the class to see what fraction of students can still hear the sound.

a.   The objective of the test is to see what fraction of people can hear a particular frequency. Once the frequency gets too high, no one will be able to hear it, or at least no humans. Cats, dogs, and other animals can hear much higher frequencies than people. Do you think the method of raising your hands is likely to give a good result? Give at least one reason why you think the method is either good or bad.

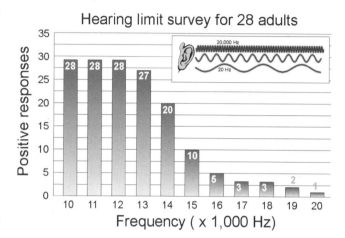

b.   Make a bar graph showing how your class responded to frequencies between 10,000 and 20,000 Hz. You should have ten bars, each one for a frequency range of 1,000 Hz. The height of each bar is the number of people who could hear that frequency of sound. If someone could hear the frequency they are counted as a positive response in the graph. This kind of graph is called a *histogram*.

3   Doing a more careful experiment

Another way to do the experiment is with a hidden ballot. The researcher running the experiment will ask if anyone can hear a certain frequency of sound and you check yes or no on a piece of paper. The researcher may play or *not* play the sound. Each frequency will be played five times, and the five repetitions will be all mixed up so there is less chance for error. Every one in the class does one response survey.

Collect the data from the survey sheets and record it in the chart below.

Survey		
#	Yes	No
1	✓	
2		✓
3		✓
4	✓	
5	✓	
6		✓
7	✓	
8		✓
9	✓	
10	✓	
11		

Key		Played	
#	Frequency	Yes	No
1	12,000	✓	
2	16,000		✓
3	10,000		✓
4	12,000	✓	
5	14,000	✓	
6	14,000		✓
7	18,000	✓	
8	20,000		✓
9	10,000	✓	
10	20,000	✓	
11	16.0		

Table 2: Frequency survey data

# Right	10,000 Hz	12,000 Hz	14,000 Hz	16,000 Hz	18,000 Hz	20,000 Hz
5						
4						
3						
2						
1						

Plot another histogram showing only those people whose choices matched the yes/no on the key for all five times at each frequency. It is hard to fake a response or get it right by chance because you have to choose correctly five times for each frequency. This kind of experiment is called a double-blind test since neither you nor the researcher can see anyone else's response. The results from a double-blind experiment are much more reliable that other forms of surveys. Doctors use the double-blind method to test new medicines.

4 Perceiving differences in frequency

Can you tell the difference between a sound with a frequency of 400 Hz and a sound at 401 Hz? The next experiment on hearing is to test people's ability to distinguish if one sound has higher frequency than another.

In this experiment the researcher will play two frequencies and you mark which one is higher.

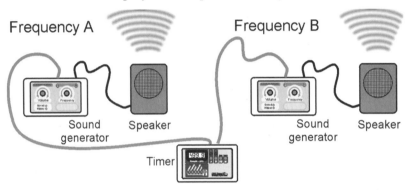

To analyze the results you need to know how many people got the right answer for each frequency range. Make a data table like the example below that is large enough to hold all of your results.

Table 3: Comparative frequency data

Frequency A (Hz)	Frequency B (Hz)	Frequency difference (Hz)	Percent difference	# of correct responses
1,000	995	5	0.5%	1
1,000	1,050	50	1%	15
1,000	1,001	1	.1%	0

a. Calculate the percent difference in frequency for each test.

b. There are two ways to look at sensitivity. In one way, we hear *absolute* differences in frequency. If the ear was sensitive to absolute differences, we would hear a 5 Hz difference no matter if the two frequencies were 500 Hz and 505 Hz, or 5,000 Hz and 5,005 Hz.

The second possibility is that we hear relative differences. We might be able to hear a 1 percent difference which would be 5 Hz at 500 Hz. But we could not hear the difference between 5,000 Hz and 5,005 Hz because the percentage difference is only 0.1 percent. To hear a similar difference at   5000 Hz, Frequency B would have to be 5,050 Hz, which is 1 percent higher.

Which model does the data support?

5 Chance and experiments

A very good way to ensure accurate results in a survey test is to make it improbable that anyone could get the correct response by guessing. A single test is almost never enough to rule out this possibility. Consider that on each test you have a 50 percent chance to guess right. That means one out of every two times you could get the right response just by guessing. This is not very reliable!

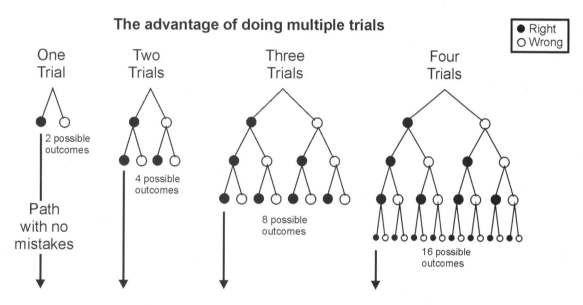

The diagram shows a decision tree for an experiment with multiple trials. There is only one path with no mistakes. With each additional trial, the total number of possible outcomes increases by 2. With two trials you have one right path out of 4 choices. That means there is only a 1 in 4 chance someone could guess twice correctly. With three trials there is only a 1 in 8 chance of guessing. With four trials the chance of guessing is down to 1 in 16.

a. What is the chance of guessing correctly with five trials?

b. If 100 people did a test with five trials, and everybody guessed, how many people would be likely to make five correct choices in a row?

Question: Does sound behave like other waves?

In this Investigation, you will:

1. Listen to beats and show how they can be explained if sound is a wave.
2. Create interference of sound waves.
3. Demonstrate resonance.

Sound is one of the most important of our senses. We use sounds to express the whole range of human emotion. Scientifically, sound is one of the simplest and most common kinds waves. But, what a huge influence it is on our everyday experience! Sound is a rich and beautiful palette from which musicians create works of joy, excitement and drama.

1   Beats, consonance, and dissonance

Our ears are capable of hearing many thousands of frequencies at a time. Suppose you have two sound waves traveling toward your ear. What reaches the ear is the addition of the two waves.

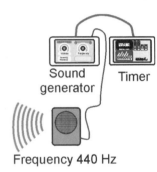

Sound generator   Timer

Frequency 440 Hz

1. Set up two sound generators close together on the same table.
2. Tune one to 440 Hz and the other to 441 Hz.
3. Stand back and listen to the sound when both are at equal volume.
4. Turn down the 440 Hz sound and listen only to the 441 Hz sound.
5. Turn down the 441 Hz sound and listen to the 440 only.
6. Turn both back up equal again and listen to the combination.
7. Keep one sound generator at 440 Hz and adjust the frequency of the other one between 430 Hz and 450 Hz. Listen to the combinations of sound.

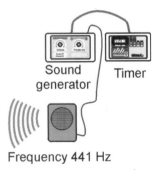

Sound generator   Timer

Frequency 441 Hz

When two waves are close, but not exactly matched in frequency, we hear beats. The beats happen because the waves drift in and out of phase with each other. sometimes they are aligned and the result is twice as loud. A moment later they are exactly opposite and they cancel out leaving periods of quiet. The alternation of loud and soft is what we hear as beats.

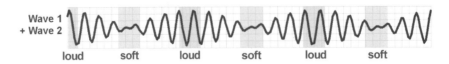

Why we hear beats

In phase

Wave 1

Wave 2

Out of phase

Wave 1 + Wave 2

loud   soft   loud   soft   loud   soft

Conduct experiments that can answer the following questions about beats.

a. What makes the beats get faster or slower? In your answer you should describe what you do to the frequencies to make the beats faster or slower.

b. Is the sound of beats pleasant to listen to, or unpleasant? The word *consonant* is used by musicians to describe sounds that fit smoothly together. The opposite of consonant is *dissonant*. Dissonant sounds tend to make people anxious and irritable. Describe the relationship between consonance, dissonance and beats.

c. How could you use beats to match one frequency to another frequency? This is done every day when musicians in an orchestra tune their instruments.

d. How much different do the two frequencies have to be before you do not hear beats any more?

2   Interference

Beats are only one way sound waves interact with each other. Suppose you have two identical sound waves and you are standing where you can hear them both. For certain positions, one sound wave reaches your ear in the opposite phase with the other wave and the sound gets softer, like in beats. Move over a little and the two sound waves add up to get louder. These effects are called interference and are easy to demonstrate.

1. Set up one sound generator with two speakers. Place one speaker about 1/2 meter behind the other.

2. Set the frequency between 400 Hz and 800 Hz.

3. Stand 3 or 4 meters in front of one speaker and have your lab partner slowly move one of the two speakers away. You will hear the sound get loud and soft and loud again when the distance between speakers has changed by one wavelength.

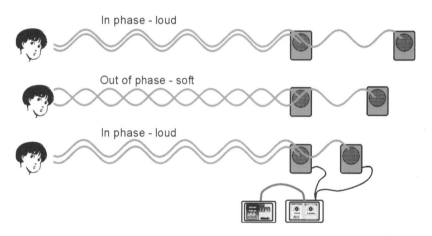

When two speakers are connected to the same sound generator they both make the exact same sound wave. If you move around a room you will hear places of loud and soft whenever your distance from each speaker differs by one wavelength.

a. Try to make an approximate measurement of the wavelength of sound by changing the separation of the two speakers. The speakers have been moved one wavelength when the sound heard by the observer has gone from loudest, to softest, and back to loudest again. For this to work you need to keep the observer and both speakers in the same line.

b. Interference can be bad news for concert halls. People do not want their sound to be canceled out after they have paid for the tickets! Why do we not usually hear interference from stereos even though they have two speakers?

3   ## Resonance

Many objects that can create sound also demonstrate resonance. When struck, played, or rubbed, these objects produce a characteristic sound at their natural frequency. A tuning fork is a good example.

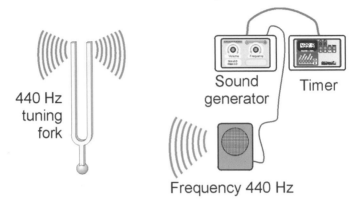

440 Hz tuning fork

Sound generator   Timer

Frequency 440 Hz

1. Select a tuning fork and tap it on your knee or another firm (but not hard) surface.

2. Listen to the sound. Does it change in frequency or do you hear a single frequency that does not change?

3. Use the sound generator to measure the frequency of the resonance by matching the frequency of the sound generator with the sound you hear from the tuning fork. The match is perfect when you no longer hear any beats.

4. Try several different size tuning forks and use the chart below to record the resonant frequency for each one.

Table 1: Resonant frequencies for tuning forks

Tuning fork description	Measured resonant frequency (Hz)	Labeled resonant frequency (if any)

4   ## Thinking about what you observed

a. Did you observe any relationship between the size (or shape) of the tuning fork and the frequency at which it was resonant?

b. What range of frequencies did you hear that seemed to match the frequency of the tuning fork? Give your answer in the form of a range written like 429 Hz - 451 Hz.

c. Strike the tuning fork and hold the bottom end against a hard, thin surface, like a window. Does the sound get louder, softer, or remain unchanged? Explain what you hear by describing what might be happening between the tuning fork and the surface you touched.

5   ## Resonance in other systems

Almost all objects show some kind of resonance. A good example is a wine glass. If you take a wine glass and rub a moistened finger around the rim you can hear a resonant sound. Adding water to the glass changes the sound. Try the following experiment.

1. Obtain a good quality wine glass, like the ones shown in the diagram.
2. Take a moistened finger and rub the rim to hear the resonance.
3. Use the sound generator to match the frequency as close as you can to the sound of the glass.
4. Fill the glass to different heights with water and use the same technique to find the resonant frequency for each different height.
5. Use the table below to record the height of water and the resonant frequency you found for each different height.

Use different heights of liquid.

Table 2: Resonant frequencies of glasses of water

Trial #	Water height	Frequency (Hz)

6. Find a tall glass bottle, like the one in the diagram.
7. You can make a resonant sound by blowing over the open mouth of the bottle, as shown. This is a little tricky and you have to find the right angle for blowing air over the mouth of the bottle.
8. Fill the bottle to different heights of water and see how the sound changes.
9. Use the sound generator to estimate the frequency of the sound you get at different heights and write the results in the table below.

Blow over the mouth of the bottle to make the sound.

Table 3: Resonant frequencies of bottles of water

Trial #	Water height	Frequency (Hz)

6   ## Thinking about what you observed

What was the relationship between the frequencies and the heights? In coming up with your answer, remember the waves on the vibrating string and how the frequency and wavelength were related. Do you see similar behavior with the sounds and heights from the glass and bottle? For each case, what might be the vibrating element that would explain your observed changes in frequency?

Music

Question: What is music and how do we make music?

In this Investigation, you will:

1. Make musical notes by choosing frequencies of sound.
2. Make a simple musical instrument called a straw kazoo.
3. Learn the foundations of musical harmony.

Music is a combination of sound and rhythm that we find pleasant. Some people like music with a heavy beat and strong rhythm. Other people like music where the notes rise and fall in beautiful melodies. Music can be slow or fast, loud or soft, happy or sad, comforting or scary.

1 **Making notes**

Musical notes are different frequencies of sound. Over thousands of years people have found combinations of frequencies that sound good together. The frequencies are different enough to not make beats but not so different that they cannot make musical melodies that flow.

1. Set up your sound generator and timer.
2. Turn down the volume so you cannot hear the sound but you can still read the frequency from the timer.
3. Each group in the class will be given a different frequency to tune to. Tune your frequency using the timer until you are within 1 Hz of the frequency you were given.

Your teacher will tell you to turn up and down different frequencies so they can be heard together. Don't change the frequency, just adjust the volume up and down when you are asked.

a. Describe the sound of the three frequencies 264 Hz, 330 Hz, and 396 Hz when you hear them together. Which three notes are these? (Look at the diagram below.)

b. Describe the sound of the three frequencies 264 Hz, 315 Hz, and 396 Hz when you hear them together.

c. Contrast the two sounds. Does one sound more happy or sad compared with the other? Does one sound spookier than the other? Which combination reminds you more of spring, which of fall?

d. Describe the effect of adding a frequency of 528 Hz to each group of frequencies.

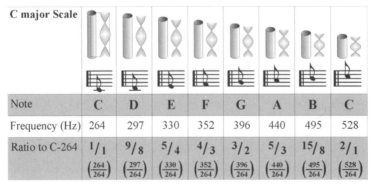

C major Scale								
Note	C	D	E	F	G	A	B	C
Frequency (Hz)	264	297	330	352	396	440	495	528
Ratio to C-264	$\frac{1}{1}$ $\left(\frac{264}{264}\right)$	$\frac{9}{8}$ $\left(\frac{297}{264}\right)$	$\frac{5}{4}$ $\left(\frac{330}{264}\right)$	$\frac{4}{3}$ $\left(\frac{352}{264}\right)$	$\frac{3}{2}$ $\left(\frac{396}{264}\right)$	$\frac{5}{3}$ $\left(\frac{440}{264}\right)$	$\frac{15}{8}$ $\left(\frac{495}{264}\right)$	$\frac{2}{1}$ $\left(\frac{528}{264}\right)$

2   Controlling frequency and wavelength

Most musical instruments use resonance. This means that when instruments are played the sounds they make are based on their natural frequencies. How do musical instruments make so many notes at different frequencies? Why does a guitar player use frets and a flute player use different fingerings?

These players are controlling the frequencies of their instruments by changing the wavelength of the vibrating string or column of air. If the wavelength is shorter, the frequency goes up. If the wavelength is longer, the frequency goes down.

The chart on the last page shows the ratios of frequency to make a musical scale. If the frequency goes up, the wavelength must go down proportionally. That means to double the frequency, the wavelength is reduced by half. To make the frequency 3/2 higher (to get the note E), the wavelength must be 2/3 because $2/3 \times 3/2 = 1$.

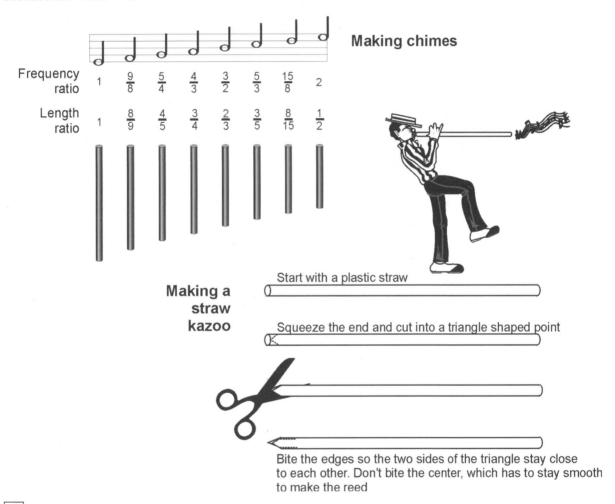

| Frequency ratio | 1 | $\frac{9}{8}$ | $\frac{5}{4}$ | $\frac{4}{3}$ | $\frac{3}{2}$ | $\frac{5}{3}$ | $\frac{15}{8}$ | 2 |
| Length ratio | 1 | $\frac{8}{9}$ | $\frac{4}{5}$ | $\frac{3}{4}$ | $\frac{2}{3}$ | $\frac{3}{5}$ | $\frac{8}{15}$ | $\frac{1}{2}$ |

Making chimes

Making a straw kazoo

Start with a plastic straw

Squeeze the end and cut into a triangle shaped point

Bite the edges so the two sides of the triangle stay close to each other. Don't bite the center, which has to stay smooth to make the reed

a.   Make a straw kazoo and make some sound with it. Take a pair of scissors and cut off the end of the kazoo. What happens to the frequency of the sound it makes?

b.   Take the scissors and cut a small hole exactly in the middle of your kazoo. Cover the hole with your finger. Blow through the kazoo and lift your finger to cover and uncover the hole. What happens to the sound? (Hint: What is vibrating in the straw is a length of air.)

c.   Identify at least three musical instruments that use vibrating objects of different lengths like the sketch of the chimes above.

Question: How can you make light and study it?

In this Investigation, you will:

1. Create light using photoluminescence.
2. Examine colors of light using diffraction grating glasses.
3. Demonstrate the polarization of light with polarizing filters.

Have you ever wondered why glow-in-the-dark materials give off light? Included in the glowing material are atoms of the element phosphorus. When light energy hits it, some of the electrons of the phosphorus atom rise to a higher energy state where they either fall right away, or wait for a while before they fall. This is called photoluminescence. The light starts it (photo) and then it gives off more light (luminescence).

The energy that is given off is in the form of light. It is light energy that begins this process in the first place. Is there a way that we could use this emitted light to cause more electrons to rise?

There are tools that allow us to study light. One of them is called a diffraction grating. When you look through a diffraction grating at a specific light source you will see all the different colors that make up that light. This leads us to the question, "What makes different colors?" If electrons falling from a high-energy state to a lower energy state cause light, what do you think would cause different colors of light? That's correct! Electrons falling from different energy levels produce different colors of light. Electrons falling a short distance produce red light and electrons falling a larger distance produce the other colors up to violet. Different atoms have different energy levels and produce different colors.

You can tell a lot about a material based on the colors of light it gives off.

 Safety Tip: Do not try to walk around while the lights are off!

1 **Examine the effects of light on glow-in-the-dark material**

1. While in a dark room, put an object over the glow-in-the-dark material.
2. Turn the lights back on, or shine a flashlight onto the glow in the dark material. Be careful to keep part of it covered.
3. Turn off the light source, remove the covering and make observations.
4. Record your observations.
5. Expose light energy to glow-in-the-dark material without anything covering it.
6. Turn off the light, and then place a piece of white paper over part of the material.
7. Remove the white paper after the glow material starts to dim, and then make observations.
8. Record your observations.

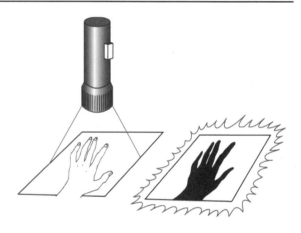

2   ## Recording and analyzing your results

a.   What happened when the light was not allowed to strike the material? Explain.

b.   What happened when light was trapped under the white paper? Explain.

In answering these questions, keep in mind that light is a form of energy. Explain what happens to the energy in both of these situations.

3   ## Examining the colors of light given off by a glowing source

1.   In this part of the Investigation, you will observe patterns generated by different light sources. Record your observations in the table below.

2.   Look through the diffraction grating. You will notice several different rainbows (these rainbows might not be very clear).

3.   Turn on the white light source and turn the room lights off. Observe the patterns generated. It is useful to limit your reporting to a single rainbow so, for consistency, refer only to the rainbow to the **left** of the center light.

4.   Record the pattern of colors, and spaces between colors, in your table. Use colored pencils, or just label the different color areas.

5.   Examine at least three other light sources around the room or building. Use the spectrum to the left of the light and record the patterns in your table. Describe the light source and record your observations in the table below.

Description of light source	Pattern observed using the diffraction grating

4   ## Analyzing your results

Are there some light sources that have identical light patterns? List and describe those here.

5   ## What did you learn?

a.   What must be happening if two different light sources have the same pattern?

b.   Could an astronomer use the techniques you used in the Investigation to identify and learn about different stars? Explain your answer.

c.   Some materials give off light when they are heated. How could a chemist use the techniques you used in the Investigation to identify and learn about different materials? Explain your answer.

6   ## Polarization of a transverse spring wave

With a transverse wave, the oscillation can be in different directions relative to the direction the wave moves. Waves on a spring are a good example of polarization.

1. Find a partner. Each of you should take one end of the spring and stretch it. Don't let go or the spring will snap back suddenly.

2. One person should hold the spring firmly without moving.

3. The other person should shake the spring up and down at a frequency to get the second harmonic wave. It has a shape like the picture below. This wave is vertically polarized since it oscillates up and down in the vertical direction.

4. Stop shaking the spring and let it settle down.

5. Shake the spring side-to-side at the same frequency and you can also get the second harmonic wave. This time the wave is horizontally polarized since the oscillations are back and forth in the horizontal direction.

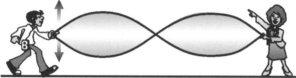
Up - down shaking produces vertical polarization

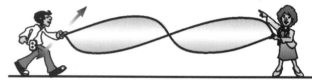
Sideways shaking produces horizontal polarization

7   ## Describing and applying what you see

a.   Describe the motion of the spring using the terms 'horizontal polarization' and 'vertical polarization'. Your description can be in words, diagrams, or both.

b.   Suppose you try to 'sandwich' your spring wave between two boards. What happens to the waves if you make them pass through the narrow space between the boards? If the boards were oriented like the picture below, discuss how the two different polarizations of waves would behave. Which one would get through the slot and which one would be blocked?

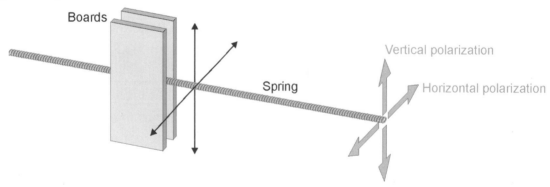

c.   Describe the polarization of water waves. Are there two polarizations (like the spring) or only one? What is it about a water surface that makes it different from a spring?

8   # The polarization of light

If you were to observe polarization, it would be strong evidence that light is a transverse wave. A material called **polarizer** has the property that it allows one polarization of light to pass through, but blocks the other polarization. A polarizer works like the two boards, except the 'boards' are really long, thin molecules. The molecules let light waves oscillate one way but absorb light that oscillates the other way.

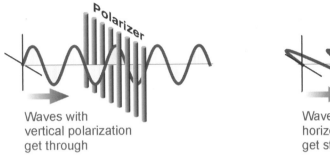

Waves with
vertical polarization
get through

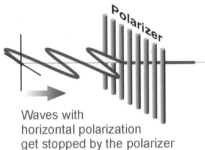

Waves with
horizontal polarization
get stopped by the polarizer

1. Take one sheet of polarizer and look through it. Observe the effect of looking through the polarizer. Try rotating the polarizer and see if it makes a difference.

2. Take a second sheet of polarizer and look through it. Observe the effects, just as with the first sheet.

3. Look through both sheets of polarizer together. Leave one fixed and rotate the other one as shown in the diagram below. Observe how much light you see through both polarizers as you rotate the second one.

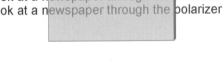

Look at a newspaper through the polarizer
Look at a newspaper through the polarizer
Look at a newspaper through the polarizer
Look at a newspaper through the polarizer
Look at a newspaper through the polarizer
Look at a newspaper through the polarizer

Look at a newspaper through the polarizer
Look at a newspaper through the polarizer
Look at a newspaper through the polarizer
Look at a newspaper through the polarizer
Look at a newspaper through the polarizer
Look at a newspaper through the polarizer

Look at something through one
polarizer.

Look at something through two polarizers
as you rotate one of them.

9   ## How do you explain what you see?

a.   The light from the sun (or a lamp) is not polarized. This means it is a mixture of light that is polarized equally in all directions. Explain why the light is reduced passing through one polarizer.

b.   When the light passes through the first polarizer it becomes polarized. We say light is polarized when it consists of only one polarization. Explain why rotating the second polarizer changes the amount of light you see coming through.

c.   The glare from low-angle sunlight reflecting from water and roads is polarized in the horizontal direction. Ordinary sunlight is not polarized. Explain how polarizing sunglasses can stop most of the glare but still allow half the regular (unpolarized) light to come through.

Color

Question: What happens when you mix different colors of light?

In this Investigation, you will:

1. Experiment with mixing different combinations of colored light.
2. Examine the effects of color filters on white light.

All the colors of visible light can be created artificially using a combination of three primary colors: red, blue and green. In this Investigation, you will use a white light source and color filters to discover what happens when you mix different colors of light. You will also learn how the filters work.

1 **Mixing primary colors of light**

1. For this Investigation, you will use red, blue, and green LEDs (light emitting diodes).

2. Attach each LED to the circuitry box and plug in the whole assembly.

3. Turn out the lights in the classroom and block light from windows.

4. Set the white box storage box from the optics kit on its edge at one short end of the optics table. It will be used as a screen in the Investigation.

5. Place the red and blue LEDs next to each other and pointing toward the screen. The red LED should be on the left and the blue LED on the right. Stack the green LED on top as shown in the graphic. To help you balance the green LED, you may want to place a 2 inch × 3.5 inch piece of a index card on top of the red and blue LEDs and then balance the green LED on top of the card.

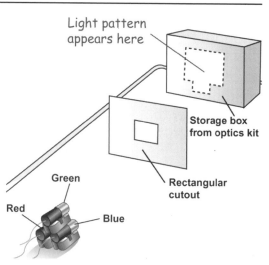

6. Your teacher will give you a cardboard cutout with a rectangular hole in the middle. Place the cutout between the three LEDs and the screen as shown in the graphic below.

7. Notice that a colorful pattern of rectangular shapes appears on the screen. Adjust the placement of the screen, cutout and LEDs until you get a very clear pattern, then answer the questions below.

a. How many colors do you see in the light pattern on the screen?

b. Use colored pencils to draw the light pattern. Pay attention to the colors of light you see when two light beams overlap.

c. What color of light do you see when two LED light beams overlap? Write your answers in Table 1.

Table 1: Mixing primary colors of light

LED color combination	Color you see
Red + Green	
Green + Blue	
Blue + Red	
Red + Green + Blue	

2   How does a color filter work?

A red laser can produce a single pure color of red which can be useful in some applications. For example, making three-dimensional images, called holograms, requires a very pure source of light which a laser can provide.

In the light and optics kit, you have three different sources of colored light; but just how "pure" are these colors? In this part of the Investigation you will examine the light produced by each colored LED, and learn how a **color filter** works. You will use the diffraction glasses to make your observations. Recall from the last Investigation that the diffraction glasses allow you to see the different colors of the spectrum that a light source produces.

1. Examine the red LED with the diffraction glasses.
2. Using colored pencils, sketch what you see in the appropriate column of table 2.
3. Repeat steps 1 and 2 for the green and blue LEDs.
4. Unscrew one of the color filter from one of the color LEDs. Examine the light produced by the white LED and record your observations in the table.
5. Answer the questions below.

Table 2: Examining LEDs

Red LED	Green LED	Blue LED
White LED		

3   Drawing conclusions

a. Compare the colors in the red LED to those in the green LED. What are the similarities and differences in the range of colors?

b. Compare the colors in the green LED to those in the blue LED. What are the similarities and differences in the range of colors?

c. How do the colors in the white LED compare to the red, green, and blue LEDs combined?

d. The red LED consists of a white LED covered with a red filter. What does the red filter do?

e. What do color filters do?

f. If you wanted to get yellow light, what part of the spectrum would the color filter have to absorb?

Seeing an Image

Question: What is magnification and how do you plot a reflected image?

In this Investigation, you will:

1. Determine the magnification of a converging lens.
2. Trace incident and reflected rays from a mirror using a laser.
3. Learn how images are formed in optical systems.

We see **images** that are formed by the eye from light that comes from objects. Because light can be bent by lenses or mirrors, the image we see can be different from the object that produced it. With a magnifying lens, we can make an image seem larger than the object. The magnification is the ratio of image size to actual object size. In this Investigation, you will learn a shortcut method for finding the magnification of a single lens. Another way an image can be different from the object is in its orientation and location. For example, the image you see reflected in a mirror is reversed left-to-right and appears to be behind the mirror. In part 2 of this Investigation, you will learn how to predict where the image in a mirror appears by tracing the incident and reflected rays of light from a laser.

1 **Finding the magnification of a lens**

1. Set your lens directly on the graph paper and count the number of *unmagnified* squares that cross the diameter of the lens. In the example, the lens is 10 squares wide.

2. Next, examine a section of graph paper with your lens held above the paper. Move the lens closer and farther away until you have the biggest squares you can still see clearly in the lens.

3. Count the number of *magnified* squares that cross the diameter of the lens. For example, the picture shows 4 1/2 squares across the lens.

4. The magnification can be calculated by dividing the number of *unmagnified* squares by the number of *magnified* squares. In the example, you see 10 *unmagnified* squares and 4.5 *magnified* squares. The magnification is 10 ÷ 4.5, or 2.22.

5. Try the experiment again using a ruler to measure the distance between the lens and the paper. Notice that the magnification changes with different distances.

6. Fill in the table by measuring the magnification of your lens for at least four different distances. The number of squares on the graph paper will be the same for all distances.

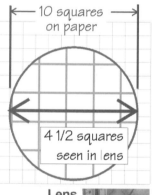

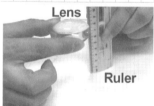

Measuring the distance from the lens to the paper

Table 1: Magnification of a lens

Distance to paper	# of squares on graph paper (unmagnified squares)	# of squares in lens (magnified squares)	Magnification

2   ## Reflections in a mirror

1. Secure a sheet of graph paper to the optics table with the magnetic strips.

2. Draw a line on the paper to mark where you will place a mirror. Place a mirror along this line.

3. Draw a 1-centimeter-long arrow on the graph paper about 3 centimeters away from your line. The arrow should be parallel to the line.

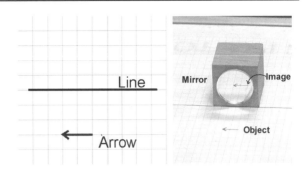

4. Move your head until you can see the reflection of the arrow in the mirror. The image of the arrow appears to be behind the mirror.

5. Hold your pencil straight up with the point on the tip of your arrow. Use the pencil to set the laser beam so it passes right over the tip of your arrow, and hits the mirror.

6. Trace the laser beam using your pencil as a guide. Trace the beam before it hits the mirror and after it hits the mirror.

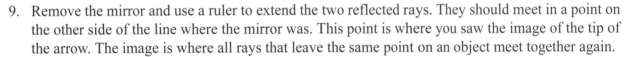

Tracing the incident ray   Tracing the reflected ray

7. Move the laser so the beam passes over the tip of your arrow from a different angle, but still hits the mirror. Trace the beam with your pencil like you did in steps 5 and 6.

8. The lines you drew represent rays of light before and after they hit the mirror. The **incident ray** shows the light before it hits the mirror. The **reflected ray** shows the path of the light after it bounces off the mirror.

9. Remove the mirror and use a ruler to extend the two reflected rays. They should meet in a point on the other side of the line where the mirror was. This point is where you saw the image of the tip of the arrow. The image is where all rays that leave the same point on an object meet together again.

Safety Tip: NEVER look directly into a laser beam. Some lasers can cause permanent damage to your eyes.

3   ## Thinking about what you observed

a. Describe how the magnification changed as you changed the distance from the paper to the lens. Does the magnification get larger or smaller with distance?

b. Could you adjust the distance between the paper and the lens to get any magnification you wanted, or was there a point where the lens could no longer create a sharp image?

c. Describe why the image formed by a mirror appears to come from the place where the reflected rays meet. In your answer, refer to the fact that each point on an object is the source of many rays of light. You might want to include a sketch.

d. Pick one pair of incident and reflected rays. Draw a straight line perpendicular to the point where the rays hit the mirror. This perpendicular line is called the **normal** in optics. Use a protractor to measure the angle between the incident ray and the normal, and between the reflected ray and the normal. From your angles, what can you say about the relationship between the direction of the incident ray and the direction of the reflected ray?

15.2 **The Human Eye**

Question: How does a lens form an image?

In this Investigation, you will:

1. Trace rays of light through prisms and lenses.
2. Find the focal length of a lens by tracing rays from a laser.
3. Learn how a lens creates an image.

The lens in your eye bends light to form an image on the retina. The lens can change shape so that we can see sharp images close up or far away.

Refraction means "bending light." Any clear material can cause refraction. The amount of bending depends on the type of material and the shape of the surface. In this Investigation, you will explore refraction with prisms and lenses.

◆**Safety Tip: Never look directly at the laser beam, or shine the laser beam at another's person's eyes.**

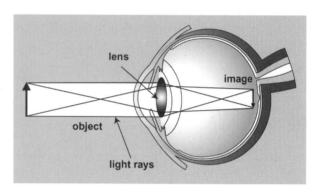

1   **Refracting light through a prism**

1. Secure a piece of graph paper to your magnetic surface. Put a prism on the center of the paper with the long flat side facing the left of the paper. Trace around the prism with a pencil.

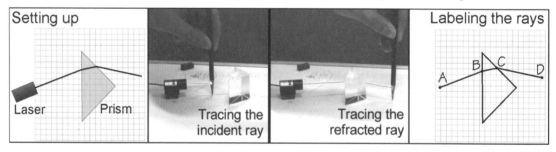

2. Put the laser on the left side of the prism.
3. Shine the laser at the prism and make sure that it comes out the other side of the prism. Use the edge of an index card to locate the beam as it enters and exits the prism. The approximate positions in the diagram will work.
4. Plot several points along the path of the laser beam as it goes into and out of the prism.
5. Remove the prism. Use a ruler to draw straight lines that follow your plot. Extend the lines until they touch the outline of your prism. Draw a third line to connect the lines through the prism. Label the points at the end of each line with the letters A, B, C, and D as shown in the diagram. Line A-B is the **incident ray**. Line B-C is the light ray inside the prism. Line C-D is the **refracted ray**.
6. Try a second time with a different angle for the laser as it approaches the prism. Not all angles will work; for some, the laser beam will not come out of the right side of the prism at all. Find a few angles for which the beam does go through the prism and trace the incident and refracted rays.

2   ## Refracting light through a lens

Like a prism, a converging lens bends light. Because the shape of a lens is curved, rays striking different places along the lens are bent different amounts. The laser allows us to follow the path of the incident and refracted rays.

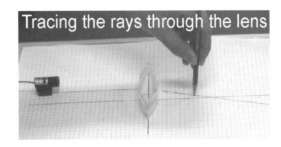

Tracing the rays through the lens

1. Take a large (11 x 17) sheet of graph paper and draw a horizontal line through the center. We will refer to this line as the **axis**. Draw a second line in the middle of the paper perpendicular to the axis.

2. Place your 'flat' lens on the intersection of the two lines as shown.

3. Place the laser to the left of the lens, so that the notch in the base is centered on the axis. Turn on the laser and shine the beam through the lens.

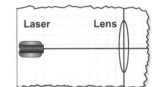

4. If the beam goes through the exact center of the lens, it will not appear to be refracted at all. Adjust the lens so that the beam goes through the exact center. Trace around the border of the lens with your pencil.

5. Now move the laser to a point 15 cm to the left of the vertical line and 2 cm **above** the axis. Shine the laser beam through the lens along a line parallel to the axis. Plot the incident and refracted rays on the graph paper.

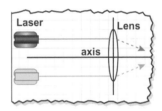

6. Repeat step 5 with the laser 2 cm **below** the axis. Plot the incident and refracted rays.

a.   Describe the path of the laser beam as it travels along the axis and through the lens. Compare the paths of the incident and the refracted rays.

b.   Describe the path of the laser beam as it travels parallel to the axis, above or below the axis. Compare the paths of the incident and refracted rays.

c.   How is the path of light through a converging lens like the path of light through a prism?

3 Finding the focal point

Rays that approach a lens *parallel to the axis* meet at a point called the **focal point**. The distance between the center of the lens and the focal point is called the **focal length**.

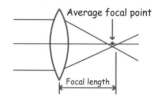

1. The two refracted rays that you traced in part 2 crossed the axis. Mark the axis where these rays crossed. This is the focal point for your lens. Due to imperfections in the lens, these two rays may not meet in exactly one point. In this case, choose the midpoint between the two points as your focal point.

2. Measure the distance between the focal point and the center of your lens. This distance is the focal length of your lens.

3. Label the focal point and focal length on your ray diagram.

4 Finding an image

When all the rays from a point on an object meet again, they form an **image**. You can use the laser to locate images formed by your lens.

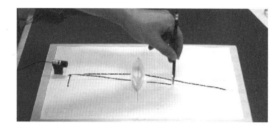

1. Tape two large (11 × 17 inches) sheets of graph paper together so that you have a new (11 × 34 inches) working surface. Draw a horizontal axis all the way across the graph paper.

2. Now draw a vertical line 20 cm from the left side of the page. Place the lens at the intersection of the lines.

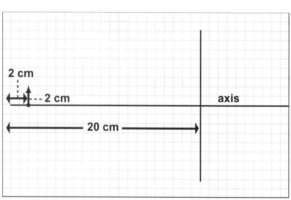

3. Use the laser to center the lens, just as you did in steps 3 and 4 of part 2. Trace around the lens with your pencil.

4. Draw a vertical arrow 2 cm from the left edge of the graph paper. The base of the arrow should be on the axis. The tip of the arrow should be 2 cm above the axis. This arrow will serve as your "object."

5. Place the laser at the tip of the arrow. Shine the beam through the lens in a line parallel to the axis. Trace the incident and refracted rays.

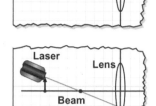

6. Check to see that the lens is still centered on the axis. On the left side of the lens, make a dot on the axis that marks off a length equal to the focal length.

7. Place the laser at the tip of the arrow. Turn the laser so that the beam passes through the dot you made in step 6. Verify that this is happening by placing the edge of your index card at the location of the dot.

8. Trace the incident and refracted rays.

9. The two refracted rays that you have drawn should intersect somewhere on the right side of the lens. Mark the intersection with an upside down arrowhead. You have just plotted the image of the tip of your arrow!

10. Draw a vertical line from your "image" arrowhead to the axis. You have now drawn the image of your arrow.

5   Characteristics of the image

Compare the image of the arrow to the original arrow.

a. Is the image larger or smaller? Calculate the magnification by dividing the length of the image by the length of the original arrow.

b. Is the image right side up, or is it inverted?

c. Is the image closer to the lens than the original arrow, or is it farther away?

Optical Technology

Question: How are optics used in everyday life?

In this Investigation, you will:

1. Find the critical angle for refracting light through a prism.
2. Learn some of the concepts about fiber optics.

Fiber optics are an important tool in optical technology. A fiber optic is like a wire for light. You can bend a fiber optic and the light will still come through!

The basis for the conduction of light by fiber optics is a phenomenon called **total internal reflection**. Once a light ray has entered the end of the fiber, it is not allowed to escape through the sides of the fiber optic. The light is "totally" reflected back into the "light pipe"(the fiber optic). This occurs if the light ray approaches the side at an angle that is larger than an angle known as the **critical angle**. In this investigation you will find the critical angle for a prism.

1   The critical angle of refraction

1. Take a piece of graph paper and draw a line about 5 centimeters from one edge. Draw an X and an O about the same distance from the line.

2. Fold the paper on the line until it makes an angle greater than 90 degrees. Place one side of the fold on the table. The other side of the fold will be off the table.

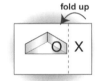

3. Place your prism on the graph paper on top of the O. The long face of the prism should be on the paper and the edge aligned with the fold.

4. Look into the prism. Move your head up and down to change the angle at which you look. Answer question 1(a).

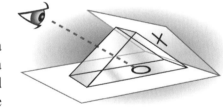

Both refraction and reflection are possible when light hits a boundary between a high index of refraction (like glass) and a lower index of refraction (like air). Whether the light is reflected or refracted depends on the angle. The critical angle is the angle at which the switch from reflection to refraction occurs.

a. What happens to the image you see through the prism? Is it an X or an O?

b. Draw a diagram showing the path of the light rays when you see the X.

c. Draw a diagram showing the path of the light rays when you see the O.

d. Is the image in the prism always reflected or refracted, or can there be both reflection and refraction at the same time?

e. Think about being outside in the bright sun looking into a glass window where it is darker inside the window. Do you see reflection, refraction, or both?

When light is reflected by the boundary between glass and air we call it total internal reflection. The same thing can happen at the boundary between water and air. A fish looking up at the surface of the water from below does not see only the sky! The fish sees reflected rays from the water from part of the surface, and refracted rays from the air from part of the surface.

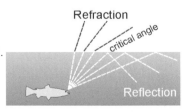

2   **Tracing the critical angle with a laser.**

You will be tracing the path of the laser light in the prism (the incident ray) and the path of the laser light leaving the prism (the refracted ray). Remember: Total internal reflection only occurs if light travels from a material that refracts (bends) light more, to a material that refracts light less.

1. Place a prism on the center of the paper on the optics table. Put the long flat side facing the left of the paper. See diagram at right. Trace the outline of the prism.

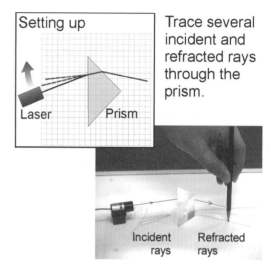

2. Put the laser on the left side of the prism. Shine the laser at the prism and make sure that the beam comes out the other side. A good way to do this is to place the laser below the level of the prism and shine it at the upper part of the prism.

3. The beam is entering the prism from the air and passing through the prism (glass) into the air again. Using your pencil, trace the path of the laser beam from the prism into the air. Observe the angles of incidence and refraction. See the diagram to the right.

4. Slowly begin to change the angle of incidence of the initial ray from the laser. Move the laser towards the top of the paper, but keep the beam hitting the prism.

5. You will see the angle of refraction increase until the beam no longer passes through the opposite side of the prism. This is total internal reflection. When the incident ray is at the critical angle, the reflected ray is at an angle of 90 degrees (that is, along the surface of the opposite side). Any increase in the incident angle (at angles greater than the critical angle), reflects the beam back into the prism.

3   **Observing internal reflection in everyday objects**

Any piece of glass or plastic can demonstrate total internal reflection.

a. Find a clear ruler or piece of clear plastic and shine the laser at the edge of it. Observe all the places where the laser beam is exiting the plastic.

b. Observe other materials around the room. Make predictions about whether they will demonstrate total internal reflection. Try out several of these materials.

? The next time that you go to a mall look at the specialty gift shops that sell interesting lamps and lights. Many of the items you will see contain fiber optic elements to help carry light from one place to another. See how many different varieties of these lights you can find.

16.1

Classifying Matter

Question: How can a homogeneous mixture be separated?

In this Investigation, you will:

1. Use a procedure called paper chromatography to separate ink into its components.

Ink is a homogeneous mixture. It consists of a **solute**, which is a collection of colored dye particles, and a **solvent**, which is the liquid that dissolves the solute(s). In this Investigation, you will use a technique called paper chromatography to separate various samples of *water-soluble* ink in order to see the dyes contained in each ink.

1 What is paper chromatography?

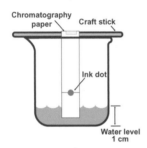

Chromatography paper   Craft stick

Ink dot

Water level
1 cm

Paper chromatography is used to separate mixtures into their components. A sample of the mixture (ink, in our case) is placed on absorbent paper. The bottom edge of the paper is placed in a liquid. As the liquid travels up the paper, it drags some of the solute particles (the dyes) with it. Different kinds of solute particles have different strengths of attraction to the liquid and to the cellulose fibers in the paper. These characteristics of the solute particles cause them to separate from each other on the paper. Some dyes travel far up the paper and some travel very little.

2 Preparing the samples

1. Cut three strips of chromatography or filter paper. Each strip should be 3 centimeters wide and a little longer than the height of the containers you will be using.

2. On each paper strip, draw a line 1.5 centimeters from one end with a pencil. This end of the paper strip will be called the "ink dot" end. On the other end of the paper, write one of the colors of ink that you will be using (black, blue or green) *and* your initials in pencil.

3. Measure the height of the cup you will be using for the Investigation. On each paper strip, mark this length (the height of the cup) with a pencil. Measure from the "ink dot" end.

4. Place a small dot of black ink (2 or 3 millimeters in diameter) in the center of the line made in step 2. On the second strip, place a blue dot, and on the third, a green dot.

5. Attach each paper strip to a craft stick by rolling the paper strip around the stick as shown in the diagram. Roll the paper until you come to the mark you made in step 3. Use your fingers to press the paper that is wrapped around the stick so that the paper does not unroll. You may want to use a small piece of tape to secure the paper to the craft stick.

3 Setting up the experiment

1. In each of the three cups, pour a small amount of water. The water level should be no higher than 1 centimeter from the bottom of the cup. Use a ruler to measure the water level.

2. Place one paper strip into each cup as shown in the diagram. The paper strip should hang straight down into the water without touching the sides of the cup. Make adjustments to the water level or the length of the paper strip to prevent the ink dot from being immersed in the water. The Investigation will not work well if the ink dot is underwater!

3. When you have achieved the proper setup, watch the water travel up each strip of paper. Remove the paper from the cup when the water is approximately 1 centimeter from the craft stick.

4. Place the paper strip on a paper towel. With a pencil, carefully mark the water line near the top of the paper strip. Allow the strip to dry.

4 Recording your results

1. In the first column of the table below, the names of the colors of ink are listed. In the second column of the table, list the colors of dye that separated from the ink dot on each of the paper strips.

2. In the third column, record the distance in millimeters from the ink dot to the highest mark made by each color of dye (Dc). Make this measurement for each color on each paper strip.

3. In the fourth column, record the distance in millimeters between the starting line and the water level line on each of your three paper strips. This is the distance traveled by the water (Dw).

4. $\frac{a}{b}$ Calculate the *retention factor* for each of the dye colors. This number shows the ratio of the distance traveled by the dye (Dc) to the distance traveled by the water (Dw). To find the ratio, you need to divide the value for Dc by Dw. Record your results in column five.

Ink color	Dye colors present	Distance traveled by dye color (Dc)	Distance traveled by water (Dw)	Retention factor (Dc ÷ Dw)
black				
blue				
green				

5 Analyzing your data

a. Which ink contained the greatest number of dye colors? Which colors did it contain?

b. Did the manufacturer use the same dye color in more than one marker? How do you know?

c. Compare your chart for the green ink with one other group's chart. Did you see the same separation of colors? Did your dye colors travel the same distance? Did your dye colors have similar retention factors? If you repeated the procedure using a 20 centimeter paper strip, would your retention factors change? Why or why not?

16.2 Measuring Matter

Question: How is matter measured?

In this Investigation, you will:

1. Measure the mass and volume of regular and irregular solids and liquids.

You have learned that matter is defined as anything that has mass and takes up space. In this Investigation, you will practice various techniques for making accurate quantitative measurements of matter. You will learn to use an indirect measurement technique: measuring volume by displacement.

1 Measuring mass

Your materials for this part of the Investigation include a large solid object, a collection of identical small objects, and a container of liquid. Develop a technique for measuring the mass of each object. Record your results in Table 1.

Table 1: Measuring mass

Object	Description of material	Mass (g)	Description of technique used to find mass
example	stick of chewing gum	3.3 g	placed directly on balance
solid object			
collection			
liquid			

2   ## Measuring volume

You have liquid in a container, a solid object with a regular shape, and in irregular solid. Develop a technique for measuring the volume of each object. Record your results in Table 2.

Table 2: Measuring volume

Object	Description of material	Volume in mL or cm^3	Description of technique used to find volume
example	cereal box	4680 cm^3	used formula: length × width × height
liquid			
regular solid			
irregular solid			

3   ## Applying your knowledge

a.   In part 1, you found the mass of a collection of identical objects. Explain how you could determine the mass of one of those objects without using the electronic balance.

b.   Imagine that you have a leaky faucet. How could you find the volume of one drop of water, using only a 100-milliliter graduated cylinder?

c.   How could you find the volume of a student? Describe your invented technique.

States of Matter

Question: How fast can you melt an ice cube?

In this Investigation, you will:

1. Observe the rate at which 15 milliliters of water changes from solid to liquid. Next, you will measure the average kinetic energy of the water molecules as they change from solid to liquid.

2. Analyze the transfer of energy which occurs when a substance undergoes a change of state.

The great ice cube race

In the first part of this Investigation, you and your teammates will race to see who can melt an ice cube in the least amount of time. Your teacher will hand you a sealed plastic bag containing an ice cube. Each cube was formed from 15 milliliters of water, measured at room temperature. It is up to you to find the best technique for melting the ice.

4 Procedure

During steps (1) to (3) hold your zipper-lock bag from the top, without touching the ice cube! If you touch the cube before the race begins, you will be disqualified!

1. Switch the CPO timer to stopwatch mode.
2. Assign one person to start the timer.
3. The first person to completely melt her or his ice cube will stop the timer.
4. Start the timer.
5. As soon as the timing begins, you may pick up your bag of ice. Try to melt the ice cube as fast as possible.
   If you open or break your plastic bag, you will be disqualified!

When the ice cubes are melted, dispose of the water and plastic bags as directed by your teacher.

5 Analyzing your results

a. List at least three techniques used in your group to melt the ice cube.

b. Which technique was most effective? Why?

c. Using what you know about potential and kinetic energy, describe the transfer of energy which occurred as your group's best technique was executed.

6 A closer look at the melting process

You have learned that molecules in a solid vibrate, but do not change position. Molecules in a liquid move over and around one another but do not spread apart. Molecules in a gas move freely, separated from one another. How do we account for this difference?

It has to do with the amount of kinetic energy in the system. As kinetic energy is added to a solid, the molecules begin to vibrate faster. When the molecules have enough kinetic energy to overcome the attractive forces holding them in place, they begin to move over and around one another. The solid begins to turn to a liquid.

How can we measure the average kinetic energy of the molecules of our water? The answer is simpler than you might expect. **Temperature** is a measure of the average kinetic energy of the molecules of a mixture or substance. In the second part of this Investigation, you will use a thermometer to gather information about the energy transfer that occurs as ice melts.

7 Procedure

1. In your lab notebook, create a data table with two columns. Label the first column "Elapsed time in minutes" and the second column "Temperature in degrees Celsius."

2. Fill a 150 mL beaker half-full of crushed ice and then add tap water to cover the ice.

3. Reset the stopwatch function of the CPO timer to zero. Place the thermometer in the ice. It should not touch the bottom or sides of the cup. Use the thermometer to gently stir the ice/water slurry.

4. Start the timer.

5. After one minute has passed, record the temperature of the ice. Continue to read and record the temperature every 30 seconds.

6. When you have readings for 3 minutes, one group member should fill a 400 mL beaker half-full of warm water. Another team member should continue to take readings every 30 seconds.

7. Just after taking the 4-minute reading, place the 150 mL beaker into the 400 mL warm water bath. Be sure that none of the warm water gets inside the 150 mL beaker!

8. Continue taking temperature readings until all the ice has melted. Note on your data table where this occurs.

9. Continue taking readings every 30 seconds for 3 more minutes AFTER all the ice has melted.

10. Dispose of the water and cup. Dry the thermometer and return all equipment to your teacher.

8 What did you learn?

a. In your lab notebook, graph the data you collected during this procedure. Label the X-axis "Time in Minutes" and the Y-axis "Temperature in degrees Celsius."

b. Where did the energy that was added to the cup of ice come from?

c. Did the kinetic energy of the water molecules increase at a constant rate throughout the experiment? Use your data as evidence to support your answer.

d. What force had to be overcome in order to change the solid to a liquid?

e. What happened to the energy that was added to the system while the ice was melting?

f. Draw a sketch of the graph you would expect to see as liquid water changes to gas. Write two or three sentences describing the energy changes that occur during this process.

17.1

Properties of Solids

Question: How can you find the density of a solid?

In this Investigation, you will:

1. Learn to find the density of various materials.
2. Use the property of density to solve a mystery.

You may be familiar with the trick question "Which is heavier: a pound of feathers or a pound of bricks?" The answer, of course, is that they have the same weight. But why do so many people blurt out "bricks" before they stop to think?

The answer lies in the amount of space occupied by a pound of each material. On the right side of the balance below, sketch a rectangular shape to represent the size of a pound of bricks. Then, on the left side, draw a second rectangle to represent the space taken up by a pound of feathers.

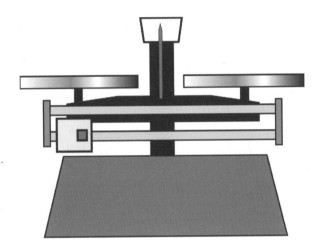

As you can see, a pound of bricks takes up a lot less space than a pound of feathers. The brick-material is squeezed together tightly, while the pound of feathers contains a large amount of empty space.

1 Setting up

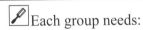Each group needs:

- graph paper and a ruler for each group member
- balance
- CPO displacement tank, disposable cup, 250-milliliter beaker, graduated cylinder
- six small identical objects (provided by your instructor), and approximately 100 pennies

2   ## Finding the relationship between the mass and volume of a substance

1. Each lab station has a unique set of six objects. Find the mass and volume of one object. Add a second object and find their combined mass and volume. Then find the combined mass and volume of three, four, and five objects. Record your data in Table 1. Note: Although your objects look identical, there may be small differences. Do not obtain your data by multiplying the mass or volume of one object by the number of objects you have.

Table 1: Mass and volume data

	one object	two objects	three objects	four objects	five objects
mass in grams (g)					
volume in milliliters (mL)					

2. Plot your data on graph paper. Label the *x*-axis "volume" and the *y*-axis "mass." Be sure to use the entire space on your graph paper for making your graph.

3   ## Analyzing your results

a. Is there any pattern to the data points on your graph? For example, the points might form a smooth curve, a straight line, a random scattering, or a cluster in a certain region. If you detect a pattern, describe it.

b. Take your ruler and move it along the points of the graph in order to find the line on the paper that is as close as possible to all of the dots. This line is called the "line of best fit." Draw the line.

Now find the slope of this line. To do so, choose any two points on the line. These will be represented as (X_1, Y_1) and (X_2, Y_2). Use the formula below to calculate the slope of the line:

$(Y_2 - Y_1) \div (X_2 - X_1)$ = slope of the line.

The slope tells how many grams of matter are contained in each milliliter of material you tested. Some substances, like lead, have quite a few grams of matter packed into each milliliter. Other substances, like styrofoam, have less than a single gram of matter packed into each milliliter.

c. Compare your slope with the result obtained by other groups. Are your slopes similar or different?

d. The relationship between a substance's mass and volume is called its density. What is the density of the material you tested?

4   ## Using your knowledge

a. Your graph includes data for five objects. Now, use your graph to predict the mass of *six* objects.

b. Next, use the balance to find the mass of six of these objects.

c. How does your value from your graph compare to the mass obtained using the balance?

d. Use the mass value that you found in step 4 (b). Find that number on the *y*-axis of your graph. Now find the point on the line which crosses that *y*-value. What is the *x*-value of that point?

e. What does the *x*-value found in step 4 (d) predict about the volume of the six objects?

f. Now, find the volume of six objects experimentally.

g. How does the *x*-value from the graph compare with the volume you obtained experimentally?

5   ## Compare class data

Collect data from each group in the class to fill in Table 2.

Table 2: Class data for density of objects

	Group1	Group 2	Group 3	Group 4	Group 5	Group 6
size of one object (mL)						
type of material						
density						

Using the data above, answer the following questions:

a. Does density depend on the size of the material? Give evidence to support your answer.

b. Does density depend on the type of material? Give evidence to support your answer.

c. Using what you have observed in this lab, do you suppose that density depends on the shape of the material? Why or why not?

6   ## Using density to solve a mystery

Many people assume that the United States' one-cent piece, the penny, is made of copper. In fact, the penny has been made from different materials at different times in its history. In 1943, for example, pennies were made of zinc-coated steel, because copper was needed for the war effort. Between 1944 and 1962, pennies were made of bronze, which is a mixture of copper, tin, and zinc. In 1962, their composition was changed to 95 percent copper and 5 percent zinc. Then, in the 1970s, the price of copper increased dramatically, reaching $1.33 per pound in 1980. This meant that the raw material in a penny was worth more than the value of the coin itself. Some members of Congress started to worry that people would collect pennies in order to melt them down and sell the copper. As a result, a bill was introduced in 1982 to change the composition of the penny to a less expensive metal with a thin copper coating.

Your job is to use the property of density to determine whether:

a. Congress decided they were overreacting to the situation, and defeated the bill.

   Or

b. Congress decided it was worth the trouble to switch to a different material, and passed the bill.

7   Procedure

a. Each lab group has been given a stack of approximately 100 pennies. Sort them into two stacks: pre-1982 and post-1982 pennies. If you find any 1982 pennies, set them aside.

b. Find the mass of your collection of pre-1982 pennies. Use the displacement tank to find the volume of the pre-1982 pennies. Repeat the procedure for your collection of post-1982 pennies. Record your results in Table 3.

Table 3: Penny data

	Pre-1982 pennies	Post-1982 pennies
mass		
volume		
density		

c. Calculate the density of each type of penny. Record your results in the third row of the table.

8   Analyze your results

Using the data you collected, answer the following questions:

a. Are the pre-1982 and post-1982 pennies made from the same material? Give evidence to support your answer.

b. Did the bill to change the composition of the penny pass or fail?

Density of Fluids

Question: Can you create a stack of liquids?

In this Investigation, you will:

1. Find the density of various liquids, and use this information to create a density column.
2. Use the density column to predict the density of a solid.

Why do you need to shake a bottle of dressing before you pour it on your salad? What does the density of liquids have to do with this? In this Investigation, you will try to stack five liquids in a graduated cylinder in order to build a density column. You will be able to use your density column to predict the density of solid materials.

1 Measuring the density of various liquids

1. You have been given 30 milliliters of each of five liquids. Using no more than 10 milliliters of each liquid, determine the density of each one. Be sure to use the most accurate techniques you have learned for finding the mass and volume of liquids.
2. Wash and dry your graduated cylinder between each measurement. Record your results in the table below.

Substance	Mass in grams	Volume in mL	Density in g/mL
molasses			
water			
vegetable oil			
light corn syrup			
glycerin			

2 Deciding how to stack your liquids

A density column is a "stack" of various liquids placed in a tall, thin cylinder. Your task is to create a density column in your 100-milliliter graduated cylinder. First, you will need to decide the order in which the liquids should be placed in the container. Use your density data from the table above to help you decide how to stack the liquids. List the order of your liquids below:

Liquid 5 (top)	
Liquid 4	
Liquid 3	
Liquid 2	
Liquid 1 (bottom)	

3   ## Constructing your density column

a.   Use the remaining 20 milliliters of each liquid to create your density column. If desired, add one or two drops of food coloring to the water, corn syrup, and glycerin to make them easier to distinguish.

b.   Carefully pour the liquids into the column. Let one liquid settle before adding the next.

4   ## Using your column to compare densities of solid objects

a.   A solid object placed in your density column will float if it is less dense than the liquid in which it is immersed, but will sink if it is more dense than the liquid. You have three objects. Predict where each object will stay when placed in the column. Write your predictions in the following table.

Material	Where will it stay?
small steel object	
cork	
rubber stopper	

b.   Gently place the objects (one at a time) into the density column.

c.   Were your predictions correct? Record your observations of each object's behavior.

5   ## Using the density column to predict the density of the rubber stopper

a.   Based on your results from above, predict the density of the rubber stopper. Use the following sentence format: The density of the rubber stopper is between __ g/mL and __g/mL.

b.   Pour the materials out of the graduated cylinder. All of the liquids may be disposed of in a sink. Clean and dry the graduated cylinder and the three objects.

c.   Calculate the actual density of the rubber stopper by obtaining its mass and volume.

d.   Does your calculated density match your predicted density based on the density column results? Explain why or why not.

Question: Can you make a clay boat float?

In this Investigation, you will:

1. Investigate how the shape of an object influences whether it sinks or floats.
2. Explore the relationship between the weight of an object and the weight of the water it displaces.

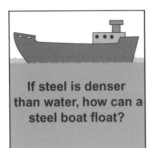

If steel is denser than water, how can a steel boat float?

In the previous Investigation, you learned that a solid material will float if it is less dense than the liquid in which it is immersed, and sink if it is denser than the liquid. You may have noticed, however, that ships are often made of steel, which is obviously denser than water. So how does a steel boat float? In this Investigation, you will experiment with modeling clay to discover how and why boats can be made of materials that are denser than water.

1 **Finding the density of your stick of clay**

1. Before molding your stick of clay, find its density. Use the formula method (length × width × height) to calculate its volume.
2. Predict: Will your stick of clay sink or float? Why?

2 **Testing your prediction**

1. Prepare the displacement tank for use. Place a dry beaker under the spout to catch the overflow.
2. Immerse your stick of clay in water. As soon as the water stops flowing, remove the clay from the water. Set it on a paper towel to dry.

   Did your stick of clay sink or float?

3 **Finding the mass and volume of the displaced water**

1. Measure the mass of the beaker + displaced water from 2.1 above.
2. Pour the water into a 100-milliliter graduated cylinder. Record the volume.
3. Dry the beaker, then measure its mass.
4. Now, calculate the mass of the displaced water.

4 **$\frac{a}{b}$ Calculating the weight of the displaced water**

Mass and weight measure two different properties of matter. Mass refers to how much matter the object contains. Weight measures the gravitational pull between the object and (in our case) Earth. The gravitational force between a 1-kilogram object and Earth is 9.8 newtons, and a 1-gram object's weight on Earth is 0.0098 newtons. You can use this information to calculate the weight of your displaced water from the mass which you found in step 3.4.

Calculate the weight of the displaced water. Use the formula: grams × (0.0098N/gram) = newtons.

5 $\frac{a}{b}$ **Calculating the weight of your clay**

From the mass of your clay (found in step 1), calculate its weight.
Again, use the formula: grams × (0.0098 N/grams) = newtons.

6 **Challenge: Can you mold your clay into a shape that floats?**

1. You know that steel can be fashioned into a shape that floats. Can you do the same thing with clay? For this part of the Investigation, you must use ALL of your clay. Mold it into a shape that you believe will float.

2. When you are ready to test a shape, lower it into a container of water approximately three-quarters full. If the clay sinks, retrieve it immediately and dry it with a paper towel. Avoid mixing water into your clay, or it will get very slimy. When your clay is dry, modify your "boat" and try again.

3. When you have successfully molded a boat that floats, take it out of the water and dry it with a paper towel. Then, prepare your displacement tank just as you did in step 2. Carefully place your boat into the displacement tank. Avoid making waves. When the water stops flowing, move the beaker away from the displacement tank spout. Retrieve your boat and set it aside to dry.

4. Find the mass of the beaker + displaced water. Subtract the mass of the beaker, which you found in step 3.3. Record the mass of the displaced water.

5. Calculate the weight of the displaced water from its mass. Use the formula given in step 4.1.

6. Pour the displaced water into a graduated cylinder. Record its volume.

7. When your boat is dry, first measure its mass, then calculate its weight.

7 **Analyzing your data**

Enter your data from this Investigation in the table below:

	weight (N) of clay	volume (mL) of displaced water	weight (N) of displaced water
stick of clay	(step 5):	(step 3.2):	(step 4):
clay boat	(step 6.7):	(step 6.6):	(step 6.5):

a. Did the weight of the clay change during the Investigation? Give a reason for your answer.
b. Which displaced more water, the stick of clay or the clay boat?
c. Which weighed more, the stick of clay or the water it displaced?
d. Which weighed more, the clay boat or the water it displaced?

8 **Drawing conclusions**

a. When you changed the shape of your clay, what happened to the amount of water it displaced?
b. Is there a relationship between the weight of a sunken object and the weight of water it displaces?
c. Is there a relationship between the weight of a floating object and the weight of water it displaces?
d. If you had a clay boat that weighed 100 newtons, how many newtons of water would it displace?

Viscosity of Fluids

Question: How can viscosity be measured?

In this Investigation, you will:

1. Learn to measure the viscosity of fluids.
2. Compare the properties of viscosity and density of fluids.

What is viscosity? As you know, it takes a lot longer to pour ketchup from one container to another than to pour the same amount of water. Ketchup has *more resistance to flow* than water. Viscosity is a measure of a fluid's resistance to flow. We say that ketchup is *more viscous* than water.

1 **Measuring viscosity**

Scientists measure viscosity in various ways. One method is to lower a paddle into a container of fluid. The paddle is attached to a motor. When the motor is switched on, the paddle turns in the liquid. The viscometer measures how much work the motor has to do to turn the paddle a certain number of times. You will measure viscosity by timing how long it takes for a marble to fall 10 centimeters through a tube filled with liquid.

The paddle and the marble viscometers work on the same principle: In order for the paddle or marble to move, the liquid must flow. As you know, two materials cannot occupy the same space at the same time. Therefore, the liquid is displaced by the paddle or marble. Your viscometer measures the relative speed of this displacement.

2 **Setting up your viscometer**

1. Attach photogate B to the CPO physics stand so that the bottom of the photogate "eye" is 7 centimeters from the physics stand base.
2. Attach photogate A so that the distance between the two photogate "eyes" is 10 centimeters.
3. Turn the CPO timer to interval mode, so that it will measure the distance between A and B. Make sure the red light on each photogate is lit.
4. Stretch a rubber band horizontally around each photogate. This will help hold the graduated cylinder in place.

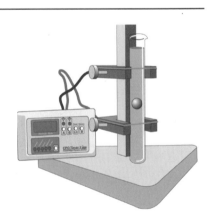

5. You will be given 150 milliliters of liquid. Pour the liquid into the graduated cylinder until it reaches 1 centimeter from the top.
6. Remove the plastic base from the graduated cylinder.
7. Slide the graduated cylinder into the U-shaped spaces created by the two photogates. Rotate the cylinder so that the photogates' light beams are not blocked by any marks on the cylinder. Check this by making sure that the red light on each photogate is still lit.
8. Reset the timer to zero, if necessary.

3   Using your viscometer

1. Carefully place an opaque glass marble on the top of the liquid. Do not drop the marble into the liquid or in any way force the marble to move.

2. Watch to make sure that as the marble starts to pass through each photogate, the red light goes off. The red light should come back on after the marble passes each photogate.

3. If the lights indicate that the marble did not break the light beam, pour the liquid back into its original container. Retrieve the marble and then pour the liquid back into the graduated cylinder. Adjust the position of the graduated cylinder. You must make sure that the light beams pass through the liquid; see "Setting up your viscometer," step 2. Then try the procedure again.

4. The timer tells you the time it took for the marble to travel between the photogates. Record this time in Table 1.

5. Repeat this procedure two more times, with your second and third marbles. Do not retrieve the marbles until you have finished all three time trials. You may need to pour off a bit of liquid each time, so that the graduated cylinder is filled up to the point one centimeter from the top.

6. Find the average velocity from the three trials and record this average in Table 1.

Table 1: Average velocity of marble in liquid

Type of liquid	Distance traveled	Time required	Average velocity of marble
Trial 1			
Trial 2			
Trial 3			
Find the average of your three values for velocity and record it here:			

4   Comparing class data

Each lab group found the data for a different substance. Record the data for each substance in Table 2.

Table 2: Class data for average velocity of marble in liquids of different viscosities

Substance	Avg. velocity of marble in substance at 20°C
group 1:	
group 2:	
group 3:	
group 4:	
group 5:	

5   Analyzing class data

a. Rewrite the table above, listing the liquids from **least** viscous to **most** viscous.

b. Compare this data with the data from the density column (Investigation 17.2). Does there seem to be a relationship between density and viscosity at room temperature? In other words, if liquids have low density, do they also have low viscosity? Provide an example to justify your answer.

18.1

Atomic Structure

Question: How was the size of an atom's nucleus determined?

In this Investigation, you will:

1. Use indirect measurement to find the radius of a circle.
2. Compare and contrast your work with Rutherford's classic experiment.

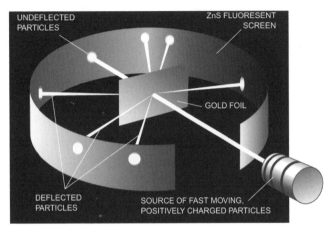

UNDEFLECTED PARTICLES

ZnS FLUORESENT SCREEN

GOLD FOIL

DEFLECTED PARTICLES

SOURCE OF FAST MOVING, POSITIVELY CHARGED PARTICLES

In 1911, British physicist Ernest Rutherford and his colleagues, Hans Geiger and Ernest Marsden, bombarded a thin sheet of gold foil with tiny alpha particles. Most of the alpha particles passed through the foil and hit a screen behind it. But to their surprise, some of the particles bounced back. They must have hit areas of the foil that were more dense! From these results, Rutherford hypothesized that an atom must be made up mostly of empty space, allowing most of the alpha particles to pass through the foil. In the center of the atom, he suggested, there was a tiny core called a nucleus, where most of the atom's mass could be found. In the gold foil experiment, the alpha particles that hit the nucleus of an atom of gold bounced back.

Rutherford and his colleagues set up a ratio of alpha particles that bounced back to total alpha particles. This allowed them to estimate the amount of space taken up by the nucleus in a gold atom. In this Investigation, you will use a similar technique to measure the radius of a circle.

1   **Using indirect measurement to determine the radius of a circle**

1. Place your sheet of carbon paper on the floor, **face up.**
2. Lay the circle-sheet, **circles side down**, over the carbon paper. You should not be able to see the circles during this activity.
3. Tape the circle-sheet to the floor in order to hold it in place.
4. Choose one person to act as the "dropper." The other person will serve as the "catcher." You will switch roles after 25 drops.
5. The "dropper" should hold the marble about 8 inches (the width of a piece of paper) above the paper. You will drop the marble onto the paper. The impact of the marble will cause the carbon paper to make a mark on the circle sheet. Your goal is to cover the paper **evenly** with marble marks. Later you will count the marks to determine the number that fell within the circles compared with the total number of marks.
6. Be sure to catch the marble before it bounces. This ensures that each drop of the marble will make only one mark on the paper.
7. Drop the marble 25 times. If the marble misses the paper, repeat the drop. Switch roles, and repeat the procedure. Continue this process until 100 successful drops have been completed.

2   Recording the data

1. Remove your circle-sheet from the floor. Discard the carbon paper.

2. Count the total number of impact marks on the paper. Do not include those that bleed off the edge of the paper. Record your data in the table below.

3. Count the number of marks that are completely within a circle. Do not include those that touch the edge of the circle. Record your data in the table below.

4. Measure the length and width of the paper in millimeters and calculate its area. Record this information in the table below.

5. We know that the circles are of uniform size and the placement of the marks was random. Therefore, we can set up a proportion:

$$\frac{\text{number of marks in circles}}{\text{number of marks on paper}} = \frac{\text{total area of circles}}{\text{total area on paper}}$$

6. Solve this equation for the total area of circles. Record your result in the table below.

number of marks on paper	number of marks in circles	area of paper in mm²	total area of circles in mm²

3 $\frac{a}{b}$ Analyzing your results

a. Divide the total area of the circles by the number of circles on your paper. This will tell you the area of one circle by *indirect measurement*.

b. Now, calculate the area of one circle by *direct measurement*. First, use your ruler to find the radius of one circle in millimeters. Use this formula to determine the area of one circle: $A_c = \Pi r^2$ where A_c, the area of a circle, is equal to pi (3.14) times the radius squared.

c. Compare this value with the radius found by the indirect method. Calculate the percent error of your results: $\frac{(\text{indirect} - \text{direct})}{\text{direct}} \times 100 = \text{percent error}$

4   Drawing conclusions

a. Write a paragraph to explain how this activity is like the gold foil experiment. Be sure to comment on **each** piece of equipment used. For example, what does the marble represent?

b. Could Rutherford and his colleagues calculate percent error in the same manner that you did? Why or why not?

c. What might Rutherford and his colleagues have done to confirm the accuracy of his findings?

d. Would your percent error have decreased if the marble were dropped 200 times? Or 1000 times?

e. Name two potential sources of error in your experiment. How could you change the procedure to minimize these errors?

f. Challenge: Calculate the number of marks that should fall inside the circles on your paper if you dropped the marble 500 times.

Question: What are atoms and how are they put together?

In this Investigation, you will:

1. Investigate the structure of the atom.
2. Identify what makes atoms of different elements different from each other.
3. Use spectral analysis to identify the elements present in different light sources.

In this Investigation, you will use the atom board to learn about atomic structure. The marbles will represent the three particles in the atom. Red marbles are protons, blue marbles are neutrons, and yellow marbles are electrons. The position of the marbles on the board shows where the real particles are in the atom. The neutrons and protons are in the nucleus (center) and the electrons are arranged in energy levels around the outside. After you have gained an understanding of atomic structure, and compared atoms of different elements, you will use a technique called spectral analysis to identify the elements present in the different light sources found in your school building.

 Neutrons (blue)

 Protons (red)

 Electrons (yellow)

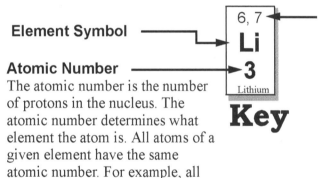

Element Symbol

Atomic Number
The atomic number is the number of protons in the nucleus. The atomic number determines what element the atom is. All atoms of a given element have the same atomic number. For example, all atoms of Lithium (Li) have 3 protons in the nucleus.

Key

Mass Number
The mass number is the total number of particles (protons plus neutrons) in the nucleus. Atoms with the same. number of protons but different mass numbers are called **isotopes.** These numbers are the mass numbers of the stable isotopes. Stable isotopes are not **radioactive.** For example, lithium has two stable isotopes, Li^6 with three protons and three neutrons, and Li^7 with three protons and four neutrons.

1   Setting up the atom board

1. Each atom board can have four players.
2. Each player should use one of the four pockets at the corners.
3. Each player should start with the following marbles in their pocket.

      6 blue marbles (neutrons)
      5 red marbles (protons)
      5 yellow marbles (electrons)

4. The remaining marbles stay in the containers and are the 'bank.' Players may need to trade marbles with the bank later in the game.

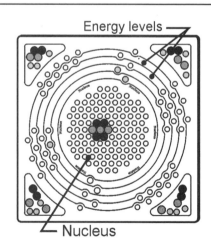
Energy levels

Nucleus

2   # The game of atomic challenge

The first player to run out of marbles wins. The object of the game is to play all your marbles by adding them to the board to make real, stable atoms from the periodic table. After each turn you must correctly identify what atom has been made. For example, you might say "Lithium six" if the marbles you added made an atom with 3 protons (red), 3 neutrons (blue) and 3 electrons (yellow).

Each player takes turns adding up to 5 marbles to the atom. The player must add the marbles according to the rules for building atoms:

1. The number of protons matches the atomic number (number of red marbles = atomic number)

2. The total number of protons and neutrons equals one of the right mass numbers for that element (number of red + blue = mass number)

3. The number of electrons and protons match (number of red = number of yellow)

4. Protons and neutrons go in the nucleus.

5. Electrons go in the energy levels.

You can add no more than 5 marbles per turn. The 5 can include any mix of colors, such as 2 red, 1 blue, and 2 yellow. You may not always be able to add 5, sometimes you will only be able to add 3 or 4 and still make a real atom. You cannot add more than 5 in one turn.

Example of a good move

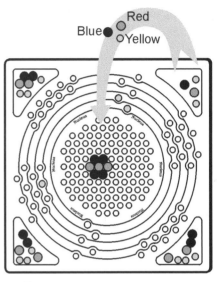

$$Li^7 + p + n + e = Be^9$$

The periodic table should be carefully consulted by all players to see whether the atom is correct or not. If the atom has been incorrectly built or identified, the offending player must take their marbles back and does not get to try again until the next turn. The next player on the right then takes a turn.

A player can trade marbles with the bank INSTEAD of taking their turn. You can take as many marbles, and of as many colors, as you need, but you must take at least as many total marbles as you put in. For example you can trade 2 yellows for 1 yellow, 1 blue, and 1 red. You put in 2 and took 3, which is OK. You cannot put in 2 and take only 1 back.

3   # What did you learn?

a. Which particles are found in an atom's nucleus? Which particles are found outside the nucleus?

b. Name one element that is always radioactive and has an atomic number less than 50.

c. What is the atomic number of sodium (Na)?

d. How many protons does Na have?

e. How many different isotopes does magnesium (Mg) have?

f. How many protons, neutrons, and electrons does Mg^{26} have?

g. If an isotope of silicon (Si) has 15 neutrons, what is its mass number?

h. What do you call an atom where the number of electrons is different from the number of protons?

i. What is the heaviest element with at least one isotope that is NOT radioactive?

j. What element has atoms with 26 protons in the nucleus?

4   What does atomic structure have to do with light and color?

Have you ever noticed differences in the colors of light given off by different light sources in your school building or at home? With your group, discuss the differences in the light given off by the light sources listed in the table below and record your observations.

Light Source	What color(s) of light is given off by the source?
Incandescent light (a regular light bulb)	
Fluorescent light (found in your classroom)	
Mercury vapor lights (the light sources found in a gym)	
Sodium lights (street lights)	

The color of light given off by different types of light sources has to do with the different elements found inside of each light source. In another unit, you learned that atoms emit light when some of their electrons gain enough energy to jump to a higher energy level. When the electrons fall back to a lower energy level, they emit electromagnetic radiation, sometimes in the form of light. Atoms of different elements emit light in characteristic regions of the electromagnetic spectrum. This is why light sources of certain types give off distinct colors of light.

In the next part of the Investigation, you will use a spectrometer to analyze the light given off by different light sources, and identify the elements found in them. Using a spectrometer is a spectral analysis technique.

5   Using the spectrometer

Hold the spectrometer so that the printed side is facing upward. In a well-lit room, hold the spectrometer so that one eye is looking through the diffraction grating and the other eye is closed. You should see a scale as illustrated below. You should also notice colors at various places inside the spectrometer. This is caused by light entering the spectrometer from different sources.

View colors here
Point this slit at the light
Look in here

Notice that the plastic disk that is attached to the diffraction grating can be turned. Looking into the spectrometer, rotate the disk until you see colors in a horizontal line to your left. The colors should appear between the two lines of numbers on the scales.

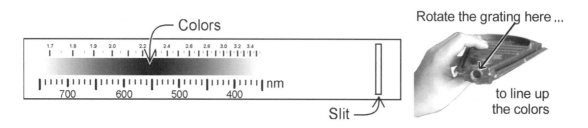

Colors
Slit
Rotate the grating here ...
to line up the colors

6   ## Observing different light sources

◆ **Safety Tips: Never look directly into any light source - especially the sun! Never aim the spectrometer directly at the sun. Instead, aim it at a cloud that is reflecting sunlight.**

1. Using the spectrometer, observe a **fluorescent light**. Aim the slit (on the right side of the spectrometer) directly at the fluorescent light and look at the spectrum on the scale. The spectrum of the fluorescent light should include several bright, vertical "lines" of different colors. These are the *spectral emission lines* of the elements found inside of the light source. Record where you see the vertical lines on the spectrometer scale in the table below. Use colored pencils to record the different colors of each vertical line you see.

2. Record the *position* for each vertical line you see, in nanometers (nm), in column three of the table.

3. Observe the spectral patterns of other light sources (gym lights, street lights, security lights or other light sources). For each light source: (a)write the name of the light source in the table; (b)record the positions of the vertical lines on the scale using colored pencils; and (c)record the position of each vertical line (nm) in the third column of the table.

4. Your teacher will provide you with the values, in nanometers, of spectral emission lines for various elements. Use these values to identify the elements found in each light source and write them in the last column of the table.

Light source	Spectrometer Scale (nm)		Position of each vertical line (nm)	Elements present
Fluorescent	700 600 500 400			
	700 600 500 400			
	700 600 500 400			
	700 600 500 400			
	700 600 500 400			

Question: What does atomic structure have to do with the periodic table?

In this Investigation, you will:

1. Learn about nuclear reactions.
2. Learn how the different elements of the periodic table were formed.

This Investigation is a game for two to four players called Nuclear Reactions. In order to win, you will need to become quick to figure out which nuclear reactions will make real atoms. The game is similar to the processes by which the elements of the periodic table were created inside stars. At the center of a star, nuclear reactions combine atoms to make new elements. We believe all the elements of the periodic table heavier than lithium were created inside stars through nuclear reactions. The process gives off a huge amount of energy and that is why the sun shines. The energy from nuclear reactions in the sun is what makes life on Earth possible.

Notice that the elements of the periodic table are arranged by **atomic number**, from lowest to highest. The atomic number is equal to the number of protons in the nucleus of an atom. The atomic number also indicates the number of electrons an atom has. Each element has a unique atomic number.

Isotopes are atoms with the same number of protons, but different numbers of neutrons. Isotopes are the same element, but have a different **mass number**. The mass number indicates how many protons and neutrons are in the nucleus of the isotope. The periodic table below shows the mass numbers of the stable isotopes of each element.

1   Introduction to Nuclear Reactions

If you were to add one, two or four extra neutrons to lithium-7 you would have created lithium-8, lithium-9, and lithium-11, respectively. Each of these isotopes of lithium is **radioactive**. These means that the atomic force in the nucleus (called **strong nuclear force**) is not strong enough to hold these atoms together. The nuclei of these atoms fly apart.

The goal of Nuclear Reactions is to earn points by creating atoms that are stable (not radioactive) and neutrally charged (not ions). Remember that **ions** are atoms that have different numbers of protons and electrons so they have a charge.

Each player starts with 8 protons, 8 electrons, and 8 neutrons in their pocket of the Atomic Building Game board. The game will last for about a half-hour. The first player to 20 points wins.

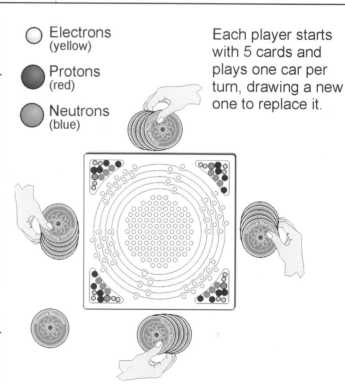

Electrons (yellow)

Protons (red)

Neutrons (blue)

Each player starts with 5 cards and plays one car per turn, drawing a new one to replace it.

2   Playing Nuclear Reactions

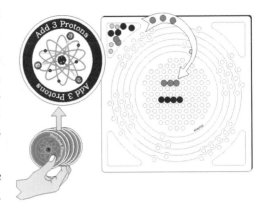

To begin play, each player is dealt five cards from the deck of Nuclear Reactions cards. These are held and not shown to anyone else.

Players take turns, choosing which card to play each turn, and adding or subtracting particles from the atom as instructed on the card. For example, playing an "Add 2 Electrons" card would mean you place two yellow marbles in the atom.

Sub-atomic particles that are added or subtracted from the atom must come from, or be placed in your own pocket. You may not play a card for which you do not have the right marbles. For example, a player with only 2 protons left cannot play an "Add 3 Protons" card.

Each time you play a card, draw a new card from the deck so you always have five cards. Played cards can be shuffled and re-used as needed

3   Scoring points

1. The number of points scored depends how many of the conditions below are satisfied by the atom you create. You can use the periodic table to determine strategy and points. In particular it is useful to know which cards to play to get to stable isotopes, neutral atoms, or stable and neutral atoms.

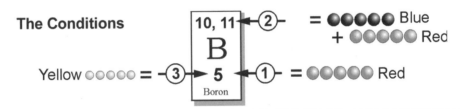

The Conditions

Condition #1: The number of protons (red marbles) matches the atomic number.
Condition #2: The number of protons (red marbles) plus the number of neutrons (blue marbles) equals one of the correct mass numbers for the element of Rule #1. This creates a stable nucleus.
Condition #3: The number of electrons (yellow marbles) equals the number of protons (red marbles). This creates a neutral atom.

You score 1 point if your move creates or leaves a stable nucleus. For example, you score 1 point by adding a neutron to a nucleus with 6 protons and 5 neutrons. Adding a neutron makes a carbon 12 nucleus, which is stable. The next player can also score a point by adding another neutron, making carbon 13. Points cannot be scored for making a stable nucleus by adding or subtracting electrons, because electrons do not live in the nucleus! To get the nucleus right you need to satisfy conditions #1 and #2.

You score 1 point for adding or taking electrons or protons from the atom if your move creates or leaves a neutral atom. A neutral atom has the same number of electrons and protons. Because neutrons have no charge, points cannot be scored for neutrality by adding or subtracting neutrons. Getting the electrons and protons to balance satisfies condition #3.

You score 3 points (the best move) when you add or take particles from the atom and your move creates a perfect, stable and neutral atom. Both adding and subtracting can leave stable, neutral atoms. For example, taking a neutron from a stable, neutral carbon 13 atom leaves a stable, neutral carbon 12 atom, scoring 3 points. You get 3 points if your turn makes an atom that meets all 3 conditions.

4   Miscellaneous rules

Taking a turn
When it is your turn you must either

1. Play a card and add or subtract marbles from the atom.

2. Trade in your cards for a new set of five.

Trading in cards
You may trade in all your cards at any time by forfeiting a turn. You have to trade all your cards in at once. Shuffle the deck before taking new cards.

Using the periodic table
All players should be allowed to use the special periodic table of the elements (on the next page) in the course of the game.

The marble bank
You may choose to play two versions of the marble bank.

Version 1: Players may take marbles from the bank at any time so they have enough to play the game.

Version 2: Players must lose a turn to draw marbles from the bank, and may draw no more than 5 total marbles (of any colors) in one turn.

5   Applying what you learned

Nuclear Fusion

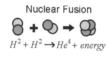

$$H^2 + H^2 \rightarrow He^4 + energy$$

Nuclear Fission

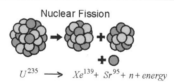

$$U^{235} \longrightarrow Xe^{139} + Sr^{95} + n + energy$$

a.   There are two basic kinds of nuclear reactions, fission and fusion. Fission splits heavy elements up into lighter elements. Fusion combines lighter elements to make heavier elements. Both can release energy, depending on which elements are involved. What element do you get when you fuse lithium six and boron 11 together? It is stable or radioactive?

b.   Write down a nuclear reaction using only two elements that would allow you to build Fluorine 19 starting with Boron 10.

c.   Suppose you split a uranium 238 atom. If you have to break it into two pieces, name two elements that could be formed. Be sure that your two elements use up all the neutrons and protons in the uranium. Are either of your two elements stable or is one (or both) radioactive?

Periodic Table of the Elements
with Atomic Numbers and Mass Numbers of Stable Isotopes

Key

Mass Numbers of Stable Isotopes

6, 7 — Li — Element Symbol
3 — Lithium — Atomic Number / Element Name

Group 1	Group 2												Group 13	Group 14	Group 15	Group 16	Group 17	Group 18
1, 2 **H** 1 Hydrogen																		3, 4 **He** 2 Helium
6, 7 **Li** 3 Lithium	9 **Be** 4 Beryllium												10, 11 **B** 5 Boron	12, 13 **C** 6 Carbon	14, 15 **N** 7 Nitrogen	16, 17, 18 **O** 8 Oxygen	19 **F** 9 Fluorine	20, 21, 22 **Ne** 10 Neon
23 **Na** 11 Sodium	24, 25, 26 **Mg** 12 Magnesium												27 **Al** 13 Aluminum	28, 29, 30 **Si** 14 Silicon	31 **P** 15 Phosphorus	32, 33, 34, 36 **S** 16 Sulfur	35, 37 **Cl** 17 Chlorine	36, 38, 40 **Ar** 18 Argon
39, 41 **K** 19 Potassium	40, 42, 43, 44, 46, 48 **Ca** 20 Calcium	45 **Sc** 21 Scandium	46, 47, 48, 49, 50 **Ti** 22 Titanium	51 **V** 23 Vanadium	50, 52, 53, 54 **Cr** 24 Chromium	55 **Mn** 25 Manganese	54, 56, 57, 58 **Fe** 26 Iron	59 **Co** 27 Cobalt	58, 60, 61, 62, 64 **Ni** 28 Nickel	63, 65 **Cu** 29 Copper	64, 66, 67, 68, 70 **Zn** 30 Zinc		69, 71 **Ga** 31 Gallium	70, 72, 73, 74, 76 **Ge** 32 Germanium	75 **As** 33 Arsenic	74, 76, 77, 78, 80, 82 **Se** 34 Selenium	79, 81 **Br** 35 Bromine	78, 80, 82, 83, 84, 86 **Kr** 36 Krypton
85 **Rb** 37 Rubidium	84, 86, 87, 88 **Sr** 38 Strontium	89 **Y** 39 Yttrium	90, 91, 92, 94, 96 **Zr** 40 Zirconium	93 **Nb** 41 Niobium	92, 94-100 **Mo** 42 Molybdenum	none **Tc** 43 Technetium	96, 104, 98-103 **Ru** 44 Ruthenium	104 **Rh** 45 Rhodium	102, 108, 11 0104-106 **Pd** 46 Palladium	107, 109 **Ag** 47 Silver	106, 108, 114, 110-112, 116 **Cd** 48 Cadmium		113 **In** 49 Indium	112, 114-120, 122, 124 **Sn** 50 Tin	121 **Sb** 51 Antimony	120, 122, 123, 124-126, 130 **Te** 52 Tellurium	127 **I** 53 Iodine	124, 126, 134, 128-132, 136 **Xe** 54 Xenon
133 **Cs** 55 Cesium	130, 132, 134-138 **Ba** 56 Barium	139 **La** 57 Lanthanum	174, 176-180 **Hf** 72 Hafnium	180, 181 **Ta** 73 Tantalum	180, 182, 183, 184, 186 **W** 74 Tungsten	185 **Re** 75 Rhenium	184, 192, 186-190 **Os** 76 Osmium	191, 193 **Ir** 77 Iridium	192, 198, 194-196 **Pt** 78 Platinum	197 **Au** 79 Gold	196, 204, 198-202 **Hg** 80 Mercury		203, 205 **Tl** 81 Thallium	204, 206-208 **Pb** 82 Lead	209 **Bi** 83 Bismuth	none **Po** 84 Polonium	none **At** 85 Astatine	none **Rn** 86 Radon
none **Fr** 87 Francium	none **Ra** 88 Radium	139 **Ac** 89 Actinium	none **Rf** 104 Rutherfordium	none **Db** 105 Dubnium	none **Sg** 106 Seaborgium	none **Bh** 107 Bohrium	none **Hs** 108 Hassium	none **Mt** 109 Meitnerium										

136, 138, 140 **Ce** 58 Cerium	141 **Pr** 59 Praseodymium	142, 143, 145, 146, 148, 150 **Nd** 60 Neodymium	none **Pm** 61 Promethium	144, 152, 154, 148, 149, 150 **Sm** 62 Samarium	151, 153 **Eu** 63 Europium	152, 160, 154-158 **Gd** 64 Gadolinium	159 **Tb** 65 Terbium	156, 158, 160-164 **Dy** 66 Dysprosium	165 **Ho** 67 Holmium	162, 164, 166, 167, 168, 170 **Er** 68 Erbium	169 **Tm** 69 Thulium	168, 176, 170-174 **Yb** 70 Ytterbium	175 **Lu** 71 Lutecium
none **Th** 90 Thorium	none **Pa** 91 Protactinium	none **U** 92 Uranium	none **Np** 93 Neptunium	none **Pu** 94 Plutonium	none **Am** 95 Americium	none **Cm** 96 Curium	none **Bk** 97 Berkelium	none **Cf** 98 Californium	none **Es** 99 Einsteinium	none **Fm** 100 Fermium	none **Md** 101 Mendelevium	none **No** 102 Nobelium	none **Lr** 103 Lawrencium

19.1 Bonding and Molecules

Question: Why do atoms form chemical bonds?

In this Investigation, you will:

1. Build models of atoms to gain an understanding of the arrangement of electrons.
2. Identify how atoms form chemical bonds and the role of electrons in bonding.

Most of the matter on Earth is in the form of compounds. Even when a substance exists as a pure element, it tends eventually to combine with other elements. For example, if you leave an iron nail outside in the rain, it will quickly combine with the oxygen in the air to form iron oxide, better known as rust. In this Investigation, you will build models of atoms and discover one of the fundamental ideas in chemistry: how electrons are involved in the formation of chemical bonds.

1 Reviewing atomic structure

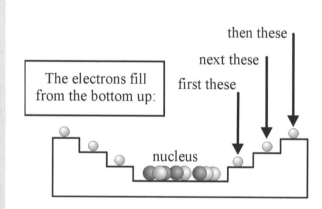

The electrons fill from the bottom up:

then these

next these

first these

nucleus

Let's review what you already know about atoms:

- A neutral atom has the same number of electrons and protons.

- The electrons occupy energy levels surrounding the nucleus.

- Since electrons are attracted to the nucleus, they fill the lower energy levels first.

Once a given level is full, electrons start filling the next level.

2 How many electrons are in the outermost level?

Using the atom building game, build each element in the table. For each element, record the number of electrons in the outermost energy level and the number of unoccupied spaces in the outermost energy level.

element	atomic number	electrons in outermost level	unoccupied spaces in outermost level
hydrogen			
helium			
lithium			
fluorine			
neon			
sodium			
chlorine			
argon			
potassium			

3   What are valence electrons?

Examine the table you just completed and record the answers to the following questions:

a. What do lithium, sodium, and potassium have in common?

b. What do fluorine and chlorine have in common?

c. What do neon and argon have in common?

The electrons in the outermost energy level of an atom are called **valence electrons**. These are the electrons involved in chemical bonds. Lithium, sodium, and potassium each have one valence electron.

4   Modeling a chemical bond

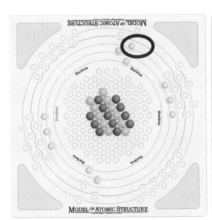 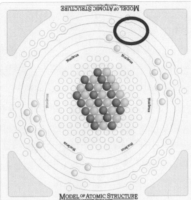

Atoms that have a complete outermost energy level are stable. If there are empty holes, an atom will either gain, lose, or share electrons with another atom in order to complete its outermost level and become stable. When atoms gain, lose, or share electrons with another atom, they form **chemical bonds**.

Using two atom building games, build a sodium atom and a chlorine atom. Put them next to each other and answer the questions below.

a. In order to complete its outermost energy level, do you think sodium will tend to lose its only valence electron, or gain seven? Explain your answer.

b. In order to complete its outermost energy level, do you think chlorine will tend to lose all of its valence electrons or gain one electron? Explain your answer.

c. Why might these two atoms bond together to form a molecule? In your answer, describe what you think might happen when sodium and chlorine form a chemical bond.

5   Determining oxidation numbers

An element's **oxidation number** is equal to the charge an atom has when it **ionizes**, that is, gains or loses electrons.

Use your models of sodium and chlorine to answer the questions below.

a. Remove the valence electron from sodium. What has happened to the balance of positive and negative charges? What is sodium's oxidation number?

b. Move the electron you took from sodium into the chlorine. What happens to chlorine's charge when it gains the electron from the sodium atom? What is chlorine's oxidation number?

c. When sodium and chlorine form a chemical bond, what is the overall charge of the molecule? Why do you think sodium and chlorine combine in a 1:1 ratio?

19.2   Chemical Formulas

Question: Why do atoms combine in certain ratios?

In this Investigation, you will:

1. Discover the relationship between elements, their placement on the periodic table, and chemical formulas.
2. Build models of compounds using the periodic table tiles and write their chemical formulas.

Chemists have long noticed that groups of elements behave similarly. The periodic table is an arrangement of the elements grouped according to similar behavior. In this Investigation, you will discover how the arrangement of electrons in atoms is related to groups on the periodic table. You will also learn why atoms form chemical bonds with other atoms in certain ratios.

1   Oxidation numbers and ions

An element's **oxidation number** indicates how many electrons are lost or gained when chemical bonding occurs. The oxidation number is equal to the charge an atom has when it **ionizes**, that is, gains or loses electrons to become an **ion**. The partial periodic table below shows the most common oxidation numbers of the elements. The oxidation numbers are written above the group number above each column on the table. Groups 1, 2, and 13 to 18 are called the **main group elements.**

Predicting Oxidation Numbers from the Periodic Table
Partial Table

1+ 1	2+ 2	Transition Metals - Variable Oxidation Numbers										3+ 13	4+ 14	3- 15	2- 16	1- 17	0 18
H 1																	He 2
Li 3	Be 4											B 5	C 6	N 7	O 8	F 9	Ne 10
Na 11	Mg 12	3	4	5	6	7	8	9	10	11	12	Al 13	Si 14	P 15	S 16	Cl 17	Ar 18
K 19	Ca 20	Sc 21	Ti 22	V 23	Cr 24	Mn 25	Fe 26	Co 27	Ni 28	Cu 29	Zn 30	Ga 31	Ge 32	As 33	Se 34	Br 35	Kr 36
Rb 37	Sr 38	Y 39	Zr 40	Nb 41	Mo 42	Tc 43	Ru 44	Rh 45	Pd 46	Ag 47	Cd 48	In 49	Sn 50	Sb 51	Te 52	I 53	Xe 54

a. How are elements grouped according to the number of valence electrons in their outermost levels?

b. Why do elements in group 2 have an oxidation number of 2+?

c. Why do elements in group 17 have an oxidation number of 1-?

d. Why do the oxidation numbers in the first two groups tend to be positive?

2   Predicting chemical formulas

Compounds that are formed from ions are called **ionic compounds**. Predict the chemical formulas for ionic compounds that are made up of the pairs of elements in the table below. Use the following steps:

1. Using the periodic table on the previous page, determine the ion formed by each element.
2. Figure out how many periodic table tiles of each element will be needed to make the compound electrically neutral.
3. Form the compound with your tiles and write the chemical formula for each compound based on the number of tiles of each element

element 1	element 2	ion 1	ion 2	number of tiles of element 1	number of tiles of element 2	chemical formula
hydrogen	fluorine					
magnesium	sulfur					
calcium	bromine					
aluminum	oxygen					
potassium	chlorine					
lithium	argon					

3   Naming ionic compounds

Naming ionic compounds is very simple if you follow these rules:

1. Write the name of the element with a positive oxidation number first.
2. Write the root name of the element with a negative oxidation number second. For example, chlor- is the root name of chlorine. Subtract the -ine ending.
3. Add the ending -ide to the root name. Chlor- becomes chloride.

Using these rules, write the name of each of the compounds in the table above.

19.3

Comparing Molecules

Question: What is the meaning of a chemical formula?

In this Investigation, you will:

1. Use nuts and bolts to model different combinations of atoms to form compounds.
2. Determine the percent composition of the compounds made out of nuts and bolts.
3. Determine the chemical formula of your compounds based on percent composition of nuts and bolts.

 You have learned that atoms combine in whole-number ratios to form chemical compounds. In fact, the same two elements may form several different compounds by combining in different ratios. Chemical formulas show the ratios in which elements combine to form a compound. In this Investigation, you will use nuts and bolts to illustrate the meaning of chemical formulas.

1 ## Find the mass of the individual atoms

Your teacher has given you a set of nuts and bolts. Let's assume that the nuts represent atoms of the element **Nu**. Bolts represent atoms of the element **Bo**. Find the mass of one **Nu** atom and the mass of one **Bo** atom and record below:

Mass of **Nu** atom (g):   Mass of **Bo** atom (g):

2 ## How many different compounds can you make?

Using the nuts and bolts, build the three different molecules listed in the table below. Then build two molecules of your own. Write the chemical formula for these molecules in the table. Using a balance, measure the mass of each molecule. Next, calculate the percent composition of each element in the molecule by using the formulas provided. Finally, calculate the ratio of **Nu** atoms and the ratio of **Bo** atoms in the molecule using the formulas provided.

chemical formula Nu_xBo_y	mass of 1 molecule	% **Nu** $\dfrac{\text{mass of nuts}}{\text{mass of molecule}} \times 100$	% **Bo** $\dfrac{\text{mass of bolts}}{\text{mass of molecule}} \times 100$	ratio of **Nu** $\dfrac{\text{\% of nuts}}{\text{mass of 1 nut}}$	ratio of **Bo** $\dfrac{\text{\% of bolts}}{\text{mass of 1 bolt}}$
1. Nu_4Bo_2					
2. Nu_2Bo_1					
3. Nu_2Bo_2					
4.					
5.					

3 $\frac{a}{b}$ Determining the empirical formula of your compounds

As you have learned, elements can combine in many different whole-number ratios to form different compounds. The simplest whole-number ratios by which elements combine are written in a form called the **empirical formula**. The actual number of atoms of each element in the compound is written in a form called the **molecular formula**. For example, H_2O_2 is the molecular formula for hydrogen peroxide. Its empirical formula, or the smallest whole-number ratio is H_1O_1, or simply HO. Determine the empirical formulas for each of your compounds using the following method:

Divide the larger of the two ratios of Nu and Bo by the smaller one. And divide the smaller one by itself to get 1. The result will be the ratio of Nu to Bo. Write the empirical formula for each of your compounds in the table below. If your ratios are not whole numbers, convert them to whole numbers. For example, $Nu_{1.5}Bo_1$ would become Nu_3Bo_2. Finally, write the molecular formula of the compound you made.

ratio of Nu	ratio of Bo	largest ratio / smallest ratio Nu or Bo?	smallest ratio / smallest ratio Nu or Bo?	Empirical formula Nu_xBo_y	Molecular formula Nu_xBo_y
1.					
2.					
3.					
4.					
5.					

4   Challenge!

What is the empirical formula and number of molecules of the compound in this box?

$\frac{a}{b}$ Your teacher has handed you a box with a certain number of molecules of Nu_xBo_y in it. Your teacher will share the following information with you: (a) percent Nu; (b) percent Bo; (c) mass of one molecule of the mystery compound; and (d) mass of empty box. Can you figure out the empirical formula and number of molecules of the mystery compound in the box? For this activity, assume the empirical and molecular formulas of your mystery molecule are the same. Show all of your calculations. You may use a balance to find the mass of your box of mystery molecules.

Percent Nu: Percent Bo:

Mass of one molecule of Nu_xBo_y: Mass of box:

Present your findings, and the methods you used, to the class.

Chemical Changes

Question: What is the evidence that a chemical change has occurred?

In this Investigation, you will:

1. Carry out and observe a series of chemical reactions.

2. Develop a set of rules for determining the occurrence of chemical changes.

Chemical changes are occurring around you all of the time. One way to know that a chemical change has occurred is that the chemical properties of reacting substances are different from the products formed. In this Investigation, you will make a list of the evidence for chemical change by carefully observing a series of chemical reactions.

Safety Tip: Wear goggles and an apron during the entire Investigation.

- Your teacher will provide you with the materials and equipment you need to carry out each chemical reaction.

- You will complete a total of six chemical reactions for this Investigation.

- Carefully follow the directions provided for each reaction below.

- Record detailed observations for each reaction.

- Record descriptions of what each substance looks like before and after the chemical change takes place.

- Properly dispose of all of your reactions after the Investigation.

1 Reaction #1

1. Put 5 grams of epsom salts into a baggie.
2. Add 50 milliliters of ammonia solution to the baggie and close it.
3. Feel the baggie with your hands as the reaction proceeds.
4. Record all observations.
5. Let the baggie sit until you are finished with the other reactions and record any further observations.

2 Reaction #2

1. Place a potato slice into a baggie.
2. Add 50 milliliters of hydrogen peroxide to the baggie and close it.
3. Feel the baggie with your hands as the reaction proceeds.
4. Record all observations.
5. Let the baggie sit until you are finished with the other reactions and record any further observations.

3 **Reaction #3**

1. Put 5 grams of baking soda into a baggie.
2. Add 10 milliliters of red cabbage juice and 50 milliliters of vinegar. Close the baggie.
3. Feel the baggie with your hands as the reaction proceeds.
4. Record all observations.
5. Let the baggie sit until you are finished with the other reactions and record any further observations.

4 **Reaction #4**

1. Put 10 grams of calcium chloride and 5 grams of baking soda into a baggie.
2. Add 50 milliliters of red cabbage juice and close the baggie.
3. Feel the baggie with your hands as the reaction proceeds.
4. Record all observations.
5. Let the baggie sit until you are finished with the other reactions and record any further observations.

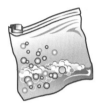

5 **Reaction #5**

1. Activate a glow stick as instructed by your teacher.
2. Feel the glow stick as the reaction proceeds.
3. Record all observations.

6 **Reaction #6**

1. Activate a heat pack as instructed by your teacher.
2. Feel the heat pack with your hands.
3. Record all observations.

7 **Interpreting your observations**

1. Look over your observations for each reaction.
2. Categorize your observations using terms such as: bubbles, color change, etc.
3. Identify the evidence of a chemical change for each observation category.
4. Make a table like the one below and record your observations. An example has been provided.

observation category	evidence of chemical change
bubbles/gas formation	The formation of a gas indicates that a new substance that exists as a gas at room temperature was probably produced.

8 **Developing your set of rules**

☑ Use your table to develop a set of rules for determining when a chemical change has occurred. Write your rules down and share them with the class.

20.2 **Chemical Equations**

Question: How do you balance chemical equations?

In this Investigation, you will:

1. Investigate how atoms are conserved in a chemical reaction.
2. Use the periodic table tiles to learn how to balance equations.

A chemical reaction involves changes in substances that react to form new products. This process involves the breaking of chemical bonds and the formation of new ones. A chemical equation shows the chemical formulas of the substances that react, called **reactants**, and the chemical formulas of the substances that are produced, called **products**. The number and type of atoms in the reactants must be exactly equal to the number and type of atoms in the products. How do you write a chemical equation so that the number and type of atoms on the reactants and products sides are balanced?

1 Writing chemical equations

Magnesium metal reacts with water to produce magnesium hydroxide and hydrogen gas.

The statement above is the word form of a chemical reaction. It tells you the names of the reactants and the products. To write it as a chemical equation, you need to determine the chemical formulas of each of the substances in the reaction:

1. Magnesium metal is an element and exists as an atom. Its chemical formula is Mg.
2. The chemical formula for water is H_2O.
3. Magnesium hydroxide is an ionic compound. To write its chemical formula, you need to find out the charges of each ion it is made out of. The magnesium ion is Mg^{2+}. The hydroxide ion is OH^-. You need 1 Mg^{2+} and 2 OH^- to make a neutral compound so the formula is $Mg(OH)_2$.
4. Pure hydrogen gas always exists as a diatomic molecule so its chemical formula is H_2.

The chemical equation is written as:

magnesium metal	reacts with	water	to produce	magnesium hydroxide	and	hydrogen gas
Mg	**+**	H_2O	⟶	$Mg(OH)_2$	**+**	H_2

2 Trying out the reaction with periodic table tiles

Use periodic table tiles to make the reactants above.

Rearrange the reactants to make the products. Is there any problem? What are you missing?

_____

_____

_____

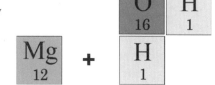

3   ## Balancing the reaction

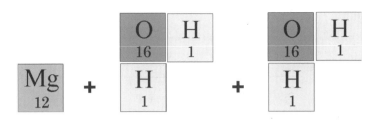

Chemical equations must always balance. This means that you must use all of the atoms you start with and you cannot have any leftover atoms when you are finished. If you need more atoms to make the products, you can only add them in the form of a chemical formula.

You cannot simply add the extra atoms that you need, unless the chemical formula is a single atom - like Mg. Which atoms did you need more of for the reaction you tried? Since you needed more oxygen and hydrogen atoms, you can only add them in the form of another water molecule. Try adding another water molecule to the reactants and rearrange them to form the products again. Did the reaction work this time?

4   ## Writing balanced chemical equations

To balance the equation for this reaction, you needed to add another water molecule to the reactants side. You ended up with the correct amount of products. Since one magnesium atom reacted with two water molecules to form one magnesium hydroxide molecule and one hydrogen gas, the proper way to write the balanced chemical equation is:

$$Mg + 2H_2O \longrightarrow Mg(OH)_2 + H_2$$

The **2** in front of water is called a coefficient. This number tells you how many water molecules are needed in the reaction. The rest of the reactants and products in the reactants show no coefficients. This is because when the coefficient is **1**, there is no need to write it.

5   ## Try balancing these chemical equations

The following chemical equations have the proper reactants and products. Try to balance each using the following steps:

1. Assemble the reactants out of the appropriate tiles.
2. Rearrange the reactants to form the products.
3. Figure out the number of each reactant and product required to make the equation balance and write the numbers (the coefficients) in the boxes.

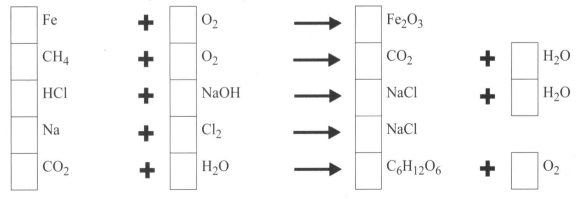

20.3 Conservation of Mass

Question: How can you prove that mass is conserved in a reaction?

In this Investigation, you will:

1. Design an experiment to prove that mass is conserved in a reaction.
2. Collect and analyze data.
3. Present the results of your experiment to the class.

Two hundred years ago, Antoine Laurent Lavoisier, a French chemist, established the **law of conservation of mass** based on his experiments. Lavoisier was the first to recognize that the total mass of the products of a reaction is always equal to the total mass of the reactants. How can you prove his statement to be true? In this Investigation, you will design your own experiment to prove that mass is conserved in a reaction.

1 Testing the reaction

The reaction you will use to prove conservation of mass is one you have probably used before. Have you ever taken an effervescent tablet for indigestion? Before swallowing the tablet, you drop it into a glass of water and allow a reaction to occur before you take the medicine.

Safety Tip: Wear goggles and an apron during the Investigation.

*   Obtain an effervescent tablet and a beaker of water from your teacher. Do not swallow it!
*   Follow the procedures below and record your data as you go.

	Step	Data and observations
a.	*Mass of effervescent tablet.* Use a balance to find the tablet's mass. Record it here.	
b.	*Mass of beaker and water.* Find the mass of the beaker and water. Record it here.	
c.	*Mass before the reaction.* Add the two masses and record the result.	
d.	*Observations.* Drop the tablet into the beaker of water. Record your observations.	
e.	*Mass after the reaction.* Let the reaction finish, then tap the beaker gently to release as many bubbles as you can. Find and record the mass of the beaker again.	
f.	*Mass difference.* Subtract e. from c. Record the result.	

2   Was there a difference in mass?

Does this experiment agree with the law of conservation of mass? Explain why or why not based on your results.

3   Proving that mass is conserved in a reaction

According to the law of conservation of mass, the mass of the products of the reaction should be exactly equal to the mass of the reactants. Can you design an experiment to prove this is true for the reaction you just observed?

Examine the materials your teacher has given you. These include:

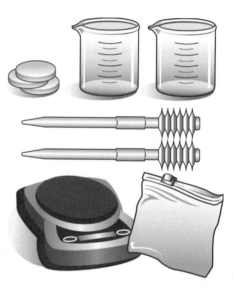

- **effervescent tablet**
- **2 beakers**
- **beaker of water**
- **2 plastic pipettes**
- **2 baggies with zippers**
- **electronic balance or mass scale**

1. Working with your lab partner, devise an experiment that will prove that mass is conserved in the reaction of the tablet and water. You may request additional materials if your teacher has them available.

2. List the materials you will need and their use in the experiment.

3. List the steps you will follow in the experiment.

4. Before you try out your experiment, request approval from your teacher.

5. If your experiment does not work, adjust your procedures and/or materials and try it again.

6. Record your procedures, data, and results.

4   Presenting your results to the class

Prepare a brief presentation for the class about your experiment. Use the following format for your presentation:

    a. Purpose   What questions were you trying to answer?

    b. Materials   What materials and equipment did you choose and why?

    c. Procedures What were the steps you followed? You may demonstrate your procedures if time and materials allow.

    d. Data   What was the data you collected?

    e. Conclusions What does your data prove? If your experiment did not yield satisfactory results, what would you change in your procedures or materials and why?

Question: How can you predict the amount of product in a reaction?

In this Investigation, you will:

1. Follow careful procedures and take accurate measurements of mass.
2. Develop a rule for predicting the mass of product given the mass of the limiting reactant.

Manufacturers of chemical products need to be able to predict how much product will be made given a certain amount of reactants. In order to harvest the greatest amount of product, they need to make sure that at least one of the reactants is completely used up. To do this, they *limit* the amount of one of the reactants (usually the more expensive one) and add the other reactant in *excess*. The reactant that is used up is called the *limiting reactant*. If manufacturers know the mass of the limiting reactant, they can predict the mass of the products. In this Investigation, you will discover the mathematical relationship that allows them to make this prediction.

1   **Writing the balanced equation for the reaction**

In this experiment, you will react sodium hydrogen carbonate (baking soda) with acetic acid (vinegar) to produce carbon dioxide gas, water and sodium carbonate. The equation for this reaction is written below. Balance the equation by writing coefficients in front of the reactants and products:

$$\underline{\hspace{1cm}}NaHCO_3 + \underline{\hspace{1cm}}HC_2H_3O_2 \longrightarrow \underline{\hspace{1cm}}CO_2 + \underline{\hspace{1cm}}H_2O + \underline{\hspace{1cm}}NaC_2H_3O_2$$

2   **What does the balanced equation tell you?**

Use your balanced equation to complete the table below:

reactants				products				
$NaHCO_3$	+	$HC_2H_3O_2$	yields	CO_2	+	H_2O	+	$NaC_2H_3O_2$
coefficient	+	coefficient	yields	coefficient	+	coefficient	+	coefficient
formula mass	+	formula mass	yields	formula mass	+	formula mass	+	formula mass

3   ## Doing the experiment and recording the data

For this experiment, you will need to label two beakers, "A" and "B." You will fill beaker B completely with $HC_2H_3O_2$ (vinegar). In the experiment, you will determine the mass of the limiting reactant, $NaHCO_3$ and the mass of one of the products, CO_2. Since CO_2 is a gas, you will obtain its mass through subtraction. It is important to add the reactants slowly and carefully to obtain good results.

Safety Tip: Wear goggles and an apron during the Investigation.

Follow the procedures below and record in the table your data for all four trials.

data and procedures	trial 1	trial 2	trial 3	trial 4
1. *Mass of beaker A*. Find and record the mass of your empty beaker (beaker A).				
2. *Mass of beaker A + NaHCO₃*. Add about 2.0 grams of $NaHCO_3$ to beaker A. Find and record the mass of beaker A + $NaHCO_3$.				
3. *Mass of NaHCO₃ used*. Subtract number 1 from number 2. This is the mass of $NaHCO_3$.				
4. *Mass of beaker B with HC₂H₃O₂ before the reaction*. Find and record the mass of the 250 mL beaker full of $HC_2H_3O_2$ (beaker B).				
5. *Mass of beaker B after HC₂H₃O₂ is used in the reaction*. Slowly add $HC_2H_3O_2$, a little at a time, to beaker A. As you add, gently swirl beaker A to dissipate the bubbles of CO_2. Add $HC_2H_3O_2$ until the bubbling stops. Find and record the mass of beaker B again.				
6. *Mass of HC₂H₃O₂ used*. Subtract number 5 from number 4. Record the result.				
7. *Mass of beaker A before the reaction*. Add numbers 2 and 6. This will give you the mass of beaker A before the reaction occurred. Record your answer.				
8. *Mass of beaker A after the reaction*. Let beaker A sit for a few minutes. Tap it gently to release as much of the CO_2 as you can. Find and record the mass of beaker A.				
9. *Mass of CO₂ produced*. Subtract number 8 from number 7. This will give you the mass of CO_2 produced. Record your answer.				

4   ## Identifying relationships between reactants and products in a reaction

How is the amount of CO_2 produced in the reaction you just carried out related to the amount of $NaHCO_3$ used? One way to find out is to determine the relationship between three variables: the **coefficients** (from the balanced equation); the **formula mass**; and the **actual mass** (from the data table). Fill in the table and identify a relationship between the variables by trying out different calculations (multiplying, dividing, adding, and subtracting). You may need to round decimals to the nearest tenth in order to identify relationships in your answers.

Trial 1	reactant $NaHCO_3$	product CO_2	Trial 2	reactant $NaHCO_3$	product CO_2
coefficient			coefficient		
formula mass			formula mass		
actual mass			actual mass		
Trial 3	reactant $NaHCO_3$	product CO_2	Trial 4	reactant $NaHCO_3$	product CO_2
coefficient			coefficient		
formula mass			formula mass		
actual mass			actual mass		

5   ## Writing your rule for predicting the amount of product in a reaction

$\frac{a}{b}$ From your work, you have discovered the relationship between number of molecules, formula mass and actual mass. Now write a mathematical formula that will allow you to predict the amount of product given the amount of the limiting reactant in a reaction. Your formula should have the limiting reactant variables on one side and the product variables on the other side. Use the following variables in your rule:

Limiting reactant	Product
C_r = coefficient in front of the limiting reactant	C_p = coefficient in front of the product
F_r = formula mass of limiting reactant	F_p = formula mass of product
A_r = actual mass of limiting reactant	A_p = actual mass of product

Your rule:

combination of reactant variables		combination of product variables
	=	

6 Testing your rule

Does your rule work? Test it by carrying out the same reaction again, using a different amount of $NaHCO_3$. Record your results below.

$NaHCO_3$ used in reaction

Predicted yield of CO_2   _____

Actual yield of CO_2   _____
                                                                       _____

7 Calculating percent yield

$\frac{a}{b}$ The predicted yield of a reaction is rarely exactly equal to the actual yield. Why do you think there might be differences? The predicted amount of product assumes the reaction will occur under perfect conditions. The percent yield is the actual yield divided by the predicted yield.

$$\text{percent yield} = \left(\frac{\text{actual yield}}{\text{predicted yield}} \right) \times 100$$

Calculate the percent yield for the reaction you just completed.

8 Analyzing the Investigation

a. Why was it necessary to measure the amount of carbon dioxide produced in the reaction instead of one of the other products?

b. Why do you think it was necessary to round off your calculations to the nearest tenth in order to identify a relationship between the variables?

c. How could your mathematical relationship be useful to a company that uses chemical reactions to manufacture products?

9 Challenge!

You use products made with aluminum metal everyday, but do you ever wonder where this metal comes from? To obtain pure aluminum, aluminum ore is treated with large amounts of heat to produce pure aluminum metal. Oxygen gas is another product in this reaction. The balanced equation for this reaction is:

$2Al_2O_3 + \text{heat} \rightarrow 4Al + 3O_2$

If you heat 50.0 grams of aluminum ore, and the reaction is completed, how many grams of pure aluminum will you get?

Classifying Reactions

Question: How can you predict the products in a reaction?

In this Investigation, you will:

1. Predict the products in a double-displacement reaction.
2. Deduce the rules for solubility of an ionic compound.

A double-displacement reaction is a chemical reaction in which the ions from the two reactants change places. One of the new compounds formed is sometimes insoluble and forms a cloudy precipitate. In this Investigation, you will develop a set of rules for solubility that will allow you to make predictions about the solubility of the products of double-displacement reactions.

Safety Tip: Wear goggles and a lab apron during the Investigation.

1 **Writing the chemical formulas of the reactants**

Write the chemical formulas for the compounds you will react (Table 19.2 on page 327 of the Student Edition).

compound	positive ion	column # of periodic table (if monoatomic)	negative ion	chemical formula
ammonium hydroxide				
calcium chloride				
magnesium sulfate				
sodium chloride				
sodium hydroxide				
sodium phosphate				

2 **Deducing your rules for solubility - part 1**

All of the compounds in the table above are soluble. You know this because the solutions you have in front of you are clear. Rules for the solubility of ionic compounds have to do with the combination of positive and negative ions. The solubility of ionic compounds also has to do with the group on the periodic table to which the positive ion belongs. For example, one rule you could deduce from the table is:

If an element from Group I is the positive ion and a phosphate is the negative ion, then the compound is soluble.

Write your rules on a separate sheet of paper. You may include the rule above.

3 Determining products and writing the equations

For each pair of reactants in the table below: (1) Write the possible products into the middle column; (2) Put a few drops of each reactant into a small beaker or spot plate and observe the reaction; and (3) Note whether or not a precipitate has formed as a result of the reaction.

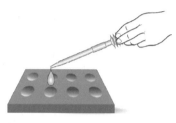

reactants	possible products	precipitate? yes or no
$CaCl_2$ + NaOH		
$CaCl_2$ + Na_3PO_4		
NaOH + Na_3PO_4		
NaCl + NH_4OH		
NaOH + $MgSO_4$		
Na_3PO_4 + $MgSO_4$		
$MgSO_4$ + $CaCl_2$		
$CaCl_2$ + NH_4OH		
NaCl + $MgSO_4$		
NH_4OH + $MgSO_4$		

4 ☑Finalizing your solubility rules

1. Look at the rules you wrote before and circle all of the products above that you know are soluble.
2. Identify the products that you absolutely know are the precipitates.
3. Based on your findings, add additional rules to your list.

5 Applying your rules

Now that you have your own rules for determining solubility, predict the precipitate for the reactions your teacher writes on the board.

21.2

Energy in Reactions

Question: How can you classify reactions based on energy?

In this Investigation, you will:

1. Measure energy changes in three different reactions.
2. Determine whether the reaction is exothermic or endothermic.
3. Write complete balanced equations that show the energy changes in each reaction.

You know that when a chemical reaction occurs, chemical bonds are broken in the reactants to make new products. Breaking bonds requires energy. Energy is released when new products are formed. In **endothermic reactions**, more energy is required to break the bonds in the reactants than is given off when the products are formed. In **exothermic reactions**, more energy is given off when new products are formed than is required to break the bonds in the reactants. In this Investigation, you will measure the energy changes in reactions and categorize the reactions as endothermic or exothermic.

 **Safety Tip: Wear goggles and a lab apron for this Investigation.**

1   **Measuring energy changes in reactions**

You will use a thermometer to measure energy changes in each reaction.

In each reaction, it is important that you measure and record the temperature of the liquid in the beaker before you add another substance.

After you add a substance, record the highest or lowest temperature you observe.

a. What does a change in temperature tell you about the energy in a reaction?

b. If a reaction occurs and no temperature change can be measured, what might that indicate about the reaction?

2   **Reaction #1 Dissolution of ammonium nitrate**

Reaction notes: When an ionic compound dissolves in water, the ionic bonds in the compound dissolve and the ions are released into the solution. This type of reaction is called **dissolution**. In this reaction, ammonium nitrate is the ionic compound that dissolves into its positive and negative ions. Follow the steps below to complete the reaction. Record all observations.

1. Obtain a 250-milliliter beaker containing 200 milliliters of water.
2. Measure the temperature of the water and record it.
3. Add 30 grams of ammonium nitrate to the beaker.
4. Stir with a stirring rod and immerse the thermometer in the solution.
5. Record the highest or lowest temperature you observe.
6. Record any other observations.

3   ## Reaction #2 Decomposition of hydrogen peroxide

Reaction notes: A **decomposition reaction** occurs when one compound decomposes to form two or more products. Follow the steps below to complete the reaction. Record all observations.

1. Obtain a 250-milliliter beaker and add 150 milliliters of hydrogen peroxide to the beaker.
2. Measure the temperature of the hydrogen peroxide and record it.
3. Place a slice of potato in the beaker.
4. Immerse the thermometer into the beaker with the potato.
5. Record the highest or lowest temperature you observe.

4   ## Reaction #3 Dissolution of calcium chloride

Reaction notes: When calcium chloride is added to water, it dissolves into its positive and negative ions. This is another dissolution reaction. Follow the steps below and record your observations.

1. Obtain a 250-milliliter beaker containing 200 milliliters of water.
2. Measure the temperature of the water and record it.
3. Add 30.0 grams of calcium chloride to the beaker.
4. Stir with a stirring rod and immerse the thermometer in the solution.
5. Record the highest or lowest temperature you observe.

5   ## Classifying the reactions and showing energy changes

For each reaction you just observed, indicate whether it is exothermic or endothermic, based on your observations. Next, write the balanced equation for each reaction. Indicate energy changes in each reaction by following the example below.

$$2H_2 + O_2 + energy \longrightarrow 2H_2O$$

Is this an example of an exothermic or endothermic reaction?

rxn	Type of reaction (exothermic or endothermic)	Write the complete, balanced equation. Show energy changes in your equation.
#1		
#2		
#3		

22.1

Nuclear Reactions

Question: How do you simulate nuclear decay?

In this Investigation, you will:

1. Investigate the concept of nuclear decay.
2. Graph your data and interpret your results.

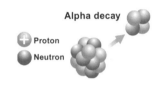

With 92 protons and 146 neutrons, the nucleus of uranium-238 has a tendency to fall apart or "decay" because it is **unstable**. In other words, the nucleus of a uranium-238 atom is **radioactive**. It emits **radiation** in the forms of particles and energy until it becomes an atom with a more stable nucleus. In this case, uranium-238 emits an alpha particle to become a thorium-234 atom. An alpha particle is composed of two protons and two neutrons.

Eventually, uranium-238 decays naturally to lead-206 which is not radioactive. The time for half of the atoms in a sample of uranium-238 to perform this entire nuclear decay process takes about 4.5 billion years! In other words, the *half-life* of uranium-238 is 4.5 billion years. In this Investigation, you will learn more about half-life and simulate the radioactive decay of a new element.

1 Discussing radioactivity

Your teacher has given you a can of pennies to represent the atoms of a sample of a newly discovered, radioactive element. Discuss and complete the following with your group.

a. With your group, decide on a name for your element.

b. Why is your element radioactive? What does this tell you about its nucleus?

c. Since your element is radioactive, what is happening to its nucleus?

d. If this were a real radioactive element, what precautions would you have to take? Why?

2 Making a prediction

You will use the pennies that you have been given to simulate the process of radioactive decay. When you have completed the simulation, you will construct a graph of your data. Sample number will be on the *x*-axis, and number of decayed atoms per sample will be on the *y*-axis. What do you think this graph will look like? Sketch your prediction. Reading over part 3 (Simulating the process of *radioactive decay*) will help you make this prediction.

3 Simulating the process of radioactive decay

To simulate the process of radioactive decay follow the steps of the procedure below.

1. Shake your can of pennies and spill them out onto a tray or table.
2. Remove all pennies that are "heads" up and count them.
3. Record these as decayed atoms in Table 1 on the next page.
4. Put the rest of the pennies back into the can, shake them again.

5. Spill them out onto the tray or table, and again, remove and count the "heads."

6. Repeat this process until you have no more pennies left.

7. If necessary, add extra rows to your table.

4   Recording the data

Table 1: Data from the experiment

sample number	number of decayed atoms	sample number	number of decayed atoms
1		8	
2		9	
3		10	
4		11	
5		12	
6		13	
7		14	

5   Graphing your data

Graph your data for number of decayed atoms per sample vs. sample number. Label the axes clearly. Be sure to provide a title for the graph. Be sure to use the entire graph in plotting your data. Use the graph paper provided by your teacher.

6   Interpreting your graph

Answer the following questions.

a. Write a paragraph that describes what your graph looks like.

b. What part of this simulation represents the half-life of this new element? Explain your answer.

c. If the half-life of your element was 430 years and you had 2000 atoms of this element, how long would it take for the element to undergo complete radioactive decay to a stable isotope? What year would it be when the element finished decaying? Note: As you work through this problem, round the number of atoms left to a whole number. For example, round 62.5 to 63.

7   Wrapping up

a. Were you correct in your prediction for what your graph would look like?

b. Make a list of pros and a list of cons regarding the uses of radioactive elements. Each list should have at least three points. As you make your lists, think about how radioactive elements are used today. You may need to do research on the Internet or in a library to make your lists.

22.2

Question: How do your choices impact the environment?

In this Investigation, you will:

1. Use consumer information to make environmentally conscious and economically responsible decisions.
2. Understand the environmental effects of using fossil fuels.

If you needed to buy a car to drive to school or work, what kind of car would you buy?

In this Investigation, you will use consumer information to evaluate how your answer to this question might affect the environment and your personal finances. For example, you will calculate how much carbon dioxide your car produces. You will also learn how the sun's energy may be used to reduce carbon dioxide in the atmosphere.

1   Choosing a car or truck

1. Prior to the Investigation, choose the car or truck you would buy to drive to work or school each day. Find three facts that justify your choice. Make a brochure that describes your car. Include in your brochure, the facts and any photographs, magazine clippings or articles you find.
2. Use the ACEEE's Green Book -- The Environmental Guide to Cars and Trucks or the Internet (http://www.fueleconomy.gov or http://www.greencars.org) to find the fuel economy for your car or truck for highway and city driving. Record this information. The unit for fuel economy is miles per gallon of gasoline (MPG).
3. Figure out how many gallons of gasoline you will need to drive 500 miles in the city and 500 miles on the highway.
4. Use the price per gallon of gas provided by your teacher to calculate the cost of enough gasoline for your car or truck to travel 500 miles in the city and 500 miles on the highway.

2   The environmental effects

a. You will use the combustion reaction for iso-octane to find out how much carbon dioxide (CO_2) your car produces. The equation for the combustion of iso-octane is:
$$2C_8H_{18}\,(l) + 25O_2(g) \dashrightarrow 16CO_2\,(g) + 18H_2O\,(g) + 10{,}900\ kJ.$$
From this equation, you can tell that you would need 2 moles of iso-octane and 25 moles of oxygen to get a complete combustion reaction that produces 10,900 kilojoules of energy.

b. Calculate the formula masses of iso-octane and CO_2. Use the periodic table to help you. Your values will be in atomic mass units. Before going to the next step, convert from atomic mass units to grams.

c. Calculate the mass of one gallon of iso-octane. The density of iso-octane is 0.69 g/ml. One gallon is equivalent to 3,840 ml.

d. $\boxed{\frac{a}{b}}$ Calculate the mass of CO_2 that will be produced to drive 500 miles in the city and 500 miles on the highway. Use the following formula:

$$\frac{\text{mass of iso-octane needed to travel 500 miles}}{(\text{formula mass of iso-octane} \times 2)} = \frac{\text{mass of carbon dioxide produced after 500 miles}}{(\text{formula mass of carbon dioxide} \times 16)}$$

3   Using the sun's energy

All plants use photosynthesis to convert the sun's energy into chemical energy. Unlike combustion which is exothermic, photosynthesis is endothermic and requires energy. The chemical equation for photosynthesis is:

$$6CO_2 + 6H_2O + 2870 \text{ kJ} \rightarrow C_6H_{12}O_6 + 6O_2.$$

Through photosynthesis, plants assimilate the carbon in CO_2 into their tissues. In this way, photosynthesis does contribute to reducing CO_2 in the atmosphere. For this Investigation, assume that one tree converts 32 pounds of CO_2 to glucose ($C_6H_{12}O_6$) each year. This figure is equivalent to 14.545 kilograms or 14,545 grams of CO_2.

$\frac{a}{b}$ Figure out how many trees you would need to plant to offset the amount of CO_2 your car or truck produces each year for driving 500 miles in the city and 500 miles on the highway.

4   Evaluating choices

Use the data from the whole class to make a list of the top five cars and trucks in each category.

a.   The best fuel economy for driving in the city.

b.   The best fuel economy for driving on the highway.

c.   The worst fuel economy for driving in the city.

d.   The worst fuel economy for driving on the highway.

e.   The least carbon dioxide produced each year.

f.   The most carbon dioxide produced each year.

5   Reaching conclusions

Answer the following questions.

a.   Was your car in any of the top five lists? If so, which one?

b.   On a scale of 1 - 5, rate the fuel economy of your car or truck. A "1" means your car is not fuel efficient and a "5" means that your car or truck is very fuel efficient. Explain your rating choice.

c.   On a scale of 1 - 5, rate your car or truck according to how much carbon dioxide it produces. A "5" means that your car or truck produces a great deal of carbon dioxide. Explain your answer.

d.   Go back to the three reasons that you chose your car or truck. Have your three reasons changed because of this Investigation? Give at least one new reason for selecting or not selecting your car or truck. Explain your answer.

e.   What are the consequences of having too much carbon dioxide in the atmosphere?

f.   Is it reasonable to say that we can plant trees to compensate for all the carbon dioxide we produce? Why or why not?

g.   Carbon dioxide (CO_2) is an end-product of a combustion reaction that occurs in car engines. Scientists believe the presence of too much CO_2 in the Earth's atmosphere is contributing to global warming. What is the economic impact of global warming on the world? What kind of extra costs would people and society have if the Earth's average temperature increased? In other words, what is the cost of producing too much CO_2? Discuss these questions with your group. Make a list of things that would cost more, or have to be paid for, if the Earth were to get warmer.

Water

Question: What are the properties of water?

In this Investigation, you will:

1. Observe the properties of water.
2. Use electrolysis to explore the molecular composition of water.

Water is a polar molecule. This means that it has a negative end (pole) and a positive end (pole). In a water molecule, the electrons are shared unequally between oxygen and hydrogen. This is because oxygen atoms attract electrons. In other words, the electrons are pulled toward the oxygen atom and away from the two hydrogen atoms. The oxygen side of the molecule (the side with the lone pairs of electrons) therefore has a partially negative charge and the hydrogen side of the molecule has a partially positive charge.

In this Investigation, you will explore the properties of water.

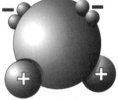

Oxygen end —

Hydrogen end +

A Water Molecule

1   The shape of a water droplet

1. For this part of the Investigation, you will have a small beaker of water with a pipette, a small piece of wax paper, a small piece of copy paper, and a glass slide.
2. Place one drop of water on the wax paper, the copy paper, and the glass slide. Write down what you observe in Table 1. For each situation, write come up with an explanation of your observations
3. Answer the questions following Table 1.

Table 1: The shape of a water droplet

	Describe shape of water droplet	Why does it look this way?
Wax paper		
Copy paper		
Glass slide		

a. Of the three surfaces—wax paper, copy paper, and glass—which is polar and which is nonpolar?

b. Fill the pipette with some water. Release water drops from the pipette so that they fall to the floor. Describe the shape of the water droplets. Come up with an explanation of the shape of these falling droplets. When you have answered this question, be sure to dry the floor with a paper towel.

c. The falling water droplets are most like which of the droplets that you placed on the three surfaces? Why do you think the shape of this water droplet resembled a falling water droplet?

2   The shape of a water molecule

In this part of the Investigation, you will build three different molecules and identify their shapes.

1. You will need some toothpicks and gumdrops for this part of the Investigation. Use these to make the three molecules. The toothpicks will represent the bonds between atoms. The gumdrops will represent the atoms.

2. As you build the three molecules, fill in Table 2 below. Write in the chemical formula for each molecule and write in the number of lone pairs of electrons. Then, determine the three-dimensional shape of each molecule and record it in the table.

3. The first atom you will build is methane. The chemical formula for methane is CH_4. Choose one color gumdrop to represent carbon (C) and four gumdrops of the same color to represent hydrogen (H).

4. A methane molecule looks like the top two graphics to the right. The arrangement shown allows the hydrogen atoms to spread out as far as possible around the carbon atom. The three-dimensional shape of a methane molecule is a *tetrahedron*. Build this molecule with your gumdrops and toothpicks as shown.

5. Starting with the methane molecule you just built, you will build an ammonia molecule. The formula for ammonia is NH_3. The carbon in the methane will now represent nitrogen (N). To build ammonia, remove one of the "hydrogen atoms" (one gumdrop) and leave the toothpick in place. This toothpick will represent one lone pair of electrons. What is the shape of this molecule?

6. Now, you will build a water molecule. As you probably know the chemical formula for a water molecule is H_2O. How can you build a water molecule from the ammonia molecule? The nitrogen will now represent oxygen (O). What is the shape of this molecule?

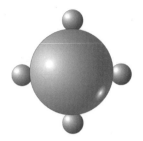

Methane

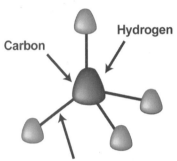

Carbon   Hydrogen

A bond between a hydrogen and carbon atom

Building methane

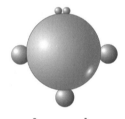

Ammonia

Table 2: Building molecules

Name of molecule	Chemical formula	Number of lone pairs	Shape of molecule
Methane			
Ammonia			
Water			

a. In each of the molecules you built, there is a center atom surrounded by four sets of electron pairs. The electron pairs are either alone, or part of a bond. How does the presence of lone electron pairs influence the shape of a molecule of water?

b. Water and ammonia are polar molecules (having positive and negative ends) while methane is nonpolar. Do you think the presence of lone electron pairs affects the polarity of a molecule? Explain your reasoning.

3   Polarity versus nonpolarity

Water is a polar substance, and oil is a nonpolar substance. This usually means that these two substances don't mix. However, detergent molecules have a polar and nonpolar end. In this part of the Investigation, you will demonstrate how detergent interacts with both water and oil.

1. Fill up your beaker with water so that it is three-fourths full.

2. Add some vegetable oil to the water's surface. Add just enough so that a thin layer covers the water's surface. Observe the thickness of this layer from the side.

3. Now, use a clean toothpick to try to see if you can mix the oil layer into the water. Observe what happens.

4. Using a fresh toothpick, dip the tip into some detergent.

5. Poke the tip of the toothpick into the center of the oil layer on the water and then pull it out. Observe what happens.

6. Now, answer the following questions.

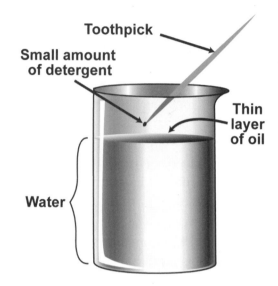

a. Describe what happened when you first tried to mix the oil and water. What evidence did you observe that proves that oil and water do not mix?

b. What happened when you added a little detergent to the oil layer? In particular, describe how the oil layer "reacted" to the detergent.

c. At the end of step 5, there are three kinds of molecules in the beaker—water, oil, and detergent. Make a diagram that shows how these molecules interact with each other in the beaker.

d. Now that some time has passed, do you notice any changes? Try to stir the oil into the water. What happens? Explain your observations.

e. ★ Having done this demonstration, do you think detergent would be useful in cleaning up an oil spill in the ocean? What would be the advantages or disadvantages of using detergent to clean up an environmental problem like an oil spill? You may do research on the Internet or in your local library to answer this question.

4 Using electrolysis to demonstrate the composition of water

In this part of the Investigation, you will split water using electricity. This process is called *electrolysis*. Follow the directions carefully.

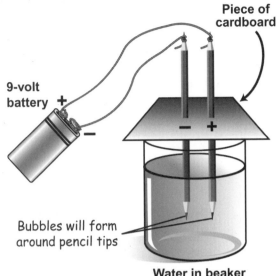

1. Obtain a clean beaker of water. The beaker should be at least three-fourths full of water. Mix a pinch of table salt into the water. You will also need two pencils with *both* ends sharpened.

2. Get a small piece of cardboard from your teacher. The size of this piece will cover the top of your beaker.

3. Carefully make two pencil-sized holes in the cardboard. The holes should be about 2 centimeters apart.

4. Place the cardboard on top of the beaker and insert the two pencils through the holes so that their tips are in the water. Make your setup exactly as shown in the diagram. The pencil points should not touch the bottom of the beaker. If your pencils will not stay in place, use pieces of masking tape to attach them to the cardboard.

5. Now, connect wires from the terminals of a 9-volt battery to the pencils. Make sure there is good contact between the wires and the graphite in the pencils. You may use tape to hold the wires in place on the battery and on the pencils. Use the diagram as a guide.

6. With a marker, write "+" on the piece of cardboard next to the pencil that represents the "+" lead. Do the same for the pencil that represents the "-" lead.

7. When you see bubbles forming in the beaker near the pencil tips, you are ready to answer the following questions.

   a. The setup you have created will result in water molecules splitting into hydrogen and oxygen atoms. Hydrogen and oxygen are both gases. Therefore, you will see small bubbles collecting near each pencil tip. Describe the number and size of the bubbles collecting near each pencil tip.

   b. Which gas is collecting near the pencil tip that is connected to the "+" lead? Justify your answer.

   c. Which gas is collecting near the pencil tip that is connected to the "-" lead? Justify your answer.

   d. How could you prove that your answers to 4b and 4c are correct? Come up with a research plan to prove your answers. Hint: It will be helpful to know the properties of both gases to prove their identity.

Solutions

Question: Can you identify mixtures as solutions, suspensions, or colloids?

In this Investigation, you will:

1. Use what you know about solutions, suspensions, and colloids to categorize six mixtures.
2. Observe the Tyndall effect.
3. Design three methods for dissolving rock salt in water.
4. Calculate the average dissolving rate obtained by each method.
5. Propose the fastest possible method you can imagine for dissolving rock salt in water.

In your reading, you learned about solutions, suspensions, and colloids. The properties of solutions, suspensions, and colloids are listed in a table in section 23.1 What is a Solution? of the student text. The Tyndall effect is one way to distinguish between solutions and colloids. In this Investigation, you will construct an apparatus to view the Tyndall effect.

1   **Preparing the Tyndall effect viewer**

Safety Tips: Wear safety goggles and a lab apron throughout the experiment. Use a utility knife with care.

1. Line a shoe box with black paper.
2. In the center of one of the long sides, cut a 3-by-3-centimeter square with scissors or a utility knife. The bottom edge of the square should be 5 centimeters from the bottom of the box.
3. In the center of one of the short sides, cut another 3-by-3-centimeter square. The bottom edge of this square should also be 5 centimeters from the bottom of the box.

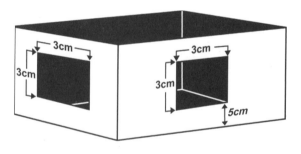

2   **Testing the Tyndall effect viewer**

1. Fill a clear glass 250-milliliter beaker with 200 milliliters of water. Grind the chalk (calcium carbonate) to a powder in your mortar and pestle. Mix about 2 grams of powdered chalk into the water. This is your colloid test solution. Place the beaker in the center of the box and put on the lid.
2. Place a flashlight against the square cut in the long side of the box. Shine the light into the box.
3. View the beaker through the square cut in the short side. The path of the light beam should be visible in your mixture. Describe what you see.
4. Fill a 250-milliliter beaker with 200 milliliters of water. Place it in the viewer. Can you see the path of the light beam now? If no beam is visible, the viewer is working correctly. Use this beaker in parts 3 through 5 of the Investigation.

3 ## Preparing the mixtures

1. Fill each of six 250-milliliter glass beakers with 200 milliliters of water. Stir one of the following substances into each of five beakers. One beaker will contain only water.

   (1) 40 milliliters corn oil; (2) 6 drops of food coloring; (3) 2.5 grams corn starch; (4) 9 grams of granulated sugar; (5) 3 grams modeling clay.

2. Label your beakers so that you remember which mixture is in each one.

3. For mixture (6), carefully heat 200 milliliters water to 100 °C. Using a hot pad, pour it into a 250-milliliter heat-resistant glass beaker. Add 2.5 grams plain gelatin. Stir the mixture.

4 ## Designing your procedure

a. Revisit the table of properties of solutions, colloids, and suspensions in section 23.1 What is a Solution? of the student text. Design a procedure that will enable you to classify your six mixtures correctly. Your procedure should include at least two tests for each mixture.

b. Observe each mixture. Write a hypothesis that explains what type of mixture you believe it is. Give a reason for each prediction.

5 ## Collecting your data

Follow your written procedure. Record your results in the table below.

Substance added to 200 mL water	results of test #1	results of test #2	solution, colloid, or suspension?
(1) corn oil			
(2) food coloring			
(3) corn starch			
(4) granulated sugar			
(5) modeling clay			
(6) gelatin			
(7) plain water			control solution

6 ## Cleaning up

1. Solutions and colloids may be washed down a sink. Clean and dry the beakers.

2. Use a coffee filter to separate the solid particles out of any suspensions. Solids may be thrown in a wastebasket. Liquids may be washed down a sink. Clean and dry the beakers.

7 ## What are your conclusions?

a. Did your two procedures help you tell the difference between solutions, colloids and suspensions? Provide evidence to support your response.

b. Were your hypotheses about each mixture correct? If not, explain why.

c. Why was plain water tested in the Investigation? What does the word *control* mean?

d. Is water a true solution? Explain your answer.

e. If you had a mixture that was not translucent, how could you determine if it should be classified as a solution, colloid, or suspension?

8   Dissolving rates

What are the factors that influence how fast a substance will dissolve? Now you have the opportunity to design an experiment in which you test the effectiveness of three different methods of dissolving rock salt in water. You may be familiar with rock salt as a substance that is used in ice cream churns.

You will design three different methods for dissolving rock salt in water. For each method, you will write a procedure. Your procedures and experiments must follow the guidelines listed below.

• You will start with approximately 5 grams of rock salt. Place whole crystals on the balance until you have as close to 5 grams as possible. You may NOT break any crystals to obtain exactly 5 grams. Record the exact mass in Table 1 (on the next page).

• You will use a graduated cylinder to measure 250 milliliters of room temperature water. Pour it into a 500-milliliter beaker or glass jar with a lid (your choice).

• You will start timing as soon as the rock salt is added to the water.

• You will follow your written procedure for getting the rock salt to enter the solution. Timing ends when all the rock salt appears to have entered the solution.

For the purposes of the Investigation, we will assume the rock salt will dissolve at a constant rate. We will call this rate the **average dissolving rate**. You will calculate the average dissolving rate in units of grams per second, using the following formula:

$$\text{average dissolving rate} = \frac{\text{amount dissolved, in grams}}{\text{time it takes to dissolve, in seconds}}$$

For example, if it took 150 seconds for 5 grams of rock salt to enter the solution, the average dissolving rate would be:

$$\text{average dissolving rate} = \frac{5 \text{ g}}{150 \text{ sec}} = 0.033 \text{ g/sec}$$

a. *Practice*: Suppose it takes 45 seconds for 3.0 grams of rock salt to enter a solution. What is the average dissolving rate?

b. Which variables do you think affect the dissolving rate of rock salt?

9   Brainstorming ideas and formulating your hypothesis

a. As a group, decide on three different methods to influence the rate of dissolving. Remember that in order to draw valid conclusions in an experiment, you can change only one variable at a time! Write a step-by-step procedure for each method. When you have finished, submit your set of procedures to your teacher for approval.

b. Write a statement describing which of your three procedures will produce the fastest dissolving rate. Be sure to explain your reasoning.

◆ **Be sure to include safety instructions in your procedures.**

10 | **Collecting your data**

Follow your written procedure for each of your three methods, recording your data and observations in the table each time.

1. Write a short description of each procedure in the first column of the table.

2. Record the mass of rock salt used for each procedure in the second column.

3. While you conduct each procedure, note any observations, problems, or changes to the procedure in the fifth column.

4. The time for dissolving the rock salt and your calculation for the average dissolving rate will be recorded in the third and fourth columns.

🪣 When you have finished this part of the Investigation, clean all of the materials used by your group.

Summary of procedure	mass of rock salt (grams)	time to dissolve rock salt (seconds)	average dissolving rate (grams / second)	notes

11 | **What did you learn?**

a. Using what you have learned in your reading, describe what was happening on a molecular level as you tried to dissolve the rock salt. You may want to use diagrams in your explanation.

b. Which method produced the fastest average dissolving rate? Did you prove or disprove your hypothesis?

c. What other, even faster, methods could you use to get 5 grams of rock salt to dissolve in 250 milliliters of water? Describe these.

Solubility

Question: What factors affect solubility?

In this Investigation, you will:

1. Observe how temperature influences average dissolving rate.
2. Develop an explanation for how temperature influences solubility.
3. Demonstrate how pressure influences the solubility of a gas.

Have you ever tried to get sugar to dissolve in a drink? You may know that you can get the job done more easily if the liquid is hot rather than cold. But why is this the case? In this Investigation, you will observe how temperature influences the average dissolving rate of a sugar cube in water. Based on your observations, you will come up with a set of ideas for how temperature influences solubility. At the end of the Investigation, you will demonstrate how pressure influences the solubility of gases.

1 **Experiment 1: temperature and solubility**

In the first experiment of the Investigation, you will observe individual sugar cubes dissolving in water at different temperatures. For each temperature of water, you will watch the cubes and make observations. Because you will not stir the water, the sugar cubes will not completely dissolve. Instead, the cubes will fall apart and become small piles of sugar at the bottom of the beakers. When one sugar cube has fallen apart and partially dissolved, you will add another one to that particular beaker. Record your data in Tables 1, 2 and 3 on the next page.

2 **Procedure**

◆ 🖐 **Safety Tip: Carefully follow your teacher's directions for working with the hot water. Take care not to spill it on yourself or others.**

1. Obtain 10 sugar cubes, three beakers, three styrofoam cups and 3 water soluble markers (one red, one blue, and one green). Use the markers to color *one* side of each of three sugar cubes. One cube will have a red side, one will have a blue side, and one will have a red side.

2. One beaker and one styrofoam cup will be used for each water temperature. Label the cups and beakers: "ice," "room temperature," and "hot." Place the sugar cube with the red in the beaker labeled "hot". The red side should face up. Place sugar cube with the blue side in the beaker labeled "ice". The blue side should face up. Place the sugar cube with the green side in the beaker labeled "room temperature". The green side should face up.

3. Obtain ice, room temperature, and hot water in your labeled styrofoam cups. Measure the temperature of the water in each cup. Record these starting temperatures in Table 1.

4. Gently transfer the water from the styrofoam cups to each of the beakers. Fill the beakers to the 50-milliliter mark with the water from the cups. *Do not disturb the cubes as you fill each beaker.*

5. Record the time as the starting time for the experiment in Table 2. Record the time in minutes and seconds.

6. First, observe how the ink from the side of the sugar cube dissolves in the water at each temperature. Record your observations.

7. Observe how the sugar cubes dissolve in each of the three beakers. Watch the cubes from the sides and tops of the beakers. Record your observations. Answer these questions:
    (a) What happens to the color on the sugar cube? (b) What happens to a sugar cube as it dissolves? and (c) What does the water above the sugar cube look like?

8. When all that is left of a cube is a small pile of sugar, write the time in Table 3. Record the time in minutes and seconds. Then, carefully add another cube to that beaker. The second and third cubes added to beakers will not have a colored side.

9. Repeat step 8 until three cubes have dissolved in one of the beakers. There may be three small piles of sugar at the bottom of this beaker. At this point, the experiment has ended. Record the ending time in Table 2.

10. Record the ending water temperature for each beaker in Table 1.

11. Gently swirl each of the beakers three times so that the sugar on the bottom is stirred up. What do you notice about the water above the sugar? Record your observations.

Table 1: Starting and ending temperatures for the experiment

Temperature range	Starting temperature (°C)	Ending temperature (°C)
Ice water (blue)		
Room temperature water (green)		
Hot water (red)		

Table 2: Starting and ending times for the experiment

Start time for experiment minute:second	End time for experiment minute:second

Table 3: Sugar cube data

Number of cubes	Time recorded when cube dissolves in ice water	Time recorded when cube dissolves in room temperature water	Time recorded when cube dissolves in hot water
1			
2			
3			

3 Analyzing your results

a. In which beaker of water did three sugar cubes dissolve the fastest? In which beaker of water did the sugar cubes dissolve the slowest?

b. Did the ice water stay colder than the room temperature water for the whole experiment? Did the hot water stay warmer than the room temperature water for the whole experiment? Why was it important to check the water temperature in each beaker at the start and at the end of the experiment?

4   ## How does temperature influence solubility?

a.   List three observations you made during the experiment. Use what you know about solubility to explain each of these observations. In other words, describe why something you observed occurred or looked a certain way.

b.   Based on your observations of the experiment and your own ideas, draw a diagram that shows how temperature influences how a substance dissolves on the molecular level.

5   ## Experiment 2: pressure and solubility

In this experiment, you will observe how pressure influences the solubility of carbon dioxide in water using a bottle of seltzer and a balloon. Each group has a bottle of seltzer water.

Observe the bottle with the cap on, before it has been opened.

a.   How do you know that the liquid in the bottle is under pressure?

b.   How do you know that the liquid contains a dissolved gas?

c.   What do you think will happen to the gas dissolved in the liquid after you take the cap off?

6   ## Procedure

👓 **Safety Tip: Wear goggles during this part of the Investigation. Work carefully.**

1. Take your balloon and blow it up to stretch it out. Release the air in the balloon. Then, stretch the mouth of the balloon over the top of the **closed** seltzer bottle. The neck of the balloon should be **below** the cap. The cap should be in the round part of the balloon so you will be able to unscrew the top more easily.

2. Now, slowly unscrew the cap (through the balloon) on your bottle of seltzer with one hand while you hold the bottle steady with your other hand. You will hear a loud fizz just as the cap begins to come off the bottle. Finish unscrewing the cap.

3. As the balloon fills, write down your observations. Answer questions 7(a) and 7(b).

4. After a few minutes, hold the bottle securely in your hands and shake it side to side to further release bubbles from the liquid. Try not to get liquid in the balloon.

5. Make final observations of your bottle of seltzer. Answer questions 7(c) - (i).

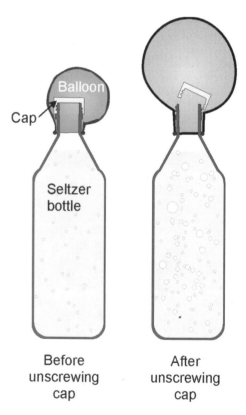

Before unscrewing cap

After unscrewing cap

7   ## Drawing conclusions

a.   What happened to the balloon as you unscrewed the cap?

b.   Are the bubbles in the liquid large or small just after you take off the cap?

c.   How has the balloon changed since you first opened the bottle? What does the change in size tell you about the amount of gas in the balloon and where did the gas come from?

d.   Has the size of the bubbles in the liquid changed since you opened the bottle? If so, come up with a reason to explain why this might have happened.

e.   Why was the balloon important in this Investigation?

f.   How did the pressure change before and after opening the bottle?

g.   How did you know the pressure changed?

h.   Based on the results and your observations from the experiment, how was the solubility of carbon dioxide gas in water affected by the pressure in the bottle? Use evidence from the Investigation in your response.

i.   Make a prediction for how the seltzer will taste a week from now if the bottle is left open. Explain your prediction using the terms pressure and solubility.

8   ## Challenge questions

a.   Soft drinks contain dissolved carbon dioxide that has been added to make a carbonated solution. The carbon dioxide is kept in solution using pressure. If you were going to start a company that makes carbonated soda, what kind of processes would you use to make and package the soda in aluminum cans? Write out and diagram your ideas. Once you have recorded your ideas, do some research at the local library or on the Internet to see how your ideas compare to real world practices for making and packaging carbonated soda. Record your findings.

b.   In this part of the Investigation, we only looked at the solubility of a gas in a liquid. How do you think pressure affects the solubility of a liquid in a liquid or a solid in a liquid? How do you think temperature would affect the solubility of a gas in a liquid? Provide evidence to support your ideas.

c.   Read "Science in the Real World: Scuba diving" in section 23.3 Solubility of the student text. Based on this reading and what you observed in the Investigation, explain why you need to understand the influence of pressure on the solubility of a gas in order to scuba dive safely.

Acids, Bases, and pH

Question: What is pH?

In this Investigation, you will:

1. Make a pH scale using a pH indicator and chemicals of known pH.
2. Use the pH scale to figure out the pH of additional chemicals.
3. Identify a "mystery" chemical with your pH scale.

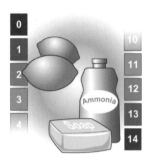

Life exists inside a certain range of pH numbers. A pH value describes whether a solution is acidic, basic (alkaline), or neutral. Acids are solutions that contain a majority of H_3O^+ ions, and bases (or alkalis) are solutions that contain a majority of OH- ions. Neutral solutions have equal numbers of H_3O^+ and OH- ions.

In this Investigation, you will learn the pH of several everyday solutions. As you measure pH of these solutions, identify some properties of acids and some properties of bases.

1 ## Setting up

1. Collect the following materials: three spot plates, permanent marker, eyedroppers or pipettes, 5 milliliters of red cabbage juice (a pH indicator), red and blue litmus paper (pH indicators). Additionally, collect 2 milliliters each of the solutions listed in the data table (solutions 1 to 12).
2. Record your data, observations, and responses during the Investigation.

Safety Tip: Wear goggles and a lab apron during the Investigation to protect your eyes and clothing from the household chemicals that you will be using.

2 ## Make a pH scale using indicators

1. To create your pH scale, you will be using solutions 1 to 7 in the table below. Place the following labels for these solutions **in order** on a spot plate. If you don't have seven wells in a row on one spot plate, place two plates side by side. The labels should describe the solution and its pH.

   Lemon, pH 2   Vinegar, 3   Soda water, 4   Red cabbage juice (the control), 6.5

   Baking soda, 8.5   Hand soap, 10   Ammonia, 11

2. Using a pipette, place three drops of red cabbage juice in each of the seven labeled wells.
3. Using a pipette, add two drops of each of the solutions to the appropriately labeled well. Use a different eyedropper or pipette for each solution. However, if you must use the same dropper or pipette, thoroughly rinse it in fresh water after each solution before using it for a new solution. Record the color changes in your data table. The color series you see on the plate(s) represents a pH scale. We will refer to it as the **pH test plate**. You will use it to identify the pH of other solutions.
4. Dip the red litmus paper and the blue litmus paper into each well of the pH test plate. Record the results according to the directions in the data table.

Name of solution	Color when mixed with red cabbage juice	Red litmus paper: If paper turns blue, write "base," or make an "x"	Blue litmus paper: If paper turns red, write "acid," or make an "x"	pH
1. lemon				2
2. vinegar				3
3. seltzer				4
4. red cabbage juice				6.5
5. baking soda solution				8.5
6. bar soap solution				10
7. ammonia				11
8. green tea				
9. antibacterial cleaner				
10. apple juice				
11. mystery solution A				
12. mystery solution B				

3   Evaluating the role of the pH test plate

a.   What is the role of a pH indicator? What is the range of pH measured by each of the indicators you used (red cabbage juice, red litmus paper, blue litmus paper)?

b.   Which of your solutions has the highest concentration of H_3O^+ ions? Which has the highest concentration of OH- ions? Explain your reasoning.

c.   The red cabbage juice used in the Investigations has two roles. It is the pH indicator and, in the series on the pH test plate, it is a *control*. Why is a control needed on the pH test plate?

4   Using pH indicators to measure unknown pH

1.   Repeat steps 2.2 to 2.4 for solutions 8 to 12. Use another spot plate for these five solutions. The labels should describe the solution. At this point, you do not know the pH of these solutions.

2.   Identify the pH of solutions 8 to 12. Compare the color reactions and the litmus paper results for solutions 8 to 12 with the pH test plate.

5   Identifying mystery solutions

Mystery solutions A and B are identical to two other solutions you used in this lab. Use your results to identify these solutions. What is the identity of mystery solution A? What is the identity of mystery B? List evidence to support your claims.

6   What did you learn?

a.   List the pros and cons of using red cabbage juice and litmus paper as pH indicators.

b.   Various professions use pH indicators. For example, photographers use stop bath in developing, and swimming pools are maintained using information from pH indicators. Find out how these pH indicators work in these (or other) situations, and what the color changes mean.

The Water Cycle

Question: What is the quality of your local surface water?

In this Investigation, you will:

1. Meet a specialist in the field of water quality testing.
2. Visit a local surface water area and perform water quality testing.

Water is one of our most important natural resources. Consequently, many careers involve studying and taking care of our water supply. Some scientists test and monitor the water supply and some study weather patterns to better understand the water cycle. People involved in government agencies, nonprofit organizations, and the media keep track of information about water and make this information available to the general public. In this Investigation, you will meet a specialist in the field of water quality testing, and perform water quality tests. As you complete the Investigation, think about what causes water pollution. What actions can you take to reduce your water usage and to improve water quality?

1 Meeting a water quality specialist

a. Before you meet the specialist, write down his or her name and occupation. Prepare three questions that you would like to ask the specialist.

b. During the meeting, take notes. Review your notes and write down at least three new things that you learned from the specialist.

2 Preparing for your field trip

As you prepare for the field trip, be sure to write down your work in your lab notebook. On your own:

1. Read *The Water Cycle* in the student text to learn about the procedures for water quality testing.
2. Familiarize yourself with the testing procedures for performing the water quality testing. Each test involves some special steps. Additionally, the field trip will be more enjoyable if you understand the tests and how they are performed.

With your group:

1. Describe the place that your class will perform water quality testing. Where is it located? What kind of surface water will be tested?
2. Make a prediction about the quality of the surface water to be tested. Will the water in this location be clean or polluted? Justify your answer.

With the class:

1. Create data sheets for collecting quantitative and qualitative data. What information needs to go on the data sheets?
2. Look at a map of the surface water that will be tested. Discuss and decide where samples will be taken. Assign locations to each group.

3   Field trip: testing surface water

Safety Tip: Wear goggles while you perform the coliform test and the tests for phosphate and nitrate. Be sure to wash your hands when you have completed the tests.

1. Make general observations about the surface water and the day's weather.
2. Use your data sheets for recording information at each sampling sight.
3. You will be using supplies from a water quality testing kit to perform this Investigation. Be sure to follow the directions and safety instructions for using these supplies while you perform the tests.

4   Follow up

1. With your group, go over your data sheets carefully and make sure that you have recorded all the observations that you wanted to make.
2. Compile the data with the class. Make data tables for each test.
3. Using the compiled data, each group should create a water quality report for the surface water tested. Be sure to address whether or not the quality of the water at this site matched your prediction. In your report, include a section that addresses what your class can do to maintain the water quality at the test site or help improve the water quality at the test site.

24.2   **Water Quality**

Question: What is the quality of your tap water?

In this Investigation, you will:

1. Learn about the composition of tap water.
2. Learn and use basic water quality tests.

If you were to take a trip across the United States, you might notice that water in different places doesn't taste the same. Why is that? The taste of water has to do with where it comes from and then how it is treated by a municipal water company before it comes out of a faucet. The taste also depends on whether or not water contains dissolved minerals from sediment in the ground or from pipes in the plumbing system. What does your water taste like? Where does it originate before it reaches the treatment plant? This Investigation will show you simple tests you can use to better understand your tap water.

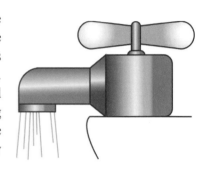

1 **Obtaining your water samples**

1. Before coming to class, collect two 500-milliliter (about 2 cups) samples of water from a faucet at your house. One sample should be of very hot water and the other sample very cold water.
2. Collect your samples in large sealable plastic bags. Be sure to label which bag has the cold sample and which the hot sample. Let the water run for 5 minutes before collecting each of your samples. Once you have your samples, place them inside a **second** larger, sealable bag. Make sure all the bags are tightly sealed! You will have to be very careful while you transport your samples. Drop them off with your teacher when you arrive at school.
3. ⭐ **Do not waste the water that runs from the faucet before you collect your sample. For example, you can use this water for watering your houseplants.**
4. While you are at home collecting your samples, look for any signs that you may have high levels of copper (blue stains), iron (orange stains), or minerals (scale on glasses) in your water. Write down your observations.
5. Find out where your water comes from. You may need to use the Internet to trace this information. A helpful Web site is http://www.epa.gov/surf.

2 **Testing your water quality**

For each of the following water quality tests, you will be pouring about 20 milliliters of each sample into small, clear beakers. Therefore, you need two clean beakers for each test. Record the results when you have completed each test.

👓 🦺 **Safety Tip: Wear goggles and a lab apron while performing the tests. When you have completed all the tests, be sure to wash your hands.**

The pH test: The pH of your tap water can affect the pipes in your house. The pH scale ranges from acids (0 to 6) to bases (8 to 14). Pure water has no dissolved substances and is neutral (pH 7). When water is acidic, it can corrode pipes and cause iron, copper, or lead to get into your drinking water. When water is basic, calcium or magnesium deposits may clog the pipes in your house.

a.   Add a pH wide-range tablet to each of your samples.

b.   Compare your results with the color series that your teacher has set up. What color is each sample?

c.   What is the pH of each of your samples?

The hardness test: Hard water has high levels of dissolved calcium and magnesium. These minerals form white deposits on drinking glasses and inside pipes. The deposits, called "scale," can clog pipes.

a.   Add a hardness-test tablet to each of your samples.

b.   Compare your results with the color series that you teacher has set up. What color is each sample?

c.   Is the water in each of your samples hard or soft?

The chlorine test: Chlorine in safe amounts is added by water treatment facilities to kill harmful bacteria and algae. Chlorine does not occur naturally in water supplies.

a.   Add a chlorine-test tablet to each of your samples.

b.   Compare your results with the color series that your teacher has set up. What color is each sample?

c.   Do your samples contain low or high amounts of chlorine?

The iron test: Iron is a natural component of tap water. However, when water is too acidic, iron may be leached from pipes into the water supply.

a.   Add an iron-test tablet to each of your samples.

b.   Compare your results with the color series that your teacher has set up. What color is each sample?

c.   Do your samples contain low or high amounts of iron?
      NOTE: Iron is unstable in water. For this reason, you may not detect iron even when it is present in your water supply.

The copper test: Copper, like iron, can be leached from pipes into the water supply when the water is too acidic. In small quantities, copper is an essential element for human health. Too much copper can make water taste bitter and cause blue stains in sinks and bathtubs.

a.   Add a copper-test tablet to each of your samples.

b.   Compare your results with the color series that your teacher set up. What color is each sample?

c.   Do your samples contain low or high amounts of copper or none at all?

3   ☑ **Analyzing results and drawing conclusions**

a.   Organize your results into a table.

b.   Write a five to eight sentence paragraph that explains the results of your testing.

c.   Is there a difference between the hot and cold tap water samples? Why or why not?

d.   How could the method of testing water quality that was used in this Investigation be improved?

e.   At a local store or in your classroom, look at the packaging for a water-filtration device. What substances -- and how much of their total presence in the water -- does the device claim to remove? Based on your testing results, would you purchase this device to improve the quality of your household drinking water? Explain your answer.

Acid Rain

Question: What is acid rain?

In this Investigation, you will:

1. Learn about the biology of the water flea (Daphnia).
2. Observe the effects of different concentrations (dilutions) of acid on Daphnia.
3. Learn about acid rain and its effects on organisms in aquatic environments.

Under normal conditions, the pH of ponds and lakes ranges from 6 to 8. When a pond or lake experiences acid rain, the pH may be lowered. At a pH value less than 5.6, numerous organisms in the pond are harmed. In this Investigation, you will be simulating the effects of acid rain on a common pond and lake organism, the water flea (Daphnia). Daphnia is a small transparent organism that is related to crabs and shrimp. This organism serves as a food source for small fish and the larvae of larger organisms. If any environmental effect harms the population of Daphnia, what do you think would happen to the other organisms in the pond or lake?

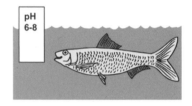

Safety Tips: Wear goggles, gloves, and a lab apron during the Investigation.

1   Observing Daphnia

Obtain a culture vial and some wide-bore pipettes. Each vial has at least six Daphnia individuals in spring water.

a. To understand how Daphnia might react to an acidic environment, it is best to figure out how it acts under normal conditions. Look carefully at this organism. Draw a detailed diagram of a single individual. It may help to use a magnifying glass to see the different parts of this small animal.

b. Once you have drawn your diagram, watch the Daphnia individuals for 5 minutes. Record the movements and behaviors of Daphnia. Be very detailed in your recording.

c. Based on your observations, label the parts of Daphnia that you included in your diagram. Next to each label, write what you think the role of each part is.

2   Making predictions

You will be exposing Daphnia to different concentrations of acid dissolved in water. Record what you think will happen as you expose Daphnia to acid. Include a list of behaviors that you think will indicate that Daphnia is being harmed by the acid. Determine the lowest concentration of acid that you think will cause harm to Daphnia. Record this hypothesis.

3   Simulating the effect of acid rain on Daphnia

1. Your teacher will give you five acid treatment solutions. Each is a different concentration, or *dilution*, of acid dissolved in spring water. These treatments are labeled 1 to 5 on the table with "1" having the lowest concentration of acid and "5" having the highest concentration of acid. You will also have a control treatment of spring water. You will be using spring water throughout the Investigation because the chlorine in tap water would kill Daphnia.

2. When you are ready to tests the effects of acid on Daphnia, remove the lid from a culture vial. Use a wide-bore pipette to transfer a single Daphnia from the culture vial to the control vial of spring water. Additionally, transfer another Daphnia from a culture vial to the vial with treatment 1 (the one with the lowest concentration of acid). Record the start time (the hour and minute) in the table below. Place the lids back on the vials.

3. Begin observing the effect of spring water and treatment 1 immediately. Compare the movements of the single Daphnia in the spring water vial with the single Daphnia in treatment 1. Record your observations.

4. Observe the two vials for 2 minutes. If the Daphnia dies in treatment 1, record the time that this happens. If the Daphnia does not die during this time, keep observing the vial. Continue to keep time on this vial, but continue with the rest of the experiment.

5. Repeat steps 3.2 to 3.4 for the next four treatments (treatments 2 - 5). Compare Daphnia in the treatments with Daphnia in the control vial. Record your observations and keep time.

6. The end time for any treatment is the point at which a Daphnia individual dies in the treatment.

7. After 30 minutes have past since the first start time that you recorded, this part of the Investigation ends. In the Observations column of the data table, record the status of the Daphnia for each vial.

8. Use pH paper or indicator tablets to identify the pH of each treatment solution and the spring water control. Record the pH value for these in the table below.

Con-centration of acid	Treatments	pH	Start time	Observations	End time
none	spring water (control)				
lowest	1				
	2				
	3				
	4				
highest	5				

4   Analyzing results and drawing conclusions

a. Write a paragraph that summarizes the results of this experiment. Do not include any conclusions in this paragraph. Simply write down what you observed.

b. Write a paragraph that explains whether or not your predictions from part 2 were correct. Include a conclusion statement that addresses what you learned by performing this experiment.

c. Was this experiment a good way to understand some of the effects of acid rain on organisms that live in a pond or lake? How could this experiment be improved to better demonstrate the effects of acid rain?

d. What is an *ecosystem*? Why is it difficult to simulate the effects of an event like acid rain on an ecosystem?

e. Write up this experiment as a lab report. Follow the format provided to you by your teacher.

Oceans

Question: How does carbon dioxide affect the oceans?

In this Investigation, you will:

1. Identify how carbon dioxide affects the pH of solutions.
2. Explore how calcium carbonate acts as a buffer in the oceans.

The oceans contain a natural *buffer* called calcium carbonate. A buffer is a substance that helps maintain the pH of a solution. When carbon dioxide (CO_2) from the atmosphere dissolves into seawater, it produces acidic conditions. However, the pH of the oceans remains relatively stable because of the calcium carbonate buffer system.

In this Investigation, you will observe what happens when CO_2 dissolves in water. You will then conduct an experiment to test how a buffer works.

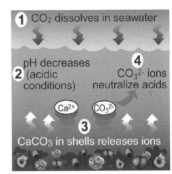

1 CO_2 dissolves in seawater
2 pH decreases (acidic conditions)
4 CO_3^{2-} ions neutralize acids
3 $CaCO_3$ in shells releases ions

1 **How does carbon dioxide affect the pH of solutions?**

1. Obtain a pH meter and two clean beakers. Choose members of your group for the following roles:
   - Bubbler - blows bubbles into the beaker;
   - Timer - keeps track of time in 10-second intervals; and
   - Recorder - records the pH reading from the meter every 10 seconds.
2. Obtain a beaker and fill it 1/2 full of tap water.
3. Immerse a pH meter into the beaker and turn it on.
4. Wait a few moments until the pH reading on the meter stabilizes. Record the pH in "initial" row under the "tap water" colum of Table 1. (Your teacher will give you a handout with a larger table.)
5. The timer should start the clock while the bubbler gently blows bubbles into the beaker with a straw. This is the source of CO_2 in the experiment.
6. Record the pH reading from the meter every 10 seconds for a total of two minutes.
7. Remove the pH meter, turn it off, and rinse it with tap water.
8. Obtain another beaker and fill it 1/2 full of tap water. Add one calcium carbonate antacid table to the beaker.
9. Repeat steps 3 through 7 and record your results in the "calcium carbonate" column of Table 1.

Table 1: The effect of carbon dioxide on pH

Time (sec)	Tap water (pH)	Calcium carbonate (pH)
initial		

a. How does adding carbon dioxide to a solution affect its pH?

b. In which beaker did the pH change the fastest?

c. How did the calcium carbonate tablet affect pH changes in the second beaker?

2   How does a buffer affect pH?

In this experiment, you will test how a buffer works. This time, you will use another buffer—sodium hydrogen carbonate (baking soda) and another acid—acetic acid (vinegar).

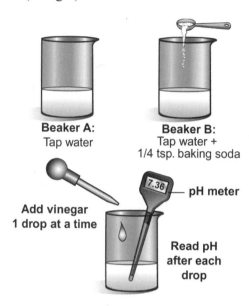

Beaker A: Tap water

Beaker B: Tap water + 1/4 tsp. baking soda

Add vinegar 1 drop at a time

7.36 — pH meter

Read pH after each drop

1. Obtain two clean beakers and fill both 1/2 full with tap water. Label one **A** and the other **B**.

2. Add 1/4 teaspoon of baking soda to beaker **B**. Stir until the baking soda is completely dissolved and set this beaker aside.

3. Immerse the pH meter into beaker A, turn it on, and wait a few moments until the reading stabilizes. Record the pH in the first row of Table 2. (A larger table is found on the handout your teacher has provided.)

4. Add one drop of vinegar to the beaker, swirl the beaker gently, and record the pH.

5. Continue adding drops of vinegar to the beaker, swirling gently, and recording the pH after each drop. Repeat until you have added a total of 60 drops of vinegar to the beaker. Record all pH measurements in Table 2.

6. Remove the pH meter, turn it off, and rinse it with clean tap water.

7. Repeat steps 3 through 6 for beaker B. Record all of your data in Table 2.

Table 2: Drops of acid and pH

Drop number	pH in beaker A	pH in beaker B
0		

3   Analyzing your results

Make a graph of the data in Table 2. Plot the number of drops of acid on the *x*-axis and pH on the *y*-axis. You should plot data for beaker **A** using one colored pencil and for beaker **B** with a contrasting color on the same grid.

a. What differences do you observe between the pH changes in beakers **A** and **B**?

b. Do your results provide evidence that buffers help stabilize the pH of solutions? Explain your answer in detail.

c. CO_2 is a greenhouse gas that has been steadily increasing in Earth's atmosphere since the Industrial Revolution. Based on your results in this experiment:

•   Do you think the oceans could help remove some of the CO_2 from the atmosphere? Why or why not?

•   What affect could an increase in CO_2 have on the amount of calcium carbonate in the oceans? Explain your answer in detail.

25.1   Measuring Heat

Question: How is temperature measured?

In this Investigation, you will:

1. Accurately measure changes in temperature.
2. Develop a way to convert between Fahrenheit and Celsius temperature scales.

In the reading you learned that materials expand as the temperature increases. You will observe this phenomenon and measure it, using both the Fahrenheit and Celsius temperature scales. You will graph the Celsius temperature scale as a function of the Fahrenheit temperature scale. From your graph you will develop a mathematical formula that you can use to convert between Fahrenheit and Celsius temperature scales.

◆ **Safety Tip: If you are using glass thermometers, remember that they are very fragile and may break. Handle them very carefully.**

1   Which beaker is warmest?

1. In front of you are four beakers of water at different temperatures, marked A, B, C, and D. By dipping your finger into the water, identify each beaker from hottest to coldest.
2. Place your right index finger in the hottest beaker. At the same time, place your left index finger in the coldest beaker. Leave them there for 30 seconds. Now place both fingers into the room temperature beaker.

a. Describe how each finger feels. Which finger feels hot? Which finger feels cold?

b. Are your fingers a reliable measuring tool for temperature? Why or why not?

2   What is the actual temperature of the water in each beaker?

1. Using your thermometer, find the temperature in each of the beakers. Do this measurement in degrees Fahrenheit. If you do not have a Fahrenheit thermometer, use the picture on the next page to convert your Celsius measurement to Fahrenheit. Record your data in the table below.
2. Now measure the water in degrees Celsius and record your data in the table.

beaker	°F	°C
A		
B		
C		
D		

3 Analyzing your data

1. Graph your Fahrenheit vs. Celsius data. Place your Fahrenheit data on the *y*-axis and the Celsius data on the *x*-axis.

2. Rather than connecting your data points dot-to-dot, draw a *trend line*. A trend line is a straight line that most closely matches your data points. It is sometimes called a "line of best fit."

3. Find the slope of your trend line by first choosing two points on the line. Then use the formula:

$$\frac{y_2 - y_1}{x_2 - x_1}$$

4. Find the equation for the trend line in the form $y = mx+b$ where *m* is the slope of the line and *b* is the *y*-intercept.

a.   Based on your graph, what is the equation that allows you to convert from Celsius to Fahrenheit?

b.   Solve the equation you just obtained, (°F = m°C + b), for °C. This will give you the formula to convert Fahrenheit to Celsius temperature.

c.   Is it possible to obtain negative values of °F? Of °C? Explain your answer.

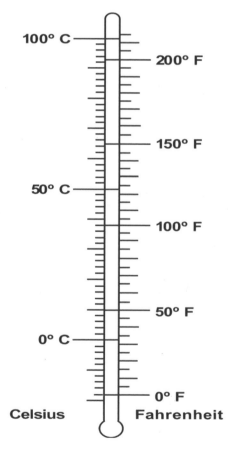

Celsius and Fahrenheit scales compared

25.2

Question: How efficient is an immersion heater?

In this Investigation, you will:

1. Calculate an increase in thermal energy, work output, work input, and efficiency.
2. Analyze the efficiency of a household appliance.

You know that when heat is added to an object it increases its temperature. This increase depends on the mass of the object and the amount of energy put into the object. In this Investigation, you will observe the heating of water as electrical energy is converted into thermal energy. You will use this data to calculate the efficiency of an immersion water heater.

1   ### Setting up

1. 👓 Put on your goggles.
2. Attach the immersion heater to the side of your beaker.
   ◆ **Warning: DO NOT plug the immersion heater in until it is immersed in water.**
3. Now you are going to fill the beaker with water. Using a graduated cylinder, measure how many milliliters of cold tap water it takes to cover the entire heating element. Record the volume of water in Table 1.
4. Calculate the mass of the water. Remember that each milliliter of water has a mass of 1 gram.
5. Your teacher will tell you the power of your heater in watts. Record this in Table 1.
6. Take an initial temperature reading of the water. Record this in Table 2.
7. Make sure your setup is near an electrical outlet.
8. Reset your stopwatch.

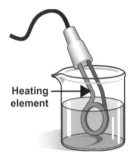

Heating element

Table 1: Initial data

Volume of water (mL)	Mass of water (g)	Heater power (watts)

👓🧤 **Safety Tip: The immersion heater will get very hot. Do not touch the metal, only the handle. Also, while heating the water, you should wear goggles.**

2   Heating the water and measuring temperature

After you plug in your immersion heater, you will take temperature readings every 30 seconds. Be sure to stir the water before each measurement. Record the time and temperature in Table 2. You will not notice a significant change in temperature for the first minute. Why do you think this is?

⬙Unplug your immersion heater when you are finished collecting data.

Table 2: Water temperature

Time (s)	Temperature (°C)
0	
30	
60	
90	
120	
150	
180	
210	
240	
270	
300	

3   Graphing your data

a.   Graph the data in Table 2. On which axis will you plot temperature? On which axis will you plot time? Explain your answer.

b.   Calculate the slope of your graph. Use the correct units.

c.   On which factors does the slope of your graph depend?

4   Calculating increase in thermal energy

$\frac{a}{b}$ Follow the directions below to calculate the increase in thermal energy of the water for each minute of the experiment. Record your answers in Table 3.

a.   Determine the change in temperature over the course of each minute and record your data in column 2 of Table 3.

b.   In the third column, record the mass of the water from Table 1.

c.   Calculate the increase in thermal energy in calories. Remember the increase in thermal energy in calories is equal to the mass times the heating constant times the change in temperature.

$$Q = mc\Delta T$$

When we are calculating the energy in calories, the heating constant is $1\frac{calorie}{gram°C}$. Record the increases in thermal energy for each minute in the fourth column of Table 3.

d.   Now convert the energy into joules. Since 1 calorie = 4.186 joules, all you need to do is multiply the energy in calories times 4.186. Record your results in the last column of Table 3.

Table 3: Increase in thermal energy of the water

Minute	Change in temperature (°C)	Mass of water (g)	Increase in thermal energy (calories)	Increase in thermal energy (joules)
1				
2				
3				
4				
5				

5   Analyzing the data

a.   If you were to change the mass of the water, what effect do you think this would have on the increase in thermal energy? What effect would it have on the increase in temperature?

b.   What effect would changing the mass have on the slope of your graph? Draw a dashed line on your graph to indicate what you think this effect would be.

c.   Does the increase in energy stay constant over the duration of the experiment or does it change? If it changes, why do you think this is?

6   ## Calculating the efficiency of the water heater

Now you are going to calculate how efficient your immersion heater is.

- **Work output** is the increase in thermal energy of the water in joules. You can get this value from Table 3. Record the values for work output for each minute in Table 4.

- **Work input** can be calculated from the definition of **power**. You are going to use the power of the immersion heater as measured in watts from Table 1. Use 60 seconds for the time value. Record your calculations in Table 4.

$$work\ input\ =\ power \times change\ in\ time$$

- To calculate the **efficiency**, simply divide work output by work input. Multiply this value by 100 to express the efficiency as a percentage.

$$efficiency\ =\ \left(\frac{work\ output}{work\ input}\right) \times 100$$

Table 4: Efficiency

Minute	Work output (joules)	Power (watts) from Table 1	Work input (watts/second = joules)	Efficiency (%)
1				
2				
3				
4				
5				

a.   How efficient would you say this method of heating water is?

b.   Is there any way to recapture the heat that is not absorbed by the water? What happens to the heat that the water does not absorb?

Heat Transfer

Question: How much heat is transferred through convection?

In this Investigation, you will:

1. Investigate natural convection through liquids.
2. Observe forced convection through liquids.

You have learned that natural convection occurs by the movement of a hot gas or liquid into a region of colder gas or liquid. Forced convection occurs when a gas or liquid is forced (by either pressure or a fan) into another gas or liquid. In this Investigation, you will observe the vertical movement of colored water due to temperature differences. You will also observe forced convection.

1 Doing the experiment

1. Have your timer ready. You will start your timer at the end of the setup.
2. Arrange the glass tubing in the stopper as seen in Figure 1.
3. Your teacher will provide you with hot water. Fill the flask with the hot water and mix in six drops of food coloring. Stir completely. Be very careful since the water might be very hot!
4. Measure the temperature of the hot water and record in Table 1.
5. Very carefully insert the glass tubing-stopper arrangement into the neck of the flask. You should hold the flask with a wet paper towel.
6. Place the hot water flask into the large beaker. Again, hold the flask with a wet paper towel.
7. Use a graduated cylinder to fill the large beaker with room-temperature water. As you fill the beaker, measure how much water you use. Fill the beaker until the water is about ½ centimeter above the higher pipette. Record the volume of water in the large beaker in Table 1.
8. Measure the temperature of the water in the large beaker. Record this information in Table 1.

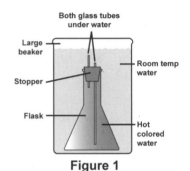

Figure 1

Safety Tip: Wear your goggles and use a potholder or a wet paper towel to hold the hot-water flask!

Table 1: Initial data

Temp. of hot water:_____ °C	Volume water in large beaker:_____ mL
	Temp. of water in large beaker:_____ °C

2 **Data and observations**

1. Record the time and temperature of the water in the outer beaker when convection starts.

2. Take temperature readings every minute until three minutes after convection stops. Record your data in Table 2. Your teacher will provide a larger version of this table. In the third column, mark (Yes/No) if convection is occurring. It is important to note at what time convection stops.

Table 2: Convection data

Time	Temp.	Y/N	Time	Temp.	Y/N	Time	Temp.	Y/N

a. Record your observations 1 minute after the onset of convection. Sketch your observations also.

b. Record your observations 5 minutes after the onset of convection. Sketch your observations also.

3 **How much heat was transferred by convection?**

$\frac{a}{b}$ Calculate the amount of heat transferred using the equation $Q = mc\Delta T$.

$m_{cold\ water}$	c_{water}	T_{final}	$T_{initial}$	ΔT	$Q_{heat\ transferred}$
	$1\frac{calorie}{gram\,°C}$				

a. What is the heat transfer rate? Divide heat transferred by the number of minutes convection occurred.

b. Does natural convection seem like a good method for transferring heat? Explain.

c. How much heat was transferred in the first minute after convection stopped? What was this heat transfer rate?

d. If convection stopped, and there was no mixing, what caused this additional heat transfer?

e. How does this other method of heat transfer compare with convection? Explain.

4 **Forced convection**

Now you are going to repeat the experiment in a different way.

1. Obtain another flask of colored water and place it in the empty large beaker.

2. Fill the large beaker with water. You do not need to measure the amount of water you put in this time. Pour in just enough water so the level of the water covers the lower pipette but not the upper pipette. The water level should be at least ½ inch below the level of the upper pipette.

3. Take your straw and place it 1 cm either inside or outside the upper pipette, depending on how it best fits. If it looks like it is not a tight seal, use a piece of tape from your teacher.

4. Now, blow *gently* through the straw. As you do this, the other members in your group can draw a picture of the resulting forced convection.

a. Describe and record your observations.

b. How is forced convection similar to natural convection? How is it different?

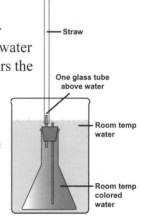

Straw

One glass tube above water

Room temp water

Room temp colored water

Figure 2

The Atmosphere

Question: Can you measure atmospheric pressure?

In this Investigation, you will:

1. Construct your own aneroid barometer.
2. Design a mechanism to amplify and measure the barometer's movement.
3. Calibrate your barometer for temperature changes.
4. Make a graph that allows you to easily convert your barometer measurements to millibars.

The atmosphere is often referred to as an "ocean of air." As weather systems interact in the troposphere, atmospheric pressure varies slightly above and below the average 1013.25 millibars at sea level. These slight changes in atmospheric pressure are one of the most useful measurements for weather prediction. But the concept of the atmosphere as an ocean goes beyond surging currents of air. The atmosphere has tides caused by the sun and moon, just like the ocean does. How are these pressure changes measured? In this Investigation, you will build your own atmospheric pressure gauge.

1 Parts of an aneroid barometer

How does an aneroid barometer work? Here is the basic principle that underlies most barometers: Common matter is classified as solid, liquid, or gas. Of the three, gas is unique in that if you put pressure on a certain volume of a gas, you can squeeze it into a space many times smaller than its original volume. Therefore, if you could measure the change in volume of a certain amount of gas, you would have a way to measure atmospheric pressure.

To build a reliable barometer, you will:

- Make a compression chamber to observe changes in atmospheric pressure.

- Construct a pointer that amplifies tiny changes and shows them on a scale.

- Contain the compression chamber in a sturdy frame so that you can move your barometer around and take readings that are consistent.

- Calibrate your barometer so that its readings are accurate even if it undergoes temperature changes.

Parts of an Aneroid Barometer

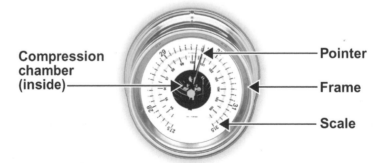

a. A compression chamber must be airtight yet flexible so that you can measure changes in volume of the gas it contains. With your group, brainstorm materials you could use for a compression chamber.

b. How will you measure your compression chamber's changes in volume?

2   Building the compression chamber

The compression chamber must be rigid except for a flexible element called a *tympanum*. The rigid part is where you will attach the chamber to a frame and where you can pick it up. You will measure the in-and-out movement of the tympanum as greater atmospheric pressure presses it in and lesser atmospheric pressure allows it to relax or bulge outward.

A wide-mouth glass jar will make a good compression chamber. The size of the jar affects the amount of movement of the tympanum. A large mayonnaise jar and a peanut butter jar have similar sized openings, but the larger volume of the mayonnaise jar will cause larger movements of the tympanum. You will form the tympanum by sealing a piece of plastic grocery bag over the mouth of the jar.

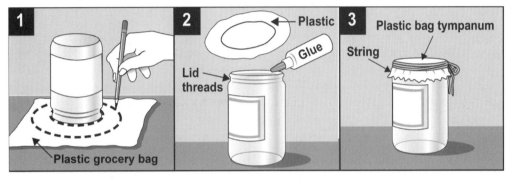

1. Cut the grocery bag in half so that you have a flat piece of plastic to spread out on your work space.
2. Place the jar upside down on an area of the plastic that is free of even the smallest holes. Use a permanent marker to trace an outline of the mouth of the jar on the plastic.
3. Remove the jar. Draw a larger circle around the first circle. Your new circle should be 6 centimeters larger in diameter than the first.
4. Cut out the larger circle with scissors.
5. Apply a generous amount of glue to the lid threads of the jar.
6. Center the plastic circle over the jar. Wind several tight turns of string around the jar's lid threads, making sure the plastic fits tightly over the jar.
7. Tie off the string. When the glue dries, cut away the excess plastic.

3   Constructing the pointer

The pointer has two purposes. It makes the small movements of the tympanum visible, and it allows those movements to be recorded as a number. Here are some suggestions:

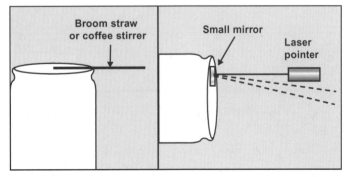

Study the pictures above. They may spark further ideas among your group. Choose one method to try.

a. Write out a step-by-step procedure for constructing your pointer.

b. As you construct the pointer, you may encounter unexpected issues that may require you to modify your procedure. When finished, revise the steps you listed in Part 3a to reflect your final procedure.

c. Test your mechanism by gently pushing on the tympanum with your finger. Could you see the pointer's movement? If not, devise a method to increase the distance moved by the pointer. Record any final changes made to your procedure.

4   Attaching a frame and scale

The frame must allow the barometer to be moved without disturbing the pointer. The frame also supports the pointer scale. The frame must be sturdy so that the positions of the pointer and scale cannot change. Movement between the pointer and the scale will cause enormous errors.

A sturdy box makes a good frame. The compression chamber with attached pointer must fit easily inside the frame. The pointer should almost touch one of the walls of the box.

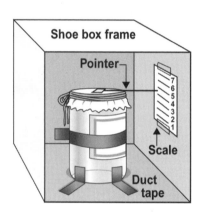

1. Attach the compression chamber to the frame. The position of the compression chamber inside the frame should not change even if the frame is moved from one location to another.

2. Create a scale to help you measure the movement of the pointer. Use a pen and a ruler to make a series of evenly-spaced marks on a piece of white paper. Number each mark 1, 2, 3, and so on.

3. Slide your scale between the pointer and the wall of your frame. Attach the scale with tape so that you can record movements of the pointer. For example, if the pointer currently points to the space between 4 and 5 on the scale, you would record the atmospheric pressure as 4.5 units.

5   Calibrating your barometer

Changing atmospheric pressure is not the only force that will cause the tympanum to bulge in and out. If your barometer warms up, the air inside will expand and that, too, will make the tympanum bulge out. Similarly, if the barometer cools, the tympanum will bulge inward. You need a way to correct readings for temperature. Commercial barometers do this with a second mechanism inside so that the displayed readings are already adjusted, or compensated, for temperature changes. To keep your barometer from becoming too difficult to build, you will read the temperature from a separate thermometer and use a graph to adjust your barometer readings for changes in temperature.

1. The first step in calibrating your barometer is to make a table of readings over the course of at least one week. Each day, record the temperature in the first column, the pointer reading in the second column, and the reading from the commercial barometer in the last column.

   If you find that the temperature varies widely over the course of the week, you may wish to take readings for a second week. Once you have at least three barometer readings at the same temperature you will be able to begin graphing your data.

Table 1: Atmospheric pressure data, Week 1

	Temperature	Scale mark on barometer	Commercial barometer reading
Sample	24°C	3	1031 millibars
Sample	26°C	4	1031 millibars
Day 1			
Day 2			
Day 3			
Day 4			
Day 5			
Day 6			
Day 7			

2. Make an easy-to-read graph to help you convert your barometer readings to millibars. First, rewrite your table, grouping together all readings at one temperature.

3. Label the x-axis of your graph with your pointer scale and the y-axis with the commercial barometer readings. Plot all of the readings *for one temperature* and draw a trend line through the points. Label that line with its temperature. Repeat this process for each group of temperatures. The end result will be a series of trend lines, one for each temperature.

4. After you have taken several sets of readings, you will be able to determine atmospheric pressure using your barometer. Find your pointer scale reading on the x-axis, and then follow that line upward until you meet the trend line for the current temperature. Then read the y-coordinate of that point to find the barometer reading in millibars. Continue to compare your barometer with the commercial one until you can read yours with confidence.

6   **Evaluating your design**

a. Use your barometer, thermometer, and graph to measure barometric pressure for an additional week. Record your data, along with data from a commercial barometer, in the table below.

Table 2: Atmospheric pressure data, Week 2

Day	Your barometer reading	Commercial barometer		Day	Your barometer reading	Commercial barometer
1				5		
2				6		
3				7		
4						

b. What is the maximum difference, in millibars, between your reading and the commercial barometer reading? Calculate the percent error of this reading.

c. Name two adjustments you could make to increase the accuracy of your barometer.

d. Look back on your barometer readings for the past week. Can you see a relationship between air pressure and the weather? Do sunny days tend to have high or low pressure? How about rainy days?

26.2 Layers of the Atmosphere

Question: How much ozone is in our living areas?

In this Investigation, you will:

1. Test four different locations for ozone.
2. Make qualitative observations of the amount of ozone present in your school environment.
3. Based on your observations, predict where else you might observe higher ozone concentrations.

Ozone is one of those compounds that has a good side and a bad side. Ozone is an important part of our protective atmospheric shield against high-energy radiation from the sun. It is also useful in water treatment and other chemical and industrial processes. However, ozone in the lower atmosphere can be harmful to human health and can damage crops and forested areas. For this reason, cities and work areas are monitored for ozone as a harmful gas. How much ozone is present in the areas you live in? Is ozone evenly distributed or are there areas that contain higher levels of the gas?

Here is a simple test you can perform that will give you answers to these questions.

1 Making Schönbein paper

Christian Friedrich Schönbein (1799-1868), a chemist, discovered ozone in 1839. He developed this technique for detecting ozone and collected the first ozone data.

1. Lay out several layers of newspaper on your work area. Do all of your work on the newspaper.
2. You will need a coffee filter or a filter disk. Use a pair of scissors to cut your filter paper into strips 1 inch wide and about 4 inches long.
3. Use a pencil to mark one end of each strip with your class, your team, and a number to identify each strip. It might look like this:

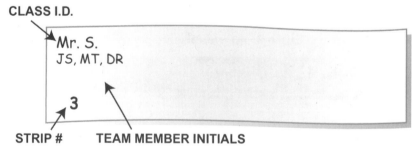

CLASS I.D.

Mr. S.
JS, MT, DR

3

STRIP #   TEAM MEMBER INITIALS

4. Lay out a square piece of wax paper. Place your paper strips on it.
5. Lay out a few paper towels to clean up any spills.
6. Your teacher will provide a small cup of ozone detecting mixture.
7. Use your finger to coat both sides of each strip with the mixture. Do not coat the labeled end. *Be sure to wash your hands after working with the mixture.*
8. Place the strips on the wax paper to dry.
9. When the strips are dry, place each in a separate zip-closing plastic bag until needed. Use a permanent marker to label each bag with the strip's number.

2   Detecting ozone

Although you can place your Schönbein paper strips in any location for ozone testing, avoid direct sunlight, and choose a place where your strips will not be disturbed.

1. Before you take your strips out of the classroom, pour a small amount of distilled water into a zip-closing bag. Take this water bag with you.
2. Save one strip as a control. Label it CONTROL and carry it along with you, but leave it in its bag.
3. At each location, first open the distilled-water bag, and dip the strip into the water. Hang the wet strip with removable tape or poster putty.
4. After placing a strip, record the strip number, location, time, and date in Table 1. Save the bag.

Table 1: Ozone detection data

Strip #	Location	Time	Date	Shade: dark, medium, light, or white	Ozone concentration rank
1					
2					
3					
4					
5					

5. Recover the strip after a period of time agreed upon by your class. One day is convenient because you can recover the strip at the same time that you put it out. Place the recovered strip in the same bag that it came from and out of direct sunlight.

3   Comparing results

You will compare all of the collected strips to determine whether there were any differences in ozone concentration. Before you collect your strip, check that the pencil markings are still clear. If not, you may have to redo them or add a tag of some kind. This is the point where most research laboratory errors are made—faulty identification and record keeping.

1. Lay out a piece of wax paper long enough for all of the class strips to be displayed at once. It may be helpful to place white paper under the wax paper to make the color comparisons easier.
2. Open the distilled-water bag and dip your strips again, one at a time. Wet your control strip too. This second dipping develops the color. You may discover that a strip that looked unchanged had detected significant ozone.
3. Drape your wet strips on the wax paper, including your control strip. Drape strips that were placed indoors on the right-hand side of the wax paper. Drape strips that were placed outdoors on the left-hand side. Make sure that the identification is visible.
4. Observe the strips as they dry. High ozone concentrations make the strips turn dark blue-purple. Middle concentrations turn a medium-purple shade, and low concentrations turn light purple or remain white. Compare strips that appear to be unchanged to your control strip. Sometimes low ozone concentrations make very small color changes that can be detected by comparing with a control strip.

4   Organizing your data

Your observations will allow you to describe ozone concentration *qualitatively*—in descriptive terms of more here and less there, rather than *quantitatively*—in a measured amount.

You will need to evaluate the indoor and outdoor strips separately, because the amount of moisture in the air can affect the sensitivity of the strips.

1. Rearrange the class set of indoor strips from darkest to lightest color. Record the shade (dark, medium, or light purple) of each of your indoor test strips in the chart on the previous page.

2. Repeat step 1 for the outdoor strips.

3. Using a permanent marker on the waxed paper, number each set of strips from highest to lowest ozone concentration. Then record the "ozone concentration rank" of each of your test strips in Table 1. For example, if there were 15 indoor test strips in your class, and yours was the third-darkest color, you would write 3/15 in the final column of the table.

4. With the help of the entire class, fill out the tables below with your class data.

Table 2: Indoor ozone data

Rank	Shade	Location
1		
2		
3		
4		
5		
6		
7		

Table 3: Outdoor ozone data

Rank	Shade	Location
1		
2		
3		
4		
5		
6		
7		

5   **Interpreting your results**

a.   Which of your group's indoor strips recorded the highest ozone concentration? Where was it located? Did any of your classmates find an indoor location with a higher ozone concentration? If so, where was the highest concentration found?

b.   Which of your group's outdoor strips recorded the highest ozone concentration? Where was it located? Did any of your classmates find an outdoor location with a higher concentration? If so, where was the highest concentration found?

c.   Using what you have learned in this activity, can you predict a location inside your home that may have a high concentration of ozone? Give a reason for your answer.

d.   Can you predict an outdoor location in your community where you may expect to find a high concentration of ozone? Why?

e.   Extension: Research the causes of ozone in the lower atmosphere. Suggest two ways that ozone concentrations in your home or community could be reduced.

Energy in the Atmosphere

Question: Which factors affect Earth's temperature?

In this Investigation, you will:

1. Model the effect of greenhouse gases on Earth's temperature.
2. Examine how glaciers act as a temperature buffer for our planet.
3. Investigate how the specific heat of water prevents temperature extremes on Earth.

Experiment 1: Greenhouse gases and Earth's temperature

You have seen that Earth's temperature results from the balance between solar energy input and energy lost into space. You have learned that a small group of atmospheric gases are important because they shift this energy balance in favor of a warmer Earth. These greenhouse gases include carbon dioxide, methane, nitrous oxide, and water vapor. Here is a simple experiment that will give you firsthand experience with a gas that behaves like a greenhouse gas.

1   Investigating the effect of greenhouse gases

Safety Tip: Wear goggles and an apron throughout this experiment.

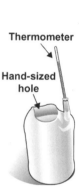

Thermometer

Hand-sized hole

1. Your teacher will provide three gallon-sized plastic jugs. A hand-sized hole has been cut into the top of each. The handle has also been cut, leaving a small stovepipe-shaped stub. Label the jugs "Dry," "Water," and "Ammonia."
2. Wrap a small piece of paper towel around a thermometer at its zero mark. Stick the thermometer snugly into the remaining stub of a jug handle. Check to be sure that you can see the thermometer fluid above the stub. Repeat for the remaining jugs.
3. Place a single paper towel in each jug. Add the following to the appropriate jug:

Dry jug:	Add nothing but the single paper towel.
Water jug:	Add 50 milliliters of room-temperature water.
Ammonia jug:	Add 50 milliliters of ammonia. *Handle the ammonia with care, preferably over a sink.*

Safety Tip: Avoid breathing the ammonia vapor. Do not touch the paper towel in the ammonia jug. Pour a small amount of vinegar into any ammonia spills.

1. Gently ease your hand into the jugs to see if you can feel a temperature difference. Do not allow your hand to touch the damp paper towels. It is important to ease your hand into the jugs because you do not want to disturb the vapor inside any more than necessary.
2. Record your sensations and the temperatures for each jug.

Table 1: Greenhouse gas simulation data

	Temperature	Sensations
Dry jug		
Water jug		
Ammonia jug		

2   Analyzing your results

a.   Which jug felt warmest?

b.   Did the thermometers measure a temperature difference between the three jugs?

c.   Why do you think one jug may have felt warmer than the others?

d.   How are the vapors in the jugs like the greenhouse gases in the atmosphere?

Experiment 2: Ice and Earth's temperature

You may have seen pictures of Antarctic ice shelves breaking away or heard about glaciers retreating around the world. Perhaps these changes signal a warming Earth. Such warming is certainly serious, but the connection between higher temperatures and melting ice seems simple enough. Why are scientists so concerned about these events? Is there more to it?

Here is an experiment that will introduce you to an important characteristic of ice that is often overlooked. It is called *latent heat*.

1   Investigating latent heat

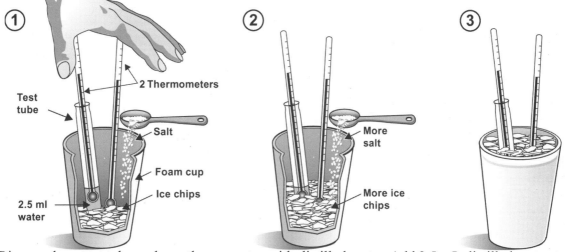

1. Rinse a clean test tube and one thermometer with distilled water. Add 2.5 mL distilled water to the test tube. Insert the thermometer into the test tube, and have a teammate hold it upright by the top of the test tube. You can use tap water if you do not have distilled water.

2. Add ice chips to a foam coffee cup until it is one-third full. Sprinkle a teaspoon of salt over the ice chips. Stand the test tube from step 1 on top of the salted ice. Also, stand a second thermometer on the salted ice.

3. Protect the open top of the test tube during this step. Add more ice chips to the foam cup until it is two-thirds full. Again sprinkle a teaspoon of salt over the ice chips. Do not allow any ice or salt to enter the test tube. If any does, you have to start over.

4. Fill the cup to the top with ice. Again, protect the open top of the test tube. Salt as before.

5. Record the temperatures of the water and ice thermometers in Table 2.

6. After 60 seconds, record a second set of temperatures. Continue recording temperatures every 60 seconds until the water temperature in the test tube reaches -10°C.

7. Graph the water and ice temperature readings as two separate lines on one graph. Label the *x*-axis "Time" and the *y*-axis "Temperature." Give your graph a title.

Table 2: Latent heat data

Elapsed time (min)	Water temp (°C)	Ice temp (°C)	Elapsed time (min)	Water temp (°C)	Ice temp (°C)
0 (start)					

2 Analyzing your data

a. What was the purpose of the ice-salt mixture in this experiment?

b. Compare the shape of the water line and the ice line on your graph.

c. Why does the line representing water temperature have a horizontal section? (Hint: Use what you know about latent heat to help you).

d. Describe the water temperature graph you would plot if you had put a piece of ice in a test tube and surrounded it with a warm-water bath.

e. Think about the contents of the test tube at the middle of the flat part of the graph you described above. What proportion of water and ice would you expect to find in the tube? Is this the same or different from what you observed at the same point in your experiment?

f. What would you expect to happen to the temperature of a test tube containing both ice and water if you placed it in a hot cup for a short time? How about if you placed it in a cold cup for a short time?

3 Applying your experience

In this experiment, you witnessed the fact that while water is changing state, its temperature stays constant. Energy was constantly leaving the test tube as the water chilled. However, the process of forming ice crystals releases energy into the test tube. We call this energy latent heat. While the energy leaving the test tube is balanced by energy added to it, the temperature does not change. This *thermal buffering* occurs only when both ice and water are present. Once all the ice crystals have formed, no more energy is released and the temperature begins dropping again.

A similar process happens when ice melts. Heat from the surrounding air adds energy to the test tube. However, it takes energy to break the bonds between water molecules in the ice crystals. While the ice is melting, the energy added to the system is balanced by energy used to break apart the water molecules, so the temperature does not change.

Let's examine how this experiment can help us understand scientists' concern about Antarctic ice shelves breaking away and glaciers retreating.

a. Would thermal buffering occur if the test tube contained only ice or only water?

b. How is our planet like the test tube?

c. What would happen to ocean temperatures in the months and years following a complete melting of all of the ice that currently serves as a thermal buffer?

Experiment 3: Water and Earth's Temperature

Everyone knows that water is crucial to life on Earth. You can probably name several ways that water makes life possible. But did you think of the *specific heat* of water? Here is an experiment that will reveal how the high specific heat of water helps regulate Earth's temperature.

1 Investigating water's specific heat

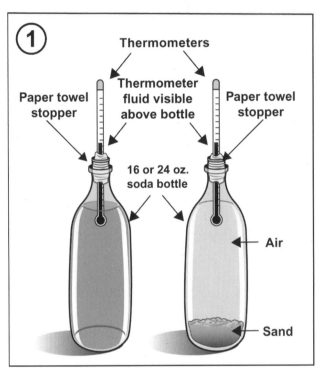
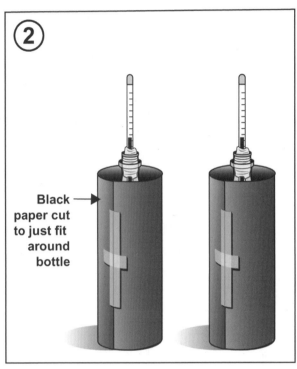

1. Fill one 16- or 24-ounce plastic soda bottle with tap water to within 2.5 centimeters of the top.
2. Pour a handful of sand into another bottle of the same size and shape. The sand has nothing to do with the experiment; it just steadies the empty bottle by adding a little weight.
3. Wrap a strip of paper towel around a thermometer at the zero mark. Stick the thermometer snugly into the neck of the water-filled bottle. The thermometer bulb must be immersed in the water. Check to be sure that you can still see the thermometer fluid above the paper towel.
4. Use the same process to insert a thermometer in the bottle filled with air.
5. Practice fitting a piece of black paper around one of the bottles so that the bottle is completely surrounded, but with no overlap. Mark the paper with your pencil and cut the paper as necessary.
6. Tape the black paper to the bottle. Wrap the paper snugly around the bottle and tape it in place.
7. Repeat steps 5 and 6 for the other bottle.
8. Place both bottles in a bright sunny window or in front of a strong lamp. Turn them so that the tape faces away from the light source.
9. Record the temperatures of the water and air bottles in Table 3.

Table 3: Specific heat data

Sunny window			Cold place		
Elapsed time (min)	Water temp (°C)	Air temp (°C)	Elapsed time (min)	Water temp (°C)	Air temp (°C)
0 (start)			0 (start)		

10. Continue recording temperatures every 60 seconds until the air temperature stops rising. This usually takes 10-15 minutes.

11. Record the time carefully and then carry both bottles to a cold place. Your teacher may suggest that you take them outside.

12. After you have the bottles positioned in the cold place, record the time and temperature again.

13. Continue recording temperatures every 60 seconds until the air temperature stops falling, or until your teacher asks you to end the data collection.

14. Graph the water and air temperature readings as two separate lines on one graph. Label the x-axis *Time*, and the y-axis *Temperature*. Be sure to give your graph a title.

2   Analyzing your data

a. Which warms more quickly, water or air?

b. Which cools faster, water or air?

c. The difference between the highest and lowest temperatures is called the temperature range. Calculate the temperature range for the water in your experiment. Then calculate the air's temperature range.

d. Each day, the surface of Earth is warmed by the energy from the sun. Seventy-five percent of Earth's surface is covered with water. If only 10 percent of the surface were covered with water, would Earth experience a greater temperature range each day, or a smaller range? Explain your answer.

3   Extension: How bodies of water affect climate

a.   Choose two cities in the world. This will work best if you avoid high polar regions and cities on or near the equator. One city must be on an ocean or sea, the other must be at least 200 miles away from any big body of water. Look up the highest monthly average temperature for both cities. This usually happens in July north of the equator. You can find this information in an encyclopedia or atlas. Or, see www.worldclimate.com on the Internet.

b.   Next, look up the lowest monthly average temperature for both cities. This usually happens in January north of the equator.

c.   Find the temperature range for both of your cities by subtracting each city's low monthly average temperature from its high monthly average temperature.

d.   Are you able to detect the effect of the specific heat of water in the temperature range of your coastal city compared with your inland city? Explain.

e.   Use the Internet to find the average daylight and nighttime temperatures for the moon and Mars. Calculate the temperature range for both of these bodies as you have done above. Compare those day-night ranges with the day-night temperature ranges that we experience here on Earth. Use this data to explain in a paragraph how water's high specific heat helps make life on Earth possible.

27.1 Variations in the Heating and Cooling of Earth

Question: What causes the seasons?

In this Investigation, you will:

1. Learn how Earth's orbit affects the seasonal variation of light intensity on Earth.
2. Learn how Earth's axial tilt affects the seasonal variation of light intensity on Earth.

Why do the seasons occur? In the summertime, it is hotter, the days are longer, and sunlight is intense. In wintertime, it is cold, the days are shorter, and the sunlight is less intense. What causes these variations in the heating and cooling of Earth so that seasons occur?

1   Developing a hypothesis about the seasons

The graphic below shows you what Earth's orbit around the sun looks like. The orbit is slightly elliptical so that at certain times of the year, Earth is a little closer to or farther from the sun than at other times. Also, Earth is tilted as it moves around the sun. Could distance or Earth's tilt be the cause of seasons?

To start the Investigation, come up with a hypothesis stating why you think the seasons occur. Do you think they are caused by Earth's distance from the sun? Do you think Earth's tilt causes the seasons? Do you think both of these factors play a role? Or do you think other factors cause the seasons?

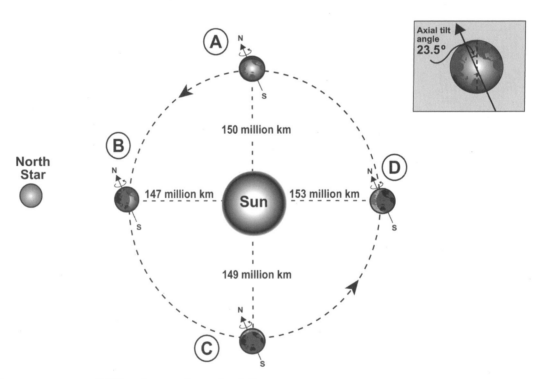

a.   Why do seasons occur? What is your hypothesis?

b.   At which point in Earth's orbit is it summer in the northern hemisphere? Draw a diagram to answer this question. Be sure to justify your answer.

2   Setting up your model of Earth's orbit around the sun

In this Investigation, you will use an electric meter and solar cell to measure the intensity of light emitted by a light bulb that will act as the sun. The solar cell will collect the light and transform it into current that will be measured by an electric meter. Using this technique, the intensity of the light will be measured in milliamps (mA).

A light source will be placed in the center of your classroom. You will use a globe to represent Earth. You will first measure the intensity of light from the bulb at different *distances* from it. In the next part of the Investigation, you will measure the intensity of light at different *places* on the globe. Relatively low light-intensity readings will represent winter-like conditions, and relatively high light-intensity readings will represent summer-like conditions. In performing these two kinds of measurements, you will determine which factors cause the seasons.

1. To get started, your teacher will place in the center of your classroom a lamp with the light bulb uncovered. This light will represent the sun. It is important that the light source emit light equally in *all* directions like the sun does.

2. With your class, choose a wall in your classroom that will represent the position of the North Star (Polaris) in the night sky. Tape a sign to this wall that says "North Star."

3. One student will move the globe, in a circle, to each position (A-D) in a counterclockwise direction around the "sun." This movement simulates *one revolution* around the sun (or one year).

4. As the globe is moved from point to point, the axial tilt at the north pole of the globe is always pointing toward the North Star.

5. As Earth revolves around the sun, it also spins on its axis. Note that the globe can also be spun on its axis.

6. After the demonstration, obtain a globe and use it to discuss the following questions with your group.

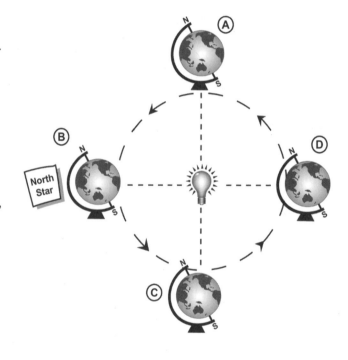

a. Although the axis of Earth is always pointing in the same way, what is happening to Earth itself as it revolves around the sun?

b. What does the side of the globe that faces the sun represent? What does the side of the globe that faces away from the sun represent?

c. Identify the following parts of your globe: equator, northern hemisphere, southern hemisphere, and latitude lines. At what latitude are you located right now?

d. In which position in the diagram is the northern hemisphere pointing towards the sun? In which position is the southern hemisphere pointing towards the sun?

3   ## How does the distance of Earth from the sun affect its intensity?

In Part 1, you read that Earth's distance from the sun varies slightly as it revolves around the sun. In this part of the Investigation, you model the distance of Earth from the sun using a scale distance. You will then measure the amount of current produced by a light source at each scale distance.

It is impossible to measure millions of kilometers in your classroom, but you can use a *scale distance* of 1 centimeter to represent 1 million kilometers. Therefore, a distance of 150 million kilometers would be represented by 150 centimeters. Using the scale distance of 1 centimeter equals 1 million kilometers, determine the scale distance for positions B, C, and D. Write the scale distance in the third column of Table 1 below.

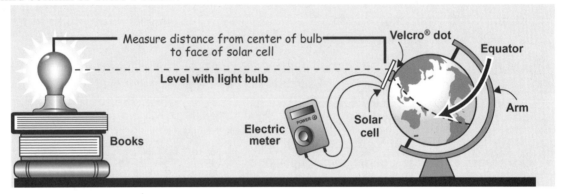

1. Gather the following materials: Earth globe, solar cell, electric meter with leads, metric tape measure. Your teacher will have a light source set up in the middle of the room. It will be at the correct level as shown in the diagram above.

    ◆ **SAFETY NOTE: The light bulb will get very hot once it is turned on.**

2. Attach the solar cell to the Velcro® dot found on the equator of the globe. Connect the leads from the electric meter to the solar cell. Set the electric meter to measure current, in milliamps (mA).

3. Place the globe so the face of the solar cell is *exactly* 150 centimeters from the center of the light bulb. You will need one student to hold the end of the tape measure at the center of the light bulb and another to move the globe into the correct distance from the bulb.

4. Measure the current, in milliamps, at the equator and record your measurement in the fourth column of Table 1.

5. Repeat steps 3 and 4 for the remaining scale distances. NOTE: Do not move the globe to simulate Earth's orbit for each position. Vary only the *distance* from the light bulb.

6. Based on your results, answer the questions below.

Position	Distance from the sun (km)	Scale distance from the sun (cm)	Light intensity (mA)
A	150,000,000	150	
B	147,000,000		
C	149,000,000		
D	153,000,000		

a. Are there big or small differences in distance as Earth revolves around the sun?

b. Based on your data, how does light intensity change as these distances change?

c. Based on your results from this experiment, do you think Earth's distance from the sun over a year causes the seasons? Why or why not?

4   How does Earth's tilt affect the sun's intensity?

In this experiment you will simulate the effect that Earth's axial tilt has on the intensity of the sun's light. This time, you will model Earth's orbit around the sun, in addition to its distance at the four positions shown below.

1. For the northern hemisphere measurement, you will place the solar cell at 45 degrees north latitude. For the southern hemisphere, you will place the solar cell at 45 degrees south latitude. For the equator, you will place the solar cell as you did in Part 3. Your globe has Velcro® dots attached at each of these positions.

2. Measure each distance from the center of the light bulb to the surface of the solar cell, as you did in Part 3.

3. At each position, make sure the north pole of the globe points **toward** the North Star. Measure light intensity in milliamps. Record your data in the blanks of the graphic. At position D, you will need to move the arm of the globe slightly to the left or right in order to place the solar cell correctly.

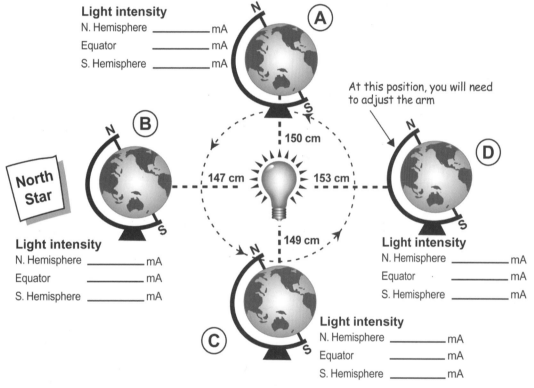

Light intensity
N. Hemisphere _____ mA
Equator _____ mA
S. Hemisphere _____ mA

At this position, you will need to adjust the arm

150 cm
147 cm   153 cm
149 cm

North Star

Light intensity
N. Hemisphere _____ mA
Equator _____ mA
S. Hemisphere _____ mA

Light intensity
N. Hemisphere _____ mA
Equator _____ mA
S. Hemisphere _____ mA

Light intensity
N. Hemisphere _____ mA
Equator _____ mA
S. Hemisphere _____ mA

a.   What role does axial tilt play in the intensity of light on Earth?

b.   At which position (A, B, C, or D) and latitude (northern hemisphere, equator, and southern hemisphere) does Earth receive the most light? The least light?

5   Applying your knowledge

a.   Of the two factors—distance from the light source and axial tilt—which plays the most significant role in causing the seasons? Was your hypothesis supported by your results?

b.   Based on your results, which position (A–D) represents the first day of summer in the northern hemisphere? Which position represents the first day of winter in the northern hemisphere?

c.   Which quarter of Earth's orbit represents summer in the northern hemisphere (from A to B, B to C, C to D, or D to A)? Explain your answer based on your results from the Investigation.

Global Winds and Ocean Currents

Question: How do temperature and salinity cause ocean layering?

In this Investigation, you will:

1. Discover how temperature and salinity create currents, underwater waterfalls, and springs in the ocean.

2. Use what you have learned to trace the currents that form the Atlantic gyre.

3. Discuss the impact on the fishing industry of changes in thermohaline currents.

The ocean contains:

In our everyday experience, liquids mix uniformly in their containers. It's hard to image a mass of ocean water as a body separate from other water in the same ocean basin. But not only do separate ocean bodies exist, there are rivers within the ocean. In some places, there are two rivers running side-by-side—in opposite directions. Now imagine underwater waterfalls and underwater springs. All of these exist in the world's oceans as a result of differences in water temperature and salinity (saltiness).

How do temperature and salinity differences cause these underwater rivers, waterfalls, and springs? It all depends on one thing: **density changes**.

1 Density and ocean currents

As global winds push ocean currents around the planet, several kinds of changes happen to the ocean water. As the current moves nearer to the equator, it warms up. As it moves toward the poles, it cools down. These changes affect the density of ocean water.

When the current moves through a warm area, there is an increase in evaporation. Since evaporation removes fresh water and leaves salt behind, the salinity of the current increases. This increases the current's density. Fresh water is added back to the ocean through melting ice, rivers, and rain. Adding fresh water to the salty ocean water decreases its density.

These changes in density cause ocean currents to float and sink at different points in their journeys. In this Investigation, you will model underwater rivers, waterfalls, and springs. Then you will use your observations to help you understand the movements of the Atlantic gyre, an ocean current system. You will also discover how these density differences play an enormous role in the life of the world's most important fishing grounds.

a. Which do you think is more dense, warm or cold ocean water? Why?

b. Explain why dissolved salt increases the density of ocean water.

2   Observing salinity-dependent layering

🪣 This Investigation requires care and preparation to keep your cleanup quick and easy. Spread newspaper over your work area to catch drips. Keep any water-filled cups over a tray or paper plate. Wipe up any spills before they get tracked around. Discard any water in the bucket provided or in the sink.

1. Make a pouring stick by cutting a cardboard circle about 4 centimeters in diameter with your scissors. Press the point of a pencil into the center of the disk so that it is stuck firmly onto the pencil.

2. Fill a clear plastic cup half-full with cool water. Add 1 teaspoon of salt to the water. Add 2 drops of green food coloring. Stir until the salt dissolves.

3. Fill a foam cup half-full with cool water.

4. Have a team member hold the pouring stick at its top, near the eraser. Lower the pouring stick into the middle of the clear cup so that the cardboard disk is just under the surface of the green water. Have a second team member hold the lip of the foam cup up to the pouring stick.

Pencil

Cardboard circle

5. Tip the foam cup so that the cool water flows slowly down the pouring stick. The first team member must move the pouring stick upward as the second team member pours so that the cardboard disk remains at the surface of the water. Continue to add water until the clear cup is almost full, and then gently remove the pouring stick. You have created two ocean layers, separated by their salinity.

a. Try slightly tipping the clear plastic cup. Are the layers stable? Do they resist mixing?

b. Tear off a small piece of foam cup. Press some staples into the foam, and place it on the surface of the clear water. Remove the foam and add more staples to it, one at a time, until the foam bit sinks. Where did the foam bit end up? Why?

c. Explain why the clear water floats over the saline water.

3   Exploring temperature-dependent layering

1. Fill a clear plastic cup half-full with cool water. Add 2 drops of blue food coloring. Stir to mix.

2. Fill a foam cup almost full from the hot-water source. Add 2 drops of red food coloring. Stir to mix.

3. Add hot red water to the clear cup using the pouring stick as you did in salinity-dependent layering. You have again created two ocean layers, this time separated by their temperatures.

a. Try tipping the cup slightly. Are the layers stable? Do they resist mixing?

b. Explain why the hot red water floats over the cool blue water.

4 ## Creating an underwater waterfall

1. Fill a clear plastic cup nearly full with cool water.

2. Fill a foam cup half-full with hot water. Add a pinch of salt. Add 6 drops of red food coloring. Stir until the salt dissolves.

3. Place the eyedropper into the hot red water to warm it up. After a minute, fill the dropper barrel with the water.

4. Hold the dropper so that it lies at a flat angle at the surface of the clear water with the tip just under the surface. Gently squeeze out a layer of hot red water onto the surface of the clear water.

5. After a short cooling time, the red layer will form little waterfalls that sink through the clear water. They may even form little smoke-ring-like structures as they fall. If this does not happen within a few minutes, add a little more salt to the hot red water, stir, and try again.

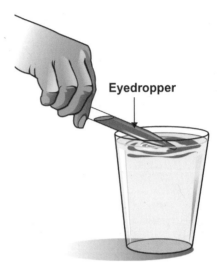

Eyedropper

a. Explain why the red water floats at first.

b. Explain why the red water eventually sinks.

5 ## Observing underwater springs

1. Fill a clear cup three-quarters full with cool water. Add a heaping teaspoon of salt to the water. Stir until the salt dissolves.

2. Fill a foam cup half-full with cool water. Add 6 drops of blue food coloring. Stir to mix.

3. Fill the eyedropper with cool blue water.

4. Gently lower the dropper into the salt water so that the tip is near the bottom. Gently squeeze the dropper so that a small stream of blue water is released.

a. Where did the blue water go? Why?

b. In this model, the blue water was less salty than the surrounding water. Think of another difference you could use to create an underwater spring. Write your own procedure, test it, and explain what happened.

6 **Applying your knowledge**

You can use these experiments to understand the Atlantic gyre, a system of currents that occupies the North Atlantic Ocean basin. After each description, fill in the experiment that applies (*salinity-dependent layering, temperature-depending layering, underwater waterfall,* or *underwater springs*), and then determine whether the current will float or sink.

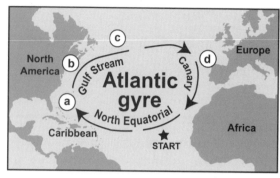

We will start with the Atlantic gyre off the coast of Africa. We will assume that the temperature of the water is cool and its salinity is low. The low salinity is dominant and the current is floating on the surface.

a. From there, the North Equatorial Current flows westward toward the Caribbean Sea. Then it turns north and becomes the beginning of the Gulf Steam. During this trip along the equator, the intense sun warms the current and evaporates a lot of water. This makes the water both warm and highly saline. The high temperature is dominant.

Experiment: _____   Float or sink: _____

b. After turning northward, the Gulf Stream flows along the United States' Atlantic Coast. The water is highly saline, but it remains warm. The high temperature remains dominant.

Experiment: _____   Float or sink: _____

c. As the Gulf Stream leaves the US coast, evaporation is not as great in the cold northern regions, but the cooling effect is very significant. The low temperature is dominant.

Experiment: _____   Float or sink: _____

d. Now part of the Gulf Stream is no longer on the surface. The water is cold and too deep to be warmed by the sun. But fresh water from ice melt may mix with these cold waters off the coast of Europe. Lower salinity is dominant.

Experiment: _____   Float or sink: _____

7 ★**Extension: Thermohaline currents and the ocean food chain**

Back in the 1960s, it was popularly believed that the key to feeding the world was the bountiful harvest that could be taken from the seas. Today, we are faced with the collapse of fisheries on both sides of the Atlantic. Why has the ocean proven to be such a modest food source?

The food paradox of the oceans is based on the nutrient cycle. For new creatures to grow, the nutrients from the old creatures must be recycled. Unfortunately, when ocean creatures die, they take their nutrients to the deep bottom. The photosynthetic plankton (*phytoplankton*) that do the recycling must live in the sunlit top-600 feet of ocean, so recyclers and the needed nutrients are hopelessly separated by thousands of feet of ocean unless something can transport the nutrients to the surface.

a. Two of the biggest fisheries in the world are off the Canary Islands and Peru. Can you explain why?

b. If global climate change eliminates all ice from the poles, how might this affect ocean currents and world fisheries?

Weather Patterns

Question: How can we measure water content in the atmosphere?

In this Investigation, you will:

1. Construct a device to indirectly measure water content in the atmosphere.
2. Look for a relationship between air temperature and water content in the atmosphere.

Temperature, air pressure, and water content in the atmosphere are three factors that influence weather patterns. In this Investigation, you will use a device called a sling psychrometer to indirectly measure the water content of the air in different locations. You will apply your experience toward understanding a term you may have heard mentioned by your local weather anchor—*relative humidity.*

1   Doing the experiment

1. Place the felt-covered bulb in room temperature water until the felt is thoroughly wet. Place the two thermometers back-to-back. Slip a rubber band over them to hold them together.

2. Slide the shoelace through the holes in the thermometer backing and tie off the end. Your sling psychrometer is now assembled.

3. In your classroom or other indoor location, gently swing the thermometers in front of you in a circular pattern for three minutes.
   ◆**Safety Tip: Be sure to provide enough space so that your classmates will not be struck by the swinging thermometers.**

4. Record the temperature of the wet-bulb and the dry-bulb thermometers in Table 1. Your teacher will give you a larger version of the table.

5. Record the difference between the two temperatures.

6. Repeat steps 1-3 in an outdoor location. If rain or other precipitation is falling, choose a covered porch, walkway, or pavilion.

7. Repeat steps 1-3 in a room in which a vaporizer has been operating for at least 30 minutes.
   ◆**Safety Tip: The steam from a vaporizer can cause serious burns. Do not put your hands or face near the steam vent.**

8. Share the data you collected with your classmates. In the remaining rows of the table, record data collected in three additional locations by other lab groups.

Table 1: Sling psychrometer data

Location description	Dry bulb temperature	Wet bulb temperature	Temperature difference

2   Analyzing your data

a. Which was generally higher, the wet bulb temperature or the dry bulb temperature?

b. Give a reason for the temperature difference between the thermometers.

c. In which location did you find the greatest temperature difference between the two thermometers? Which location had the smallest difference?

d. What environmental factors seem to be connected to large temperature differences between the two thermometers? What factors seem to be connected to small temperature differences?

e. How might the temperature difference at each location be related to the water content of the atmosphere at each location?

3   Finding relative humidity

Relative humidity is a term that you may have heard mentioned on your local weather report. It is a measure of the actual water content of the air compared to the amount in the air when evaporation and condensation are in equilibrium at that temperature. If the relative humidity is 100%, water added to the atmosphere condenses right back out again. Days with high relative humidity feel "sticky" because perspiration can't easily evaporate from your skin to cool you.

Use your data from the experiment to determine the relative humidity in each location tested.

1. Obtain a relative humidity chart from your teacher. On the left-hand column of the chart, find the dry-bulb reading for your first measurement.

2. Find the difference between the dry- and wet-bulb readings at the top of the chart.

3. Find the box where the the two readings cross. The number in the box tells you the relative humidity at this location. Record the relative humidity in the chart below.

4. Repeat steps 1-3 for each location measured.

Table 2: Relative humidity at each location tested

Location	Relative humidity

4   Analyzing your results

a. Make a bar graph which shows the relative humidity of the locations tested, in order from lowest to highest. On each bar, print the dry bulb temperature at each location.

b. Does your graph show a relationship between dry bulb temperature (the temperature of the atmosphere) and the relative humidity? Using what you know about water content in the atmosphere, explain why or why not.

c. Challenge: It takes specialized equipment to directly measure water content in the atmosphere. This equipment tells how many grams of water are present in a cubic meter of air—a measurement called absolute humidity. If the relative humidity was 100% in two cities, but one had a dry bulb temperature of 16°C and the other was at 32°C, would their absolute humidity be the same? Why or why not?

Question: How does Doppler radar work?

In this Investigation, you will:

1. Learn how Doppler radar images are produced.
2. Learn how meteorologists use Doppler radar to track a storm system.
3. Examine a set of Doppler radar images and calculate the speed of a storm system.

"The National Weather Service has just issued a severe thunderstorm warning for the following locations . . ."

Has a broadcaster ever interrupted your favorite television program with these words? In this Investigation, you will learn about one of the important tools the National Weather Service uses to track storms: Doppler radar.

1   How can we use radar to track precipitation?

You may be familiar with the radar images used by weather forecasters on the news. Did you ever wonder how these images are produced?

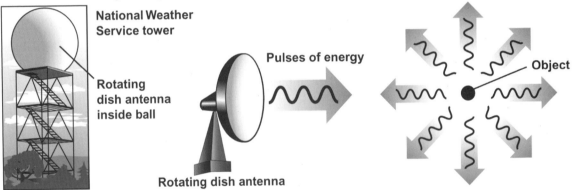

The National Weather Service has radar stations located across the United States. At each station there is a tower with what looks like a large soccer ball on top. Inside this protective ball is a 10-meter-diameter rotating dish antenna that sends out pulses of energy. If a pulse of energy strikes an object like a raindrop, the energy is scattered in all directions. A small part of the energy will bounce back to the antenna.

This reflected energy is then received by the radar during its listening period. This process of sending a signal, listening for any returned signal, then sending the next signal, takes place very fast, up to around 1,300 times each second. Computers analyze the strength of the returned signal and the time it took to travel to the object and back. They use this information to create a color diagram showing the location, amount, and movement of precipitation falling over a region. In this *reflectivity mode*, four colors are typically used to show the rainfall rate per hour. For example, green may indicate traces of precipitation; yellow, a light rain; orange, heavy rainfall; and red, severe thunderstorms or hail. A color key is usually provided on the radar image.

a.   Look at Radar Image Plate 1. Over which state is the most intense rain falling?

b.   Name two states in which mixed precipitation is falling.

2   How can we use radar to detect a tornado?

Doppler radar, developed in 1988, has a distinct advantage over earlier radar systems: It can detect the direction of air movement within a storm. Doppler radar works by detecting the difference between signals bouncing off raindrops moving away from the antenna and signals bouncing off raindrops moving toward the antenna. In *Doppler mode* (also called *velocity mode*), the radar image is presented in two colors: green represents raindrops moving toward the antenna, and red represents raindrops moving away from the antenna. Doppler radar is very useful for locating rotating columns of air within a storm. One feature meteorologists pay close attention to is the appearance of a "J" hook-shape appearing near the back of the storm. This means that air is beginning to circulate in a pattern that often leads to the formation of a tornado.

Daphne Zaras NSSL/NOAA photo

Central Oklahoma tornado, May 3, 1999

a. Look at Radar Image Plate 2. Near which interstate highway intersection is a tornado possibly beginning to form?

b. The National Weather Service issues tornado watch and tornado warning bulletins when certain atmospheric conditions are observed. Use the Internet to find out what each notice means. How does Doppler radar help meteorologists issue these bulletins?

3   Recognizing insects, birds, or airborne debris on a radar image

Of course, the pulses of energy sent by the antenna can bounce off things other than raindrops or other forms of precipitation. Interference from objects on the ground can be easily recognized because those objects do not move. However, in the spring and fall, swarms of insects or flocks of migrating birds can show up on radar images. Meteorologists practice looking at images and recognizing the characteristic patterns these creatures create, so that they do not mistake the birds and bugs for rain.

In some cases, the interference is actually important to meteorologists. In Radar Image Plate 3, locate the white spot in the center of a very intense storm. The color white represents an area that is reflecting back a large number of energy pulses—too many pulses to be bouncing off raindrops. These energy pulses are bouncing back from debris in the air thrown there by a tornado. This white area helps meteorologists locate places where the tornado is causing damage.

NOAA photo

Debris from central Oklahoma tornado, May 3, 1999

a. Near which city is the airborne debris located?

b. What safety precautions does the National Weather service recommend when conditions like these are observed?

4 How can we use radar to track a hurricane?

Hurricane Georges, a category 3 hurricane, struck the island of Puerto Rico on Monday, Sept. 21, 1998. The next six radar images are from the National Weather Service's San Juan headquarters. The radar station is located in the Guavate Forest just south of the city of Cayey. All of the hurricane images are in reflectivity mode, depicting the intensity of the rainfall through a series of colors. The color key to the right of each image tells you that blue indicates light rainfall; green moderate rainfall; and yellow, orange, red, purple, and white indicate increasingly severe rainfall, often accompanied by thunderstorms and hail.

Satellite image of Hurricane Georges as it hit Puerto Rico on September 21, 1998.

a. The hurricane's eye is the low-pressure center around which the storm rotates. Inside the eye, winds are calm and skies are blue. Look at Hurricane Image 1. Where is the eye located?

b. In the afternoon, Georges gathered strength because of the combination of the Caribbean Sea's warmer waters, the demise of some earlier wind shear, and the fact that as the storm moved over open sea between St. Croix and Puerto Rico, the wind circulating around the eye had no resistance from land objects. What evidence can you see in Hurricane Image 2 that the storm is gaining strength?

c. The National Weather Service reported that Georges made landfall on Puerto Rico at 7 p.m. local time (23:00 GMT). Landfall is defined as the time when the center of the hurricane's eye reaches land. Use the scale printed on Hurricane Image 3 to determine the diameter of the eye when it made landfall.

Airplane entering the eye of Hurricane Georges to take storm measurements. The sky above is clear and sunlight can be seen reflecting off clouds.

d. As the hurricane moved across Puerto Rico, intense rain and a possible tornado were spawned as the eye wall's heavy thunderstorms interacted with the mountainous terrain. Notice the strong bands of precipitation found in Hurricane Image 4. Why do you suppose it is harder to see the eye in this image?

USGS photo

Hurricane George's high winds tore the roof and exterior walls from this home in Puerto Rico.

e. Just after midnight on the morning of Sept. 22, 1998 (04:01 GMT), the eye of Hurricane Georges began to move off the west coast of Puerto Rico. Using the time stamps on Hurricane Image 3 and Hurricane Image 5, calculate the time it took for Georges to make its way across Puerto Rico.

Hurricane Georges' travel time (round to the nearest hour): _____

Then, using a ruler and the scale provided on the radar images, calculate the distance from the center of the eye in the third image to the center of the eye in the fifth image.

Hurricane Georges' travel distance (round to the nearest km): _____

Divide the distance traveled by the time taken in order to calculate the speed of the hurricane as it moved across the island.

Hurricane Georges' speed (round to the nearest km/hour): _____

f. By 2:51 a.m. local time (06:51 GMT) the eye of Hurricane Georges was again over water. Use information from Hurricane Image 5 and Hurricane Image 6 to calculate the speed of the storm as it moved off of Puerto Rico. Does the storm appear to be intensifying or dissipating? Explain your answer.

Distance _____ **÷ time** _____ **= speed** _____ **km/hour**

Question: How do zoos mimic an animal's natural habitat?

In this Investigation, you will:

1. Research an animal that is adapted to live in one of the six land biomes you have studied.
2. Determine what conditions would be necessary for this animal to thrive in a zoo in your community.
3. Design a scale model of a zoo habitat that would both provide for the animal's needs and teach visitors about the biome in which this animal lives in the wild.

The polar bears' native home is in the tundra biome. Their dense fur, thick blubber, and specially padded feet help them survive in temperatures as low as -45°C. A single polar bear can roam over a territory twice the size of Iceland, feeding on seals, digging shelters in snow banks, and swimming freely between ice blocks. In October, pregnant females dig a two-room den in a large snowdrift. Cubs are born in December, and they emerge from the den in March or April. Mothers are fiercely protective of their cubs, and have even been known to rear up and leap at helicopters with research scientists aboard. Cubs must be protected from adult male bears until they are about 2 years old.

Heat is a much greater problem for polar bears than is cold. Their bodies are such effective insulators that an infrared photograph taken of a bear will show nothing but a small puff from their exhaled breath. Even in their native tundra biome, polar bears cannot run more than short distances without overheating.

Imagine the difficulties faced by zoo exhibit designers as they attempt to create a comfortable home for these animals in places as far away from the tundra biome as Asheboro, North Carolina; Albuquerque, New Mexico; and San Diego, California. Beyond their basic physical needs, polar bears are intelligent, curious animals who exhibit signs of stress unless provided with an environment that poses new and interesting challenges for them.

In this Investigation, you will take on the zoo exhibit designer's role. You will choose an animal that represents your assigned biome, and design and build a scale model of a zoo habitat in which the animal would thrive.

1 Choose an animal

a. Your group will be assigned a particular biome to study. Use a library or the Internet to research the biome's characteristics. You should be able to identify the temperature range, annual rainfall, special characteristics such as alternating rainy and dry seasons, and the prominent types of vegetation in the biome.

b. Once you have a clear picture of the biome's physical characteristics, choose an animal unique to this biome that you believe could thrive in a carefully planned zoo habitat. Choose an animal that could be used to teach zoo visitors about its native environment. For example, a wildebeest's long legs are adapted to enable it to outrun the periodic fires on the savanna grasslands.

2 Plan an environment

Discuss with your group the physical conditions that would be necessary for this animal to survive in a zoo in your community. Be sure to consider any differences in temperature, humidity, and rainfall between your animal's native biome and the one in which you live. How will you keep your animal healthy and comfortable? You may wish to use the Internet to explore zoo exhibit design, or contact a zoo in your area for assistance. Here are some things to consider:

a. How many animals of this species will you have in the exhibit? Is this animal a solitary creature or does it live in a group?

b. Size of zoo habitat: Be sure to provide for both viewing areas and sheltered areas for the animal. Consider its exercise requirements as well as space for a dens, nests, etc.

c. Landscape: What type of ground surface and vegetation will make this animal most comfortable?

d. Security: How will you provide for both animal and visitor safety? Will you use fencing, a moat, a glass enclosure, or other means?

e. Feeding areas/water needs: How will you provide a clean and sanitary supply of food and water?

f. Heating and/or cooling of the exhibit: How will you meet the temperature and humidity needs of this animal?

g. Well-being of the animal: What additional features are necessary to ensure that the animal not only survives, but thrives in this environment?

h. Visitor education: What means will you use to teach visitors about this animal and the biome in which it originates?

3 Present your design

a. Decide as a group on a method of presenting your design visually. Your design must effectively show how your zoo exhibit would both provide for the welfare of the animal and teach visitors about the animal's home biome.

b. Zoo exhibit designers must present their ideas to the zoo's board of directors before plans are finalized and construction begins. Prepare a 10-minute oral presentation that highlights the important features of your design and clearly shows how it meets the goals listed in step 3a.

c. Present your project to your classmates.

Understanding Earth

Question: What story is hidden here?

In this Investigation, you will:

1. Practice reconstructing a series of events from clues.
2. Learn how to sequence events recorded in a geologic formation.

Earth is very old and many of its features were formed before people came along to study them. For that reason, studying Earth now is like detective work—using clues to uncover fascinating stories. The work of Earth science researchers is very much like the work of forensic scientists at a crime scene. In both fields, the ability to put events in their proper order is the key to unraveling the hidden story.

1 **Sequencing events after a thunderstorm**

Carefully examine this illustration. It contains evidence of following events:

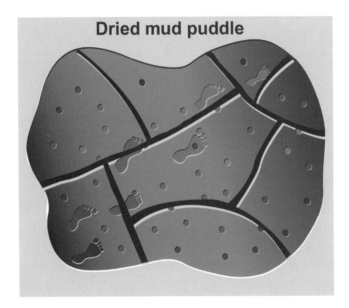

Dried mud puddle

- The baking heat of the sun caused cracks to formed in the dried mud puddle.

- A thunderstorm began.

- The mud puddle dried.

- A child ran through the mud puddle.

- Hailstones fell during the thunderstorm.

a. From the clues in the illustration, sequence the events listed above in the order in which they happened.

b. Write a brief story that explains the appearance of the dried mud puddle and includes all the events. In your story, justify the order of the events.

2 Determining the relative ages of rock formations

Relative dating is an Earth science term that describes the set of principles and techniques used to sequence geologic events and determine the relative age of rock formations. Below are graphics that illustrate some of these basic principles used by geologists. You will find that these concepts are easy to understand.

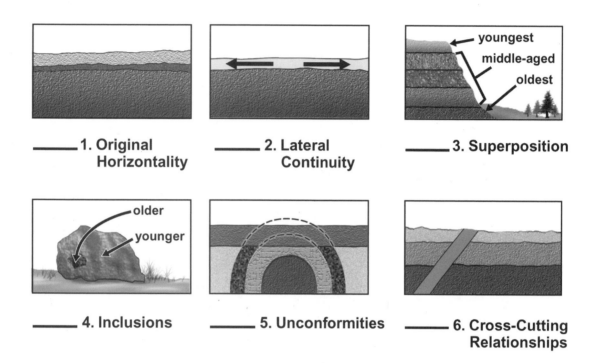

_____ 1. Original Horizontality   _____ 2. Lateral Continuity   _____ 3. Superposition

_____ 4. Inclusions   _____ 5. Unconformities   _____ 6. Cross-Cutting Relationships

Match each principle to its explanation. Write the letter of the explanation in the space provided under each graphic.

Explanations:

A. In undisturbed rock layers, the oldest layer is at the bottom and the youngest layer is at the top.

B. In some rock formations, layers or parts of layers may be missing. This is often due to **erosion**. Erosion by water or wind removes sediment from exposed surfaces. Erosion often leaves a new flat surface with some of the original material missing.

C. Sediments are originally deposited in horizontal layers.

D. Any feature that cuts across rock layers is younger than the layers.

E. Sedimentary layers or lava flows extend sideways in all directions until they thin out or reach a barrier.

F. Any part of a previous rock layer, like a piece of stone, is older than the layer containing it.

3   Sequencing events in a geologic cross-section

Understanding how a land formation was created with its many layers of soil begins with the same time-ordering process you used in Part 1. Geologists use logical thinking and geology principles like the ones described in Part 2 to determine the order of events for a geologic formation. Cross-sections of Earth, like the one shown below, are our best records of what has happened in the past.

Rock bodies in this cross-section are labeled A through H. One of these rock bodies is an **intrusion**. Intrusions occur when molten rock called **magma** penetrates into layers from below. The magma is always younger than the layers that it penetrates. Likewise, a fault is always younger than the layers that have faulted. A **fault** is a crack or break occurs across rock layers, and the term **faulting** is used to describe the occurrence of a fault. The broken layers may move so that one side of the fault is higher than the other. Faulted layers may also tilt.

a.   Put the rock bodies illustrated below in order based on when they formed.

b.   Relative to the other rock bodies, when did the fault occur?

c.   Compared with the formation of the rock bodies, when did the stream form? Justify your answer.

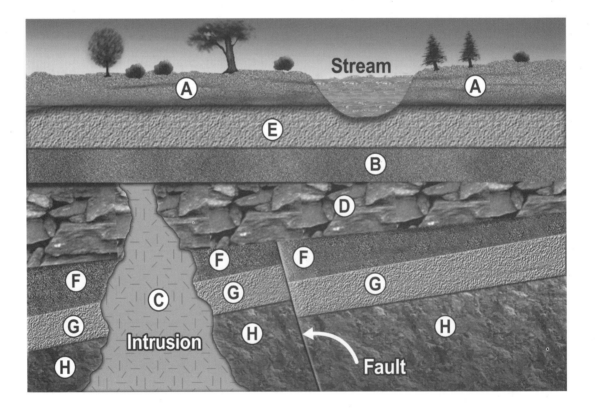

4   Creating clues for a story

Now, your teacher will provide your group with some materials. Using these materials, create a set of clues that will tell a story. Then, give another group in your class the opportunity to sequence the clues into a story. Follow these guidelines in setting up your story:

- Set up a situation that includes clues that represent at least five events.

- Each of the five events must happen independently. In other words, two events cannot have happened at the same time.

- Use at least one geology principle that you learned in this Investigation.

- Answer the questions below.

a. Describe your set of clues in a paragraph. Include enough details in your paragraph so that someone can re-create the set of clues.

b. What relative dating principles are represented with your set of clues? Explain how these principles are represented.

c. Now, have a group of your classmates put your set of clues in order. When they are done, evaluate their work. Write a short paragraph that explains how they did and whether or not they figured out the correct sequence of clues. Describe the clue they missed if they made an error.

5   The significance of stories

a. In the Investigation, you organized your thoughts into stories. How does organizing your thoughts as stories help you understand Earth science?

b. Cross-sections like the illustration in Part 3 have been used to help explain amazing events like the collision of continents or an ancient earthquake. If two continents collided, what features might you see in a cross-section of land?

c. Read about forensic science on the Internet or in your local library. How is forensic science like Earth science? Write a short paragraph that compares and contrasts these two branches of science.

28.2 Plate Tectonics

Question: What will Earth look like in 50 million years?

In this Investigation, you will:

1. Identify the most important tectonic plates of Earth's lithosphere.
2. Learn which geologic features are associated with the boundaries of plates.
3. Discover what Earth will look like in 50 million years.

The theory of plate tectonics states that large pieces of Earth's lithosphere called *tectonic plates* move on the surface. At the plate boundaries, plates move apart, collide, or slide past each other. As a result of this movement, new features emerge on Earth's surface. We know Earth is 4.6 billion years old. In the Investigation, you will move Earth's tectonic plates to where they may be 50 million years from now. You will see for yourself what our planet might look like this far into the future.

1 Reading a bathymetric map

A **bathymetric map** shows what land looks like under a body of water like the ocean.

1. Find examples of the following features on your bathymetric map: mid-ocean ridges, rises, and deep ocean trenches. Some mid-ocean ridges are labeled as rises (i.e., the East Pacific Rise). List one example of each from your map in the second column of Table 1.
2. In the third column of Table 1, list which kind of plate boundary is associated with each feature.
3. In the fourth column, there are small diagrams showing two plates and the boundary between them. Draw arrows showing how the plates move relative to each other at these boundaries.

Table 1: Features on a bathymetric map

Features	Examples from the map	Kind of plate boundary (convergent or divergent?)	How do the plates at this boundary move?
mid-ocean ridge			Plate 1 / Plate 2
rise			Plate 1 / Plate 2
deep ocean trench			Plate 1 / Plate 2

2   Starting to find plate boundaries

1. Earth has seven to 10 large pieces and a lot of small plates, especially in the western Pacific Basin. To keep things simple in this Investigation, you will identify **seven** large plates.

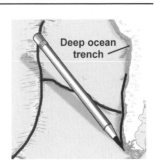

2. You will use the information you organized in Table 1 to identify the plates. With your pencil, draw a single line along the mid-ocean ridges, rises, and deep ocean trenches on your map. Draw your lines along the center of these features. Your line should trace the **bottom** of a trench. Keep in mind that the line represents the point of contact between two plates.

3   Using earthquakes to find plate boundaries

1. Once you have identified all of the trenches, ridges, and rises, notice that many of your lines will not connect. Clearly, they must connect if they represent the boundaries of a plate. The following steps will help you connect these lines.

2. Earthquakes are common along plate boundaries. Use the map of frequent earthquakes at right to help you fill in missing boundary lines for your plates.

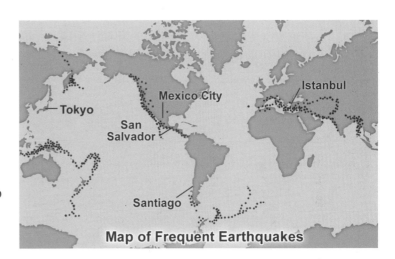

Map of Frequent Earthquakes

3. Recall that mountain ranges often occur at convergent plate boundaries. Using the globe, identify the location of the Himalayan Mountains on your map. This mountain range will help you complete a boundary line.

4. Now, make a cylinder with your map as shown at right. Notice how the pieces on the edge of your map come together the way they would on a globe. Doing this will help you see how plate pieces on the right side of your map are continuous with plate pieces on the left side of your map.

When you form a cylinder with the map, you can see how the pieces of the plates come together.

5. Continue working on completing the boundaries of each plate. Your teacher will help you distinguish any remaining areas that are hard to decipher. You will know you are done with this part of the Investigation when you can count **seven major plates** on your map. Make sure each plate has a complete boundary.

4 What direction do the plates move?

1. You will hold the African plate stationary while you move the other plates. Draw a circle on the African plate.

2. We will use two rules to determine the general direction that each of the other plates will move:

   1. Plates move apart at ridges and rises.

   2. Plates move together at trenches and mountains.

3. When you have determined the direction that a plate will move, draw an arrow in the middle of the plate to represent this movement.

5 Coloring and cutting the plates

1. Lightly color each plate a different color. Remember that the left and right edges of the map are connected and color any split plates with the same colors. Hold the map edges together, forming a cylinder, so that you can see this relationship.

2. Before cutting out the plates, make a small cut between the map and its border. Cut the border from the map in one piece.

3. Now, cut the plates apart along the boundary lines. This means cutting along trenches, ridges, rises, and along big mountain ranges.

4. Write your name and class neatly on the back of each plate piece.

5. Your teacher will give you a large backing sheet. Reassemble the map on top of your backing sheet.

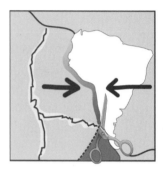

6 Moving the plates

1. At this point, you have on paper a present-day representation of the Earth's surface.

2. We will assume that in 50 million years the plates will move about 3 percent from their current positions, continuing in their current direction. This means that each plate on the bathymetric map will move about 1.5 centimeters (5/8 inch).

3. Hold the African plate stationary. Move the other plates 1.5 centimeters in the direction indicated by the arrow on each plate. Some pieces will move apart and some will move together. In some cases, *several* map pieces will move closer together.

4. At boundaries with trenches, slide the subducting plate **under** the other plate. When the convergent boundary includes oceanic crust and continental crust, the oceanic crust subducts.

5. Where continents come together, remember that continents cannot subduct, so mountain-building will take place. At these locations, use a black pen or crayon to draw in mountains (or more mountains) at these locations to represent mountain-building.

6. After you have everything positioned to your satisfaction, lift one side of each plate and apply some glue to fasten the plate to the backing sheet.

🪣Clean up: Place layers of newspaper on your table before gluing the plates to the backing sheet. The newspaper will protect your table and make clean up easier.

7   ## Reconstructing Earth

Now, you can reconstruct the 50-million-year-older Earth:

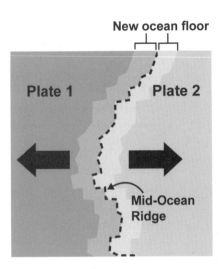

1. In some places, new ocean floor will have formed along mid-ocean ridges and rises. Blank areas on your backing sheet will show through. Draw a new plate boundary line through the middle of the blank areas and fill them in with the appropriate color on both sides of this line.

2. Make sure you have drawn mountains at locations where continents have collided.

3. Redraw the new continental margins with a black pen. Be careful not to trace the original margins unless they are unaltered.

8   ## Analyzing your map

a. Your teacher will have a completed map for you to examine. Compare your map to this map. How did you do?

b. Some of the oldest records of mankind come from the Middle East and Northern Africa. What has become of this "Cradle of Civilization" 50 million years into the future?

c. What has become of China, the islands of the western Pacific Ocean, and Australia? Do all of the maps in your class look the same in this region?

d. Where will the longest mountain range be located 50 million years from now?

e. Your map is only an approximation of the future Earth, but it is more reliable than a map that attempts to represent Earth 200 million years from now. What limits the accuracy of maps that try to project four times further into the future?

f. You know that plate movement is related to the nature of Earth's mantle. What conditions would have to be true to have movement of tectonic plates on the moon? What might the surface of the moon look like if plate tectonics **did** occur there? Hint: Review the role of the mantle in plate movement in the student reading.

Earthquakes

Question: What mechanical factors affect earthquakes?

In this Investigation, you will:

1. Create a model that simulates an earthquake.

2. Discover some of the conditions that affect the timing, duration, and intensity of an earthquake.

Most earthquakes are associated with plate boundaries. This is because the slow movement of the plates against each other causes *stress* on the rocks at the boundaries to increase. Stress results in the buildup of pressure and stored energy in objects. Earthquakes occur when the rocks that are under stress experience a release of pressure and stored energy. In this Investigation, you will use simple materials to simulate an earthquake.

1 Setting up an earthquake model

Start by gathering your materials.

1. Cut two pieces of sandpaper in half. Each half will be 9 by 5.5 inches. Turn the four halves smooth side up and place them short-end-to-short-end. Tape the halves together so that they form a 36-inch strip.

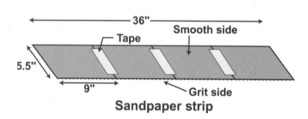

36"
Tape
Smooth side
5.5"
9"
Grit side
Sandpaper strip

2. Tape the sandpaper strip to your desk so the smooth side is down and the grit side is up.

3. Make a strain gauge by hooking two paper clips into a rubber band. Tie a long piece of kite string to one of the paper clips.

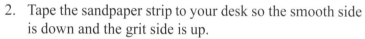

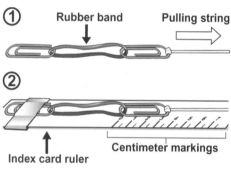

① Rubber band   Pulling string

②

Index card ruler

Centimeter markings

Strain gauge setup

4. Now, you will make a paper ruler with a a piece of index card that is 2 cm wide by 12.5 cm long. Place the card under the paper clip that is not attached to the string. Tape the card to this paper clip as shown in the diagram. The strain gauge and the paper ruler will move together in the model.

5. Once you have done this, starting with zero at the far end of the rubber band, mark off centimeters using a metric ruler until you get to the end of the card. Make your strain gauge look like the diagram. Make sure you have at least 7 centimeters marked on the paper ruler.

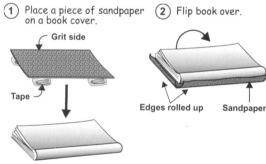

① Place a piece of sandpaper on a book cover.   ② Flip book over.

Grit side

Tape

Edges rolled up   Sandpaper

Safety Tip: To avoid injuries, do not shoot or overstretch the rubber bands.

6. Using masking tape, attach a piece of sandpaper on the outside of one cover of a book. The sandpaper should be a little larger than the cover. Once the sandpaper is on the book, fold up the overhanging sandpaper.

7. Now, tie a piece of kite string to the paper clip that is taped to the paper ruler. Then, place this string down the center of a page in the middle of the book. Use a very small piece of tape to hold the string in place on the page. Close the book. Tie the overhanging kite string to another paper clip so that it serves as an anchor to keep the string from pulling through the book. You may want to tape this paper clip to the top of the book with masking tape.

8. Place the book on the sandpaper strip at one end of the sandpaper strip. Make sure your setup matches with the setup of the earthquake model shown in the diagram below.

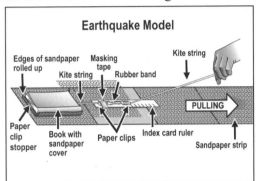

9. Next to the diagram of the earthquake model is a graphic that illustrates an earthquake occurring near a fault. Use this graphic to identify how the earthquake model represents an earthquake. Then, fill in Table 1.

Table 1: What does each item represent?

Material in setup	What does it represent?
The book	
The sandpaper strip	
The boundary between the book and the sandpaper	

2 Working with the model

Wear goggles to protect your eyes if a rubber band snaps during an experiment.

1. Place the book at one end of the sandpaper strip.

2. Gently pull on the string until the book moves a little. If the book does not move straight, move the string inside the book little off center and re-tape the string to the page.

3. Make adjustments to the setup as needed until it works well. However, do not pull the book along the sandpaper too many times. Doing this will wear down the sandpaper and change your results.

4. Now, place the book back at the end of the strip and pull the string until the edge of the rubber band moves from zero on the paper ruler to the 1-centimeter mark. This distance is related to how much *stress* is in the rubber band.

a. Did the book move when the stretch was 1 centimeter?

b. What does the movement of the book on the sandpaper strip represent in this Investigation?

Simulating the timing of an earthquake

To simulate an earthquake, you will pull the thread until the book suddenly moves along the sandpaper strip. This sudden movement, called a "slip" or a "failure," is the release of stress between the book and the sandpaper. It is also a release of energy.

1. Place the book at the far end of the sandpaper strip.

2. Pull the thread slowly and smoothly until the book slips (moves suddenly). Record the stretch just as the book slips. This is the *slip stretch.*

3. Without moving the hand holding the string, record the remaining stretch after the book stops. This is the *stop stretch.*

4. Repeat this process twice. Start with the book at the far end of the sandpaper strip for each trial. Record all data in Table 2. Find the average slip stretch and stop stretch lengths. Then, answer the questions.

Table 2: Simulating the timing of an earthquake

Trial number	Length of slip stretch (cm)	Length of stop stretch (cm)
1		
2		
3		
Average		

a. The movement of tectonic plates occurs all the time, but earthquakes do not. Why doesn't plate movement cause continual small earthquakes? Why do earthquakes occur every once in a while? Explain your answer.

b. Did all of the energy stored in the rubber band release when the book slipped? Do you think an earthquake releases all of the stored energy when it occurs?

4 Simulating the duration of an earthquake

1. In this part of the Investigation, you will simulate another earthquake. As you did in Part 3, pull the thread to move the book. However, when the book slips, continue to pull the thread just hard enough to keep the book moving. Practice your technique.

2. When you have perfected your technique, begin collecting data. Read the stretch measurement after the book first slips but while the book is still moving. Run three trials, record your data, and find the average. Then answer the questions below.

Table 3: Simulating the duration of an earthquake

Trial number	Length of stretch while the book is moving (cm)
1	
2	
3	
Average	

a. How does the data from Table 2 compare with the data from Table 3? Why do you think this is?

b. Earthquakes last longer than a few seconds. They do not simply start and quickly stop. Explain the relatively long duration of earthquakes based on the results of this experiment.

5   Simulating the intensity of an earthquake

1. Now, you and your group will simulate another earthquake by having team members drum on the table top with their fists. Each person should drum on the table with gentle to medium force.

2. While drumming is taking place, simulate an earthquake with your earthquake model.

3. Depending on what you observe in this experiment, record slip and stop stretches **or** stretch while the book is moving. Average your data. Then, answer the questions.

◆ **Safety Tip: Make sure your work table is stable before you start drumming. Use only gentle to medium force in your drumming.**

Table 4: Simulating the intensity of an earthquake

Trial number	Length of slip stretch (cm)	Length of stop stretch (cm)	Length of stretch while book is moving (cm)
1			
2			
3			
Average			

a. How does the data from Tables 2 or 3 compare with the data from Table 4? Why do you think this is?

b. How did the drumming affect the intensity of the "earthquake" in the model?

c. Do you think one earthquake can cause another earthquake? Explain your answer.

6   Simulating the damage caused by an earthquake

1. Now, you will simulate the damage caused by an earthquake. Perform each of the experiments with sugar cubes stacked on the book. Place one sugar cube alone, then have stacks of two, three, and four cubes. These stacked sugar cubes represent one-, two-, three-, and four-story buildings.

2. In the spaces of Table 5, record whether the cubes moved or the stacks fell during each simulation. Then, answer the questions.

Table 5: What happens to the sugar cubes when you simulate an earthquake?

Earthquake experiment	One cube	Two cubes	Three cubes	Four cubes
Timing simulation				
Duration simulation				
Intensity simulation				

a. Which sugar-cube building experienced the most damage? Develop a hypothesis to explain this result.

b. Which experiment resulted in the most damage? Develop a hypothesis to explain this result.

c. Given the results, propose one safety tip that would minimize structural damage during an earthquake.

7   Drawing conclusions

a. Based on your observations in this Investigation, what are some conditions that affect the timing of an earthquake? What conditions affect the duration? What conditions affect the intensity?

b. CHALLENGE! Describe what happens to cause an earthquake and what happens during an earthquake. In your answer, address these questions: How is the build up and release of stress involved in earthquakes? How are potential energy and kinetic energy related to earthquakes?

Volcanoes

Question: Why do some volcanoes erupt explosively?

In this Investigation, you will:

1. Learn how volcanoes are associated with plate boundaries.
2. Learn how volcanic eruptions are related to magma chemistry.

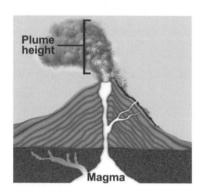

All active volcanoes erupt and release material that is very hot and therefore dangerous. But some volcanoes are especially dangerous because of the sudden, violently explosive nature of their eruptions. Less explosive volcanoes spew lava fountains and streams of melted rock, but in a gentle manner. In this Investigation, you will discover key differences between gentle and explosive volcanoes and will discover a pattern in their geographic distribution.

1 ## The Volcanic Explosivity Index

Geologists have developed a number scale that is used to describe volcanic eruptions. This number scale is called the Volcanic Explosivity Index, or VEI. The higher the VEI, the more explosive or violent the eruption of a volcano. Explosive eruptions are associated with high plumes of lava and ash escaping from the top of the volcano. Volcanoes with low VEI numbers have gentle eruptions. The plumes of these eruptions are not very high and not as much lava is released when the volcano erupts. Table 1 provides a list of examples of volcanoes and their VEI ratings.

Table 1: Examples of volcanoes and VEI ratings

VEI	Plume height	Volume (m^3)	Average time interval between eruptions	Example
0	<100 m	≥1000	one day	Kilauea
1	100-1000 m	≥10,000	one day	Stromboli
2	1-5 km	≥1,000,000	one week	Galeras, 1992
3	3-15 km	≥10,000,000	one year	Ruiz, 1985
4	10-25 km	≥100,000,000	≥10 years	Galunggung, 1982
5	>25 km	≥1,000,000,000	≥100 years	Mount St. Helens, 1981
6	>25 km	≥10,000,000,000	≥100 years	Krakatoa, 1883
7	>25 km	≥100,000,000,000	≥1,000 years	Tambora, 1815
8	>25 km	≥1,000,000,000,000	≥10,000 years	Toba, 71,000 years ago

Based on C.G. Newhall and S. Self (*Journal of Geophysical Research*, v. 87, p. 1231-1238, 1982).

a. What characteristics of a volcano might increase the plume height?

b. Would it be possible to have two eruptions with a VEI of 7 in the same year?

2   Finding a pattern of volcanoes

1. Table 2 provides the position by latitude (Lat) and longitude (Long) for eight volcanoes represented by two-letter symbols. The left-hand group are known to erupt violently. The right-hand group are known as gentle or less violent.

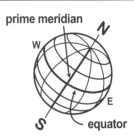

prime meridian

Lines of latitude are horizontal. Lines of longitude are vertical.

2. Plot the locations of all volcanoes on your bathymetric map. Lines of latitude are horizontal; they are described as being either north (N) or south (S) of the equator. Lines of longitude are vertical; they are described as being east (E) or west (W) of the prime meridian at 0° longitude.

3. Represent each volcano with its two-letter symbol. Represent violent volcanoes with a red marker and gentle volcanoes with a blue marker.

Table 2: Locations of volcanoes

Violent volcanoes		Gentle (less violent) volcanoes	
PN	*Lat* 15.1° N, *Long* 120.4° E	MA	*Lat* 19.5° N, *Long* 155.5° W
KR	*Lat* 16.7° S, *Long* 105.4° E	FE	*Lat* 0.4 S, *Long* 91.6 W
KA	*Lat* 58.3° N, *Long* 155.0° W	ER	*Lat* 13.6° N, *Long* 40. 7° E
BE	*Lat* 56.1° N, *Long* 160.7° E	PT	*Lat* 21.2° S, *Long* 55.7° E

a. How do the locations of the two kinds of volcanoes relate to the locations of plate boundaries?

b. What is the relationship between the nature of a volcanic eruption and plate boundary features?

3   Magma chemistry

Table 3 provides information about the magma chemistry of certain volcanoes. Study the table and think about how magma chemistry relates to a volcano's location. Then, answer the questions.

Table 3: How does magma content differ between violent and gentle volcanoes?

Volcano	Type	VEI	Magma chemistry		
			Magma type	Silica	Water
Pinatubo (PN)	Stratovolcano	6	Rhyolite	High	High
Krakatoa (KR)	Stratovolcano	7	Rhyolite/Andesite	High	High
Katmai (KA)	Complex stratovolcano	3	Andesite	Moderate	High
Bezymianny (BE)	Complex stratovolcano	2	Andesite	Moderate	High
Mauna Loa (MA)	Shield	0	Basalt	Low	Low
Fernandina (FE)	Shield	2	Basalt	Low	Low
Erta Ale (ER)	Shield	2	Basalt	Low	Low
Piton de la Fournaise (PT)	Shield	1	Basalt	Low	Low

a. How does magma chemistry differ between violent and gentle volcanoes? How does the chemistry of magma cause an explosive eruption?

b. Does magma chemistry seem to be related to the location of the volcano? Explain your answer.

c. Imagine you are asked to investigate a newly discovered volcano to find out whether it will produce a gentle or violent eruption. Develop a research plan for studying the volcano. What evidence will you need to be able to identify the nature of the eruption? Assume that you can use any resources you need.

Question: How have meteors affected Earth's surface?

In this Investigation, you will:

1. Learn about the frequency with which meteors hit the moon and Earth.
2. Calculate how often in 3.5 billion years Earth has been hit by meteors.

Fortunately, in recorded human experience, devastating meteors have not collided with Earth. Yet we know from the United States' Apollo missions to the moon (1963-72) and from modern research that the surface of both Earth and the moon have been, and will continue to be, modified by collisions with large objects from space. In Earth's billion-year history, there have been many collisions—even if they seem rare. In this Investigation, you will determine how often meteors have hit Earth's surface in the past 3.5 billion years.

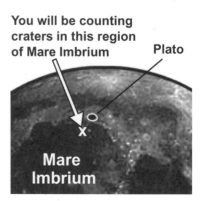

You will be counting craters in this region of Mare Imbrium

Plato

Mare Imbrium

1 Why are missions to the moon useful for understanding Earth?

Earth's surface is constantly changed by wind and water erosion and by plate tectonics. In contrast, the lack of an atmosphere or plate tectonics on the moon means that its surface only changes when something lands—like a space module or a meteor. If we assume that the number of meteors that have hit the moon is similar to the number that have hit Earth, then the moon's surface is a good research site for exploring the frequency of collisions.

Exploration of the moon began when the first man walked on its surface in 1969 during the Apollo 11 space mission. The first lunar explorers brought back moon rocks to Earth. Radioactive dating of these rocks was used to calculate the age of the moon's surface at several locations. For example, in 1971, Apollo 15 landed on the eastern edge of Mare Imbrium (Sea of Rains), a large basaltic lava flow. Rock samples from here show that the lava is about 3.5 billion years old. This means that any meteor craters in Mare Imbrium must have formed during the last 3.5 billion years.

Diagram of the Moon's Surface

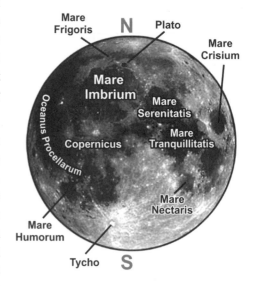

a. You have probably seen footprint marks in a cement sidewalk. How are the craters in Mare Imbrium like footprints that are preserved in cement?

b. Why can we assume that the craters happened after Mare Imbrium formed 3.5 billion years ago? Is this a form of relative dating? Explain your answers to these questions.

c. The area of Mare Imbrium is about 1,226,562 km^2. For the Investigation, you will study a section of Mare Imbrium that is 46,000 km^2. What percentage of Mare Imbrium's surface is this section?

2 Counting the number of craters in a section of Mare Imbrium

By counting the craters in a section of Mare Imbrium, we can estimate the number of collisions that have occurred on Earth during the last 3.5 billion years.

1. Your teacher will provide you with a photograph of a section of Mare Imbrium. Note that the Verrier crater and Mons Pico are labeled. You will also notice that there are lines on the photograph that divide it into seven strips.

2. Count all visible craters in each strip. Then record the number of craters for each strip in Table 1.

3. Add up the craters for each strip. Record the total number of craters in the last row of Table 1.

4. Now, write the value for the total number of craters in the fourth column of Table 2 on the next page.

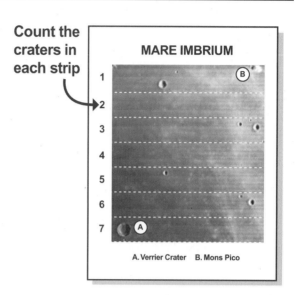

Count the craters in each strip

A. Verrier Crater   B. Mons Pico

Table 1: Number of craters in a section of Mare Imbrium

Strip number	Number of craters
1	
2	
3	
4	
5	
6	
7	
Total number of craters	

3   Estimating the effects of meteor impacts on Earth

The real diameter of the Verrier crater is 18 kilometers. In the photograph of Mare Imbrium, the diameter is 18 millimeters. This means that each millimeter in the photograph represents 1 kilometer.
one millimeter in the photograph = one kilometer in Mare Imbrium

The dimensions of the photograph are 200 mm by 230 mm. Therefore, since one millimeter equals one kilometer, the photograph represents an area of 200 km by 230 km. The area of this photograph is 46,000 km^2.

area of the section of Mare Imbrium = 200 km × 230 km = 46,000 km^2

1. Now, divide each Earth area in Table 2 by the area of the photograph (46,000 km^2). This calculation will give you a value that will be used to determine the number of collisions for each of the Earth areas. Record these values in the third column in Table 2.

2. Now, multiply the values in the third column by the total number of craters (the fourth column). Record the calculated values in the last column of Table 2. Each value equals the number of meteor impacts that may have occurred in a particular area during the past 3.5 billion years.

Table 2: Comparing the area of Mare Imbrium with various areas on Earth

Areas on Earth (km^2)	Area of the section of M. I. (km^2)	Earth area ÷ M. I. area	Total number of craters in Mare Imbrium (from Table 1)	Number of crater collisions for each Earth area
Texas = 681,239	**46,000**			
Alaska = 1,484,166				
United States = 5,708,615				
World's oceans = 361,000,000				
Earth = 510,000,000				

a. Given the number of meteor impacts that likely occurred in the last 3.5 billion years, what would the United States look like if erosion and plate tectonics had not changed Earth's surface during this time?

b. Why is the surface of Earth so much different from the moon's surface?

c. The smallest craters that you were able to count on Mare Imbrium would be catastrophic events today on Earth. But what of more frequent, smaller collisions? Exposed lunar rocks show many deep pits caused by micrometeorites smaller than the thickness of your hair. On Earth, frictional heating destroys much of what enters our atmosphere; only the largest and smallest objects reach the surface. Because micrometeorites are so tiny, they are slowed and fall to Earth as a gentle rain. About 30,000 tons of micrometeorites land on Earth *each year*. Given the volume of micrometeorites that encounter Earth's surface, chances are that you have been hit by a tiny space object more than once in your lifetime. Calculate how many tons of micrometeorites fall on Earth's surface *each day*.

4 | **Identifying meteor craters on Earth**

Due to plate tectonics and erosion, impact craters are hard to find on Earth. About 160 impact craters, including the Chicxulub crater on the Yucatan Pennisula in Mexico, have been identified so far. The meteor that caused the Chicxulub crater may have caused environmental changes on Earth that led to the extinction of the dinosaurs.

As scientists learn more about recognizing the signs of impact craters, more of the craters are being found. In this part of the Investigation, you will identify which of the following geologic features *mostly likely* was caused by a meteor. Read each scenario carefully and study the clues. Use your understanding of Earth science and the forces that shape Earth's surface to make your choice.

Table 3: Which of these geographic formations is an impact crater?

Name and age of the geographic formation	Description	Cross-section
Carolina Bays Southeast coast, U. S. 12,000 years	1. A single Carolina bay may be 60 m to 11 km across and up to 15 m deep. 2. The bays are elliptical depressions often filled with organic material and bordered with a sandy rim. 3. At least 500,000 bays exist in the southeast of North and South Carolina. 3. Aerial view of the coast shows many bays. These appear as large elliptical rings on the ground. 4. Bedrock can occurs below the bays.	
Avak Crater Alaska 95 million years	1. The diameter of this feature is 12 km. 2. Several hundred feet of overlying sediment cover this geological feature. To study it, scientists drill to collect cores of sediment. 3. Rocks in the region appear to be pulverized. 4. Breccia is present. Breccia is a type of sedimentary rock that is composed of many sharp fragments stuck together	
Crater Lake Oregon 7,000 years	1. This feature is about 1.2 km deep in its deepest part and about 9 km across. 2. A small formation called Wizard Island is in the lake. 3. Crater Lake is in the top of Mount Mazama, an ancient mountain that is part of the Cascade mountain range. 4. About 25 miles of ancient lava flows extend beyond the base of Mount Mazama.	

a. Based on the information in the table and on any research you do, describe how each of these geologic features may have formed.

b. Which of these features seems to have changed the most since it was formed? Explain your answer.

c. Of the three scenarios above, which was most likely caused by a meteor? Give three pieces of evidence that justify your answer.

Question: How can we interpret the stories inside rocks?

In this Investigation, you will:

1. Learn about igneous, sedimentary, and metamorphic rocks.
2. Identify how these rocks were formed.
3. Describe the stories hidden in rocks.

Geologists divide rocks into three groups based on how they were formed. There are **igneous**, **sedimentary**, and **metamorphic** rocks. In this multi-part Investigation, you will discover key concepts in the formation of each rock type. With these discoveries, you will be able to reveal parts of the stories hidden in many rocks and rock formations.

Section 1: Igneous Rocks

Igneous rocks form when melted rock material cools. This melt usually includes the ingredients for more than one kind of mineral. When the melt cools, minerals with the highest melting point begin to form crystals. These first-forming crystals are surrounded by the remaining fluid melt. As the temperature continues to fall, different mineral crystals form. Finally, the last of the fluid material solidifies, locking all of the crystals into a solid igneous rock. This order of crystallization results in distinct, randomly oriented, interlocking crystals. Granite is an example of an igneous rock. The different minerals in granite are easily visible.

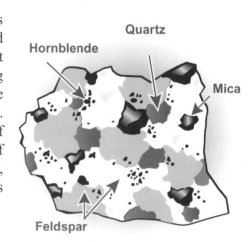

GRANITE

1   Prepare a crystal-growing solution

1. Add 4 heaping teaspoons of salt to a plastic beverage cup half-filled with water.
2. Stir this mixture for 1 minute. Not all the salt will dissolve because you have formed a saturated solution, meaning that the water has dissolved all the salt it can hold in solution.
3. Pour a little of the salt solution into two dishes. Label one dish "Warm" and the other "Cool."
4. Place the dish labeled "Warm" in a warm place such as over a radiator or near a sunny window. Alternatively, you can use a hair dryer to warm the liquid in this dish until it dries up.
5. Place the dish labeled "Cool" away from sources of warmth and light.

a. Making a prediction: How do you think the crystals will look in each dish after the water has evaporated? Describe your prediction in a few sentences.

b. Draw a picture to illustrate your prediction.

2 Observing the size of crystals that form

Crystal growth is slow and will take more than one day.

1. Examine both dishes from time to time for the next few days until all the water has evaporated. You may want to record the temperature at each dish's location.

2. Make a table to record your observations.

3. Record the date, time, and the amount of water left in each dish at each observation. Describe the crystals in each dish. Use relative terms such as *slightly*, *more*, and *most* to record these observations. Measure and record the size of the largest crystal in each dish.

3 Interpreting the size of crystals that form

1. When the water has evaporated from one of the dishes, make a final inspection of both dishes. Both dishes will have large and small crystals, but one will have the largest crystals. Usually these largest crystals will form near the edges of the dish.

2. Record your final observations in the table you made in Part 2.

a. In which dish did the liquid crystal solution remain for a longer time?

b. Which dish had more time to grow crystals?

c. Which dish grew the biggest crystals?

d. Write a conclusion statement about the time available for crystals to form and the size of the crystals that form.

4 Applying your conclusion to igneous rock formation

The size of a rock crystal depends on the amount of interaction among the materials in the rock melt. More time allows more interaction; slow-growing crystals tend to be bigger than fast-growing crystals. Anything that might slow the cooling of a rock melt will provide that time.

a. List two events or conditions (other than the methods you used in this Investigation) that might slow the cooling of a rock melt.

b. List two conditions that might speed up cooling of a rock melt.

c. What would the crystals from a rapidly cooled melt look like? Explain your answer in terms of your conclusion statement from 3(d).

d. Find samples of granite, gabbro, rhyolite (felsite), and basalt in your rock kit. Compare the appearance of each sample. Based on your work in this part of the Investigation, which rocks formed slowly and which rocks formed relatively quickly? Explain your answer to this question.

e. Igneous rocks that form on Earth's surface are *extrusive* and those that form underground are called *intrusive*. Based on your observations of the igneous rocks in 4(d), which of them are likely to be extrusive? Which are likely to be intrusive? Explain your answer.

Section 2: Sedimentary Rocks

Sedimentary rocks begin as separate particles. These particles are usually loose or fragmented bits of other rock, or they may form directly as a result of chemical changes in water. Telltale patterns often develop as these particles settle and accumulate. These patterns are preserved when layers of accumulated particles are converted to sedimentary rock by compaction and cementing. Geologists use the patterns to understand the conditions during which the material was deposited. This part of the Investigation will allow you to interpret the patterns commonly found in sedimentary rocks.

1 Preparing sedimentary deposits

This Investigation requires a little care to shorten your cleanup time. Start by assembling all the items needed for the Investigation. Lay out newspaper over your work area. After you have finished, you can roll the newspaper inward and easily dispose of any loose material.

1. Your will need two plastic beverage bottles for your group. One will be cut in half and is for mixing. The other bottle will still have some of its top remaining and will hold your sediments.

2. Add water to the sediment bottle to a depth of 5 centimeters.

3. Add dirt to the mixing bottle to the depth of 3 centimeters. Then, add water to the mixing bottle and mix it to make a mud slurry. Add just enough water to make it the thickness of a thick milk shake.

4. With the slurry well-stirred, pour it into the sediment bottle, and mix it into the water. Allow the sediment bottle to stand undisturbed for two minutes or until you can see layers forming.

a. Once you see layers in the sediment bottle, make a sketch of the layers. Add labels to your sketch to help describe what you see. Where is the coarsest sediment? Where is the finest sediment?

b. Is there a change in color from bottom to top? If so, shade your sketch to show the change.

2 Additional sedimentary deposits

You are now going to add more layers in the sediment bottle. The procedure is slightly different for the extra layers, so read these instructions carefully.

1. Examine the water level in your sediment bottle. You only need 5 centimeters of water over the settled slurry for this Investigation. **Carefully** pour off excess water into a wastewater container. Repeat this step after each addition so that spilling is not a problem.

2. Now, add 1 centimeter of sediment to the mixing bottle. Then, add water until the new mud slurry is dilute and much thinner than the first slurry.

3. BEFORE you add this second slurry to the sediment bottle, we need to introduce turbulence in the sediment bottle. The next two steps need to happen one right after the other. Before you start step 4, have a team member stir the second slurry continuously to keep it in suspension.

4. Pull your spoon through the water in the sediment bottle just over the surface of the settled slurry, a little off-center. Do this just once.

5. Immediately add the new slurry to the sediment bottle while the water is still turbulent.

6. After two minutes, repeat steps 1 through 5 until you have added three slurries to the original for a total of four slurries added to the sediment bottle. Stop this process if your sediment bottle gets too full.

3   Final observations

a.   Gently wipe off the side of the sediment bottle. Turn the bottle, and look for where a layer of settled slurry has been cut, or added to, by a new layer. Use your first observations to detect where an earlier slurry ends and a newer one begins. You will probably find several places where the bottom of a newer layer has broken the top of an earlier layer. Is each slurry represented by a distinct layer?

b.   Observe, sketch, and label the appearance of these layers. Try to sketch clearly the appearance of an earlier slurry *top* cut by a new slurry *bottom*. Use shading to show color changes. You may want to make multiple views (front view, side views, and back views) of the sediment in the bottle.

4   Applying your experience

Flowing water greatly influences the formation of sedimentary rocks. Rock is denser than water and sinks in still water. However, the turbulence of rapidly flowing water can keep rock particles suspended despite their greater density. The faster water is flowing, the larger the rock particles that will be transported. When this water begins to slow, the largest particles will settle first, followed by smaller particles, and finally, as the water slows to a stop, the finest particles will settle.

a.   In Part 2, you saw that when a turbulent mixture of different soil particles is added to water, the largest particles settled first and the smallest particles settled last. Can you explain why this happens based on the effect of flowing water described above?

b.   Imagine that 2 million years ago there was a valley surrounded by foothills. In the middle of the valley lay a large, shallow lake. Rainstorms would cause small streams to run hard into the lake for a few days, but usually the streams ran gently. A million years later, volcanic ash covered the valley, including the streams and the lake. Later, glaciers scraped away the ash, exposing the sedimentary rock that was once the lake and the streams. Your geology team has collected samples of sedimentary rocks from three sites in the valley. Describe and sketch what each rock would look like in the table below. Then, explain why these samples look the way they do.

c.   Examine a sample of conglomerate and shale (preferably oil shale) from your rock kit. Come up with an explanation for how each of the rocks was formed based on their appearance. How do you know they are sedimentary rocks?

Site where samples were collected	What do these rock samples look like?	Why do these rock samples look the way they do?
Stream bed		
Stream mouth		
Lake center		

Section 3: Metamorphic Rocks

Metamorphic rocks are formed when great heat and pressure act on already existing rock—of any kind. The word *metamorphic* means *of changed form*. Sedimentary, igneous, and metamorphic rocks all can undergo metamorphism. A metamorphic rock can be forced to a higher level of metamorphism, or it may be changed structurally by later periods of metamorphism.

**Metamorphic rock
with many folds**

The process of forming a metamorphic rock involves squeezing, deep submergence below the Earth's surface, and heating. In this Investigation, you will discover how squeezing causes rock to fold like soft dough.

It is hard to imagine rock folding like dough. In our everyday experience, rock seems hard and brittle. How can it fold at all? The answer lies in the heating that softens the rock and the thousands of centuries taken for the folding event. It is important to note that in this Investigation, you will apply force to play dough quickly—instantaneously— compared with actual metamorphism. That is because play dough is very soft, and you do not have a few hundred thousand years to spend making a rock!

1 Preparing a metamorphic rock

1. Cut a file card into six pieces. First, cut the card in half **lengthwise**. Then cut the halves into thirds. Each piece will be about 4-by-4-centimeters. You will need only five of the card pieces.

2. Prepare six pieces of play dough by forming them into balls about 3 centimeters in diameter. Use different colors of dough for the layers.

3. Use your fingers to form each ball into a slab of dough that is the same shape as a file card piece.

4. Build a model section of layers by alternating play dough slabs with file card pieces. Alternate colors of dough as you build. The finished model has alternating layers of play dough and card with play dough on both outer surfaces. Gently press this package together with the palm of your hand.

2 Simulating metamorphism

1. On a piece of newspaper, stand the package so that the layers are vertical.

2. Wrap newspaper around a small, hardcover book. Hold the book level over the play dough package.

3. Create *compression* on the package by pressing the book down on the package. You do not need to press down hard. Press the package until it is about 3 centimeters high.

4. Take your metamorphic package to your teacher to slice so that you can see the folding.

5. Sketch the folded layers in your notebook. This is a simple fold representing **low metamorphism**. Show the compression by drawing arrows pointing inward in the direction of compression.

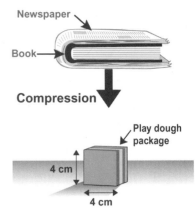

3   ## Making and interpreting complex folds

For the following steps, refer to Parts 1 and 2 to make the play dough packages.

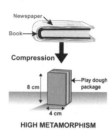

1. **High metamorphism:** You have shown a single fold in the play dough. Sometimes folds in rock go back and forth and look more like an accordion. To see this for yourself, cut file cards into six pieces that are 4-by-8 centimeters. Make a layered package using five pieces of card and six pieces of dough. Stand the layered package tall-end-up before applying pressure to create folds. It may take more than one run before you get good results. Make a sketch of this fold.

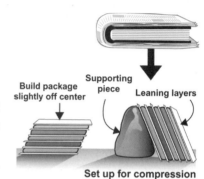

2. **Angled metamorphism:** Usually, layers of rock are not perpendicular to the direction of metamorphic pressure. When this happens, the folds are uneven. To see this, build your package slightly off-center by placing each layer a little to one side. You can do this with the original size (4x4) file card pieces or the longer (4x8) pieces. After you have made your package, set it up as shown in the diagram at right. The package should lean to one side. Press a piece of triangular piece of play dough on one side to support the leaning package. Apply compression as shown in the graphic at right. Make a sketch of this fold.

3. **Extension:** Repeat the process using different techniques. For example, change the number of layers or the amount of pressure used. In each case, carefully record your techniques for building each package and compressing it. Finally, sketch the appearance of the folded package.

4   ## Applying your experience

a. How can the shape of metamorphic folds allow geologists to reconstruct the direction of metamorphic compression?

b. It is common to find folds of folds. Some of these refolded folds seem to have been formed by two different directions of compression. How might a refolded fold occur? Write a short description of events that might cause a refolded fold in rocks.

c. In small metamorphic rocks, it is difficult to see folding. However, it is possible to see some effects of metamorphism. Compare a sample of shale from your rock kit to a sample of slate, a metamorphic rock made from shale (a sedimentary rock). Do you see evidence of metamorphism?

Section 4: Interpretation of Rock Formations

Now, you will use all that you have learned in this unit on Earth science to interpret the history of five rock formations. On the back of each photograph of a rock formation, you will find: a map of the United States showing the location where the photograph was taken, a brief description, a set of questions, and a list of activities. For each photograph, answer the questions and accomplish the activities on your own paper. When you have finished these, answer the following questions.

a. Evaluate your ability to interpret the photographs of the land formations. How did you do? Write your evaluation of your efforts in one to two paragraphs.

b. Describe a land or rock formation near your home or at a place you have visited. Using what you have learned, write an interpretation of how it formed and provide its history.

30.1

Cycles on Earth

Question: How do we keep track of time?

In this Investigation, you will:

1. Build a sundial to keep track of daily time.
2. Simulate the lunar cycle.

Measurment of days and months depends on the cycles between Earth and the moon and Earth and the sun. Therefore, it is not surprising that some of the first clocks were sundials based on the movement of shadows as the sun appeared to move across the sky. A sundial is a large timepiece on the ground. The "hand" of the clock to the right is a shadow created by an obelisk. In this Investigation, you will build a sundial, and then calibrate it so that you use it to accurately tell the time. You will also model the lunar cycle and then observe it over the course of a month.

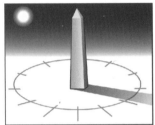

An obelisk allowed ancient Eqyptians to divide up the day into parts.

1 Building a sundial

1. Obtain a cardboard folder from your teacher. To build your sundial, measure and cut out a 20-by-26 centimeters size piece of the folder. First, draw one line dividing the piece in half. This will be the *noon line*. Then, draw a perpendicular line 2.5 centimeters from one edge: The place where the two lines intersect will be called the *vertex*.

2. Next you need to make the part of your sundial that casts a shadow. This part is called the **gnomon**. On another piece of the folder, mark off a baseline that is 10 centimeters long. Then, using your protractor, make an angle with this line that is equal to the angle of your particular location's latitude on Earth. Your teacher will give you the correct latitude. Then, draw a second line, perpendicular to the baseline and making a right triangle. Write the angle for your latitude in the position shown on the diagram.

3. Cut out your gnomon. Then, attach the gnomon so that it is perpendicular to the base of the sundial. To keep the gnomon upright, cut out two rectangular tabs. Tape these to each side of the gnomon and fold them out in opposite directions. Then, tape them to the base of the sundial as shown.

4. Bring your sundial outside on a sunny day. Use a compass to help you point the noon line to the north.

a. Do you see a shadow on the sundial? Where is it located?

b. What will happen to the shadow as the day progresses? Explain your answer.

c. Can you tell the time by looking at the location of the shadow on the sundial? What do you need to do in order to be able to tell the time?

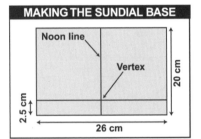

MAKING THE SUNDIAL BASE

Noon line

Vertex

20 cm

2.5 cm

26 cm

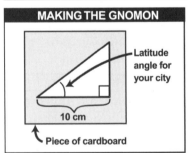

MAKING THE GNOMON

Latitude angle for your city

10 cm

Piece of cardboard

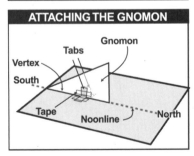

ATTACHING THE GNOMON

Gnomon

Tabs

Vertex

South

Tape

Noonline

North

2   Calibrating the sundial

In order to tell the time accurately with your sundial, you need to calibrate it. You will need a few hours on a sunny afternoon to complete this part of the Investigation.

1. Take your sundial outside at noon on a sunny day. Use a navigational compass to point the noon line on the sundial toward the north.

2. Move the sundial slightly to the right or left until the point of the gnomon's shadow is resting on the noon line.

3. Use the compass to determine the exact direction that the noon line is pointing, and write it down.

4. Leave your sundial for exactly one hour. Go back and mark where point of the gnomon's shadow is located on the sundial. Write the time (1:00 pm) next to this mark.

5. Repeat the fourth step five more times (until the actual time is 6:00 pm). You should have a mark for each hour after noon from 1:00 until 6:00.

6. Take your sundial indoors. Use a ruler to connect each point to the vertex as shown. You have now calibrated your sundial to measure time from noon until 6:00 pm.

7. Use a protractor to measure the angle between the noon line and the 1:00 line. Record this angle in the table below.

8. Measure the other angles from the noon line to each of the other marks and record the angles in the table.

9. To calibrate the morning hours, you will use the same angles you measured for the afternoon hours. The table below will help you determine which angle to use for each morning hour.

10. Test your sundial on another sunny day. To do this, make sure you use a compass to point the noon line in the direction you recorded earlier.

Afternoon hour	Angle from noon line	Corresponding morning hour
1:00 pm		11:00 am
2:00 pm		10:00 am
3:00 pm		9:00 am
4:00 pm		8:00 am
5:00 pm		7:00 am
6:00 pm		6:00 am

a. Can you use your sundial to tell the time? How accurate is your sundial?

b. How could you improve the accuracy of your sundial so you could tell the time within fifteen minutes?

c. What variables affect the accuracy of your sundial? List as many variables as you can think of.

d. What effect do you think that the time of year will have on the accuracy of your sundial? Explain your answer.

e. How do you think Daylight Savings Time will affect the accuracy of your sundial? How could you adjust the sundial for this?

3   Modeling the lunar cycle

A sundial is an instrument that allows you to keep track of time during the day. Ancient civilizations used the moon to keep track of the passage of each month. The moon revolves around Earth in a counterclockwise direction. As it revolves, its appearance from Earth changes in a repeating pattern called the *lunar cycle*. In this part of the Investigation, you will model the lunar cycle using a flashlight and a foam ball on a stick. You will work with another student, as shown in Figure 1.

✎ **Your teacher will turn out the classroom lights once you have gathered your materials are are ready to begin.**

1.   Place a foam ball on a pencil or stick. This ball represents the moon.

2.   Have another student hold a flashlight. The flashlight represents the sun. Your head represents Earth.

3.   Hold the ball above your head, at arm's length from your face. Stand about one meter from the flashlight, which is held at the same level as the ball.

4.   Observe the moon in each of the positions shown in Figure 2. Face the ball at each position.

5.   For each position, indicate how much of the ball is dark and how much is illuminated, in the table below. Use a pencil to show the shaded regions.

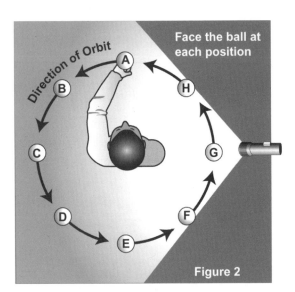

Figure 2

Position	Appearance	Position	Appearance
A	○	E	○
B	○	F	○
C	○	G	○
D	○	H	○

a.   Compare your observations to the diagram of the moon phases in the reading, *Cycles on Earth*. Based on your observations, what do the terms **waning** and **waxing** mean?

b.   During what position on Figure 2 would a solar eclipse occur? During what position on Figure 2 would a lunar eclipse occur?

4   Long-term project: Constructing a lunar calendar

Now, you will track time by following the phases of the moon. In the chart below, draw the moon as it appears in the sky each night for 28 nights. Record the date of your observation, the time, and illustrate the shape of the moon for each night. Identify the phase of the moon for each night. Refer to *Cycles on Earth* in your student text for a graphic that shows each phase. Use the following two-letter symbols to represent each phase: new moon (NM), waxing crescent (XC), first quarter (FQ), waxing gibbous (XG), full moon (FM), waning gibbous (NG), third quarter (TQ), waning crescent (NC).

SUN	MON	TUE	WED	THUR	FRI	SAT
○ Date ___ Time ___ Phase ___	○ Date ___ Time ___ Phase ___	○ Date ___ Time ___ Phase ___	○ Date ___ Time ___ Phase ___	○ Date ___ Time ___ Phase ___	○ Date ___ Time ___ Phase ___	○ Date ___ Time ___ Phase ___
○ Date ___ Time ___ Phase ___	○ Date ___ Time ___ Phase ___	○ Date ___ Time ___ Phase ___	○ Date ___ Time ___ Phase ___	○ Date ___ Time ___ Phase ___	○ Date ___ Time ___ Phase ___	○ Date ___ Time ___ Phase ___
○ Date ___ Time ___ Phase ___	○ Date ___ Time ___ Phase ___	○ Date ___ Time ___ Phase ___	○ Date ___ Time ___ Phase ___	○ Date ___ Time ___ Phase ___	○ Date ___ Time ___ Phase ___	○ Date ___ Time ___ Phase ___
○ Date ___ Time ___ Phase ___	○ Date ___ Time ___ Phase ___	○ Date ___ Time ___ Phase ___	○ Date ___ Time ___ Phase ___	○ Date ___ Time ___ Phase ___	○ Date ___ Time ___ Phase ___	○ Date ___ Time ___ Phase ___
○ Date ___ Time ___ Phase ___	○ Date ___ Time ___ Phase ___	○ Date ___ Time ___ Phase ___	○ Date ___ Time ___ Phase ___	○ Date ___ Time ___ Phase ___	○ Date ___ Time ___ Phase ___	○ Date ___ Time ___ Phase ___

30.2

Tools of Astronomy

Question: How does a telescope work?

In this Investigation, you will:

1. Identify the parts of a refracting telescope and describe the function of each part.
2. Make observations of the moon's surface.

A **telescope** is a device that makes objects that are faraway appear to be closer. Telescopes work by collecting the light from a distant object with a lens or mirror and bringing

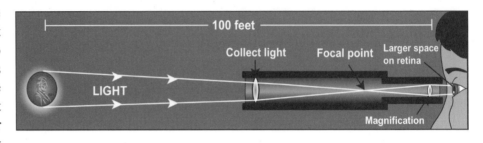

that light into a concentrated point, called a **focal point**. The bright light from the focal point is then magnified by another lens (the eyepiece) so that it takes up more space on your retina (the light-sensing membrane of the eye). This makes the object appear to be larger and closer. In this Investigation, you will identify the parts of a simple telescope and learn how it works. You will then use your telescope to observe features on the moon including craters and maria (the Latin word for "seas").

1 Learning the parts of a refracting telescope

For this Investigation you will use a small **refracting** telescope. This type of telescope uses a lens to gather light into a focal point, and another lens to magnify the image. Use the diagram below to identify the parts of your telescope. You may take your telescope apart and reassemble it to learn the parts. The function of each part is listed next to the diagram. Place the letter of each function next to the correct part.

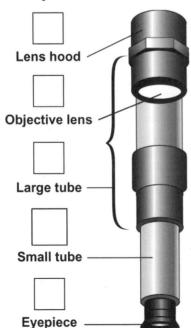

Lens hood

Objective lens

Large tube

Small tube

Eyepiece

A. Moves in or out to focus image

B. Magnifies image

C. Reduces glare

D. Holds the light-gathering lens

E. Gathers light

2 Focusing a telescope

⬦**Safety Tip: Never look at the sun or a bright object through your telescope! You will cause damage to your eye.**

1. Pull the small tube all of the way out of your telescope and place a piece of masking tape lengthwise along the tube.

2. Write the letter "e" to measure 1 centimeter tall on a 3-by-5-inch card. Place the card at eye level on a wall in a large room (your classroom, the library, etc.).

3. Starting at the wall, lay a tape measure on the floor. Pull 10 meters of tape out from the wall. This will be your distance scale, 0-10, with zero at the wall.

4. Stand at the 10-meter mark and use your telescope to observe the letter on the card on the wall. Pull the small tube in or out until the letter comes sharply into focus. Record your observations in the table below. For your observations, describe the appearance of the image in terms of orientation and apparent size.

5. Draw a pencil line on the masking tape where the short tube enters the long tube. Write "10 m" (your distance from the card) next to the mark.

6. Repeat steps 4 and 5, moving closer to the wall by one meter for each trial. Continue to move 1 meter closer to the card, while repeating steps 4 and 5, until you cannot bring the letter into focus.

7. Use a ruler with millimeter markings to measure the length of the small tube, from your marks to the edge of the tube, as shown. Record your measurements in the table below.

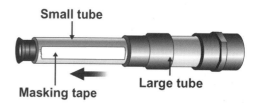

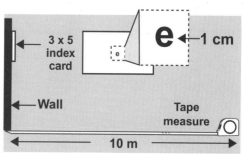

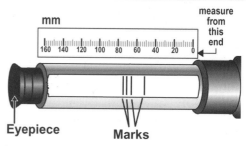

Distance from card (m)	Observations	Length of small tube (mm)
10		
9		
8		
7		
6		
5		
4		
3		
2		
1		

a. In general, as you move closer to an object, how should you adjust the small tube?

b. When you view the letter "e" through your telescope, why does the image appear upside down? (HINT: Trace the light rays coming from the penny in the picture at the top of page one.)

c. Make a graph of distance versus length of the small tube. Would you describe the relationship as direct or inverse? Explain your answer.

3   **a/b Determining the magnification of a telescope**

The **magnification** of a telescope is a measure of the number of times the image being viewed is enlarged. If your telescope has a magnification of 10x, this means that it magnifies the image of an object 10 times. The magnification of a telescope is the relationship between the objective lens and the eyepiece you are using. Since eyepieces in most telescopes can be interchanged, the magnification of a telescope can vary. The magnification of a telescope is determined using the following equation:

$$\text{magnification} = \frac{\text{focal length of objective lens}}{\text{focal length of eyepiece}}$$

The **focal length** of a lens is distance between the center of the lens and the focal point. The focal length of a lens is directly related to its diameter. The larger the diameter, the greater the focal length. Here is how the focal length of a lens is measured:

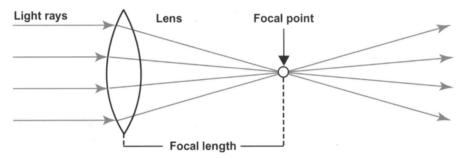

Popular focal lengths for eyepieces are 10 millimeters and 25 millimeters. Suppose your telescope has an objective lens with a focal length of 200 mm and an eyepiece with a focal length of 25 mm. What is the magnification of your telescope?

$$\text{magnification} = \frac{200 \text{ mm}}{25 \text{ mm}} = 8\text{x}$$

a.   If you wanted to increase the magnification of the telescope in the problem above, which eyepiece would you choose—10 mm or 40 mm? Explain your answer and show your solution to the problem.

b.   Calculate the magnification of the following telescopes:

Objective lens	Eyepiece	Magnification
1200 mm	10 mm	
1200 mm	25 mm	
800 mm	20 mm	

c.   A telescope with an 800 mm objective lens can gather more light than a telescope with a 200 mm objective lens. Does this mean that the 800 mm telescope has greater magnification than the 200 mm telescope? Explain your answer.

d.   The focal lengths of two telescopes are shown below. Which telescope would have the greater magnification? Through which telescope would you expect to see a brighter image? Explain your answers.

   Telescope A: 800 mm objective lens; 20 mm eyepiece
   Telescope B: 200 mm objective lens; 5 mm eyepiece

4   Observing the moon

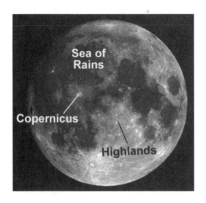

If you look at the moon through a telescope (or even without one), you can see the three main features of the lunar surface: craters, highlands, and maria. Craters are large, round pits that cover much of the moon's surface. One of the moon's largest craters, named for Copernicus, is hundreds of kilometers across.

When you look at the moon, some areas appear bright, others dark. The brighter areas are called **highlands** because they are higher in elevation. The darker areas are called **maria** (a single area is called a *mare*) because early observers believed they were oceans. Maria are low, dry areas that were flooded with molten lava billions of years ago when the moon was formed. Among the maria you can see through a telescope is a large one named Mare Imbrium, or Sea of Rains.

1. Find out on which evenings the moon will be full, or at least 80 percent of its surface illuminated. This will be the best time for observing lunar features.

2. If you hold the telescope as steady as you can, what happens to the image of the moon in your telescope over a few minutes, and why?

3. The diagram to the right shows the names of some of the craters, highlands, and maria you can observe. Study the diagram, then try to locate as many of the features as you can. Record all of the features you observe in a notebook.

4. As you observe the moon, answer the questions below.

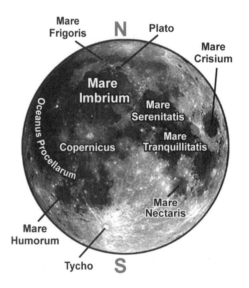

a. How many craters can you see? Do they overlap? What do you believe this tells you about their age? Make sure you can locate Tycho, an 85-kilometer-wide crater on the lower part of the moon that is the hub of a system of bright streaks.

b. How many maria (Latin for seas, remember?) can you see?

5   CHALLENGE! Observing Jupiter and its moons

When it is visible, Jupiter is the third brightest object in the night sky—after the moon and Venus. Though you will not be able to see any of Jupiter's features through your telescope, you may be able to see four of its moons.

a. Find out when Jupiter is visible in the night sky and the best time for viewing. Good resources include your local newspaper (the weather page) and the Internet.

b. Use a telescope to view Jupiter. How many moons do you see?

c. Why is Jupiter visible from Earth only during certain periods of time?

Earth and the Moon

Question: What does the length of a year have to do with Earth's distance from the sun?

In this Investigation, you will:

1. Simulate an object in orbit.
2. Investigate how orbital period varies with distance.

You have learned that an **orbit** results from the balance between *inertia* (the forward motion of an object in space) and **gravitational force** (the attractive force between two objects). **Orbital speed** is the speed required to achieve a balance between inertia and the pulling force of gravity. For example, the moon's orbital speed is approximately 3,700 kilometers per hour. If it were moving any slower, it would fall toward Earth because of gravity. If it were moving any faster, it would break free of gravity and travel in a straight line away from Earth.

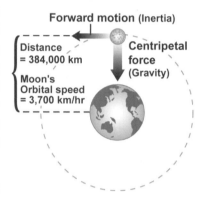

In this Investigation, you will use a ball and a string to simulate a planet or moon in orbit. In this model, the string will act as a *centripetal* (pulling) force on the ball just as gravity acts as a centripetal force on orbiting planets and moons. Through the experiment, you will discover the relationship between orbital speed and distance.

1 **Setting up**

1. Obtain a ball with a 1.5 meter string threaded through it.
2. Hold the string between your thumb and forefinger so that there is about 20 to 30 centimeters of string between the ball and your thumb.
3. Swing the ball in a circle so that it "orbits" around your head. Be sure to move your hand at a constant speed.
4. Try slowing down the speed until the ball just stays in orbit without falling down. This will represent the "orbital speed" of the ball.

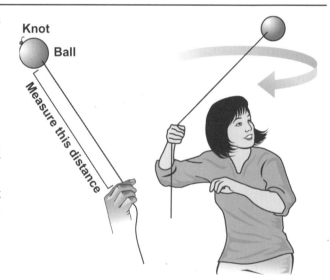

🔷 **Safety Tip: Make sure that others stay out of the path of the ball's orbit.**

a. What forces keep the ball in orbit? How are these forces similar to those that keep a planet in orbit?

b. What would happen to the ball if you cut the string while it was in orbit?

c. What information would you need to determine the orbital speed of the ball?

2   Doing the experiment

1. Choose members of your group for each of the following tasks:
    - Spinner: twirls the ball on the string so that it stays in orbit.
    - Counter: counts the number of revolutions the ball completes in 60 seconds.
    - Timer: measures 60 seconds for each trial.
    - Recorder: records data.
2. Measure 0.10 meter (10 centimeters) of string between the center of the ball and the tip of your thumb. This will be the **distance** of the ball from your thumb (the first column of the table below).
3. Twirl the ball until it remains in orbit without falling back down.
4. Count the number of revolutions the ball completes in exactly 60 seconds and record this number in the **revolutions** column in the table.
5. Repeat steps 2 through 4 for the distances in the table below.
6. Calculate the **orbital speed** of the ball for each distance using the following equation, and record in the table:

$$\text{orbital speed} = \frac{(2\pi r) \times (\text{number of revolutions})}{60.0 \text{ seconds}}$$

where r = distance of the ball from the tube

Distance (m)	Revolutions	Orbital speed (m/sec)	Distance (m)	Revolutions	Orbital speed (m/sec)
0.10			0.60		
0.20			0.70		
0.30			0.80		
0.40			0.90		
0.50			1.00		

3   Analyzing the results

a. Make a graph of distance versus orbital speed. What does the curve of the graph reveal about the relationship between these two variables?

b. According to the equation of universal gravitation, the gravitational force between two objects decreases inversely with the distance between them. How would you state the mathematical relationship between orbital speed and distance?

c. Explain why the relationship between orbital speed and distance is the same as that between gravity and distance.

4   Applying your knowledge

a. How do the results from this experiment compare with the orbital speeds of the planets?

b. The **orbital period** of a planet is the amount of time (in Earth years) it takes to make a complete revolution around the sun. Based on the results of your experiment, which planet has the shortest orbital period? Which has the longest orbital period?

31.2 Solar System

Question: How big is the solar system?

In this Investigation, you will:

1. Set up a scale model of the solar system based on distances you can measure.
2. Investigate the scale of the planets relative to distances between planets in the solar system.

It is difficult to comprehend great distances. For example, how great a distance is 140,000 kilometers (the diameter of Jupiter) or 150,000,000 kilometers (the distance from the sun to the Earth)? An easy way to compare these distances is to create a **scale model**. For instance, a globe is a scale model of Earth and road maps are scale models of geographic regions. These scale models help us visualize the true sizes of objects and the distances between them.

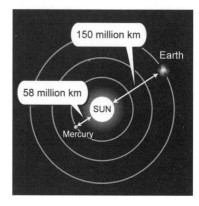

In this Investigation, you will compare an astronomical distance—like the distance from the sun to Pluto—to a measurable distance—like the length of a football or soccer field. Using proportions, you will make a scale model of the distances of the planets from the sun. Then, you will investigate how the sizes of the planets compare with the distances between them in the solar system. The results may surprise you.

1 $\frac{a}{b}$ Using proportions to determine scale distances

Pluto is an average distance of 5.9 billion kilometers from the sun. We can use a *proportion* to determine a scale distance for our model. Assume the largest distance you can measure is 100 meters. The length of a soccer field is usually between 90 and 120 meters long. For this Investigation, we will use 100 meters as the scale distance between the sun and Pluto.

$$100 \text{ m} = 5,900,000,000 \text{ km}$$

If the distance from the sun to Pluto equals 100 meters, where would you find the other planets? You can answer this question by setting up the following proportion where x is the distance from the sun to any planet, in meters:

$$\frac{x}{\text{Distance from the sun to planet}} = \frac{100 \text{ m}}{5,900,000,000 \text{ km}}$$

Mercury is 58,000,000 kilometers from the sun. Using our proportion, we can find the scale distance:

$$\frac{x}{58,000,000 \text{ km}} = \frac{100 \text{ m}}{5,900,000,000 \text{ km}}$$

Cross-multiply and rearrange the variables to solve for x:

$$x = \frac{100 \text{ m}}{5,900,000,000 \text{ km}} \times 58,000,000 \text{ km} = 0.98 \text{ m}$$

Mercury is 0.98 meters from the sun using this scale.

2   Determining scale distances for the other planets

Based on the example in Part 1, you would place Mercury 0.98 meters or 98 centimeters from the sun in your 100-meter scale model. Use this example to help you calculate the placement of the other planets. Write the distance in meters for each planet in Table 1.

Table 1: Distance from the sun

Planet	Actual distance to sun (km)	Proportional distance from the sun (m)
Mercury	**58,000,000**	**0.98**
Venus	108,000,000	
Earth	150,000,000	
Mars	228,000,000	
Jupiter	778,000,000	
Saturn	1,430,000,000	
Uranus	2,870,000,000	
Neptune	4,500,000,000	
Pluto	5,900,000,000	

3   Setting up the scale model

1. To begin, make signs for each of the planets and one for the sun. In your scale model, a student in your class will hold the sign at each position of the planet.

2. In an area that is at least 100-meters long, identify the location of the sun. A student will stand in this position with a sign that says "Sun."

3. Measure 100 meters from the position of the sun. At the 100-meter mark, a student will stand with a sign that says "Pluto." In this model, 100 meters is the scale distance from the sun to Pluto.

4. Now, use the scale distances from Table 1 to find the locations of each planet. At the location of each planet, a student will stand with the appropriate sign. Then, answer the questions.

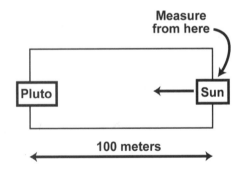

a. After constructing a model of it, what is your impression of our solar system?

b. Describe some disadvantages and advantages to this model of the solar system.

c. Alpha Centauri is the closest star to Earth at 274,332 AU. One astronomical unit is equal to 150 million kilometers. Where would you place this star in the 100-meter scale model?

d. The diameter of the Milky Way galaxy is known to be about 100,000 light years. One light year is 63,000 AU. How does the Milky Way compare with the size of the model solar system?

4   Determining scale sizes of the planets

What would the planets look like in this scale model of the solar system? For example, Mercury has a diameter of 4,880 kilometers. How big would Mercury be in your 100-meter scale model? You can use the same method to determine the scale diameter of Mercury that you used in Part 2:

$$\frac{x}{4{,}880 \text{ km}} = \frac{100 \text{ m}}{5{,}900{,}000{,}000 \text{ km}}$$

Cross-multiply and rearrange the variables to solve for x:

$$x = \frac{100 \text{ m}}{5{,}900{,}000{,}000 \text{ km}} \times 4{,}880 \text{ km} = 0.000078 \text{ m}$$

Based on the example above, the diameter of Mercury in a 100-meter scale solar system would be 0.000078 meters or 0.078 millimeters. For comparison purposes, a single human hair is about 0.1 millimeters in diameter or one-tenth of a millimeter.

Use the above proportion to calculate the diameters of the other planets as well as the sun and Earth's moon. Write these values in units of meters in the third column of Table 2. Then answer the questions that follow the table.

Table 2: Diameters of the planets, our moon, and sun

Planet	Actual diameter (km)	Scale diameter (m)	Scale diameter (mm)
Sun	1,391,980		
Mercury	4,880	**0.000078**	
Venus	12,100		
Earth	12,800		
Moon	3,475		
Mars	6,800		
Jupiter	142,000		
Saturn	120,000		
Uranus	51,800		
Neptune	49,500		
Pluto	2,300		

a.   How big is the sun in this model in units of centimeters?

b.   How much larger is the sun's diameter compared with Earth's? How much larger is Earth's diameter compared with the moon's?

c.   The smallest object that the human eye can see without magnification is 0.100 millimeters. Given this information, which planets would be visible to the human eye? Would you be able to see the sun or the moon on this 100-meter scale model of the solar system?

d.   What is your impression of how the size of the planets and the sun compare with the size of the solar system?

5   ## Extension: Making a larger scale model of the solar system

In this part of the Investigation, you will use common objects to compare the diameters of planets, the sun, and Earth's moon in our solar system. For example, we could use an Earth globe to represent the scale size of Earth. The diameter of the globe we will use is 30 centimeters.

1.   If an Earth globe is used to represent the size of Earth, what would the sizes of the sun and the other planets be? How big would the moon be? Use what you have learned in this Investigation to calculate the scale diameters of the other planets, the moon, and the sun. Fill in the third column of Table 3 with these values.

2.   What objects could be used to represent each of the planets, the moon, and the sun? Fill in the fourth column of Table 3 with your answers to this question.

3.   Answer the questions that follow the table.

Table 3: A scale model of the solar system

Planet	Actual diameter of planet (km)	Scale diameter of sun or planet (cm)	Representative object and its diameter or length (cm)
Sun	1,391,980		
Mercury	4,880		
Venus	12,100		
Earth	**12,800**	**30 cm**	**Earth globe, 30 cm**
Moon	3,475		
Mars	6,800		
Jupiter	142,000		
Saturn	120,000		
Uranus	51,800		
Neptune	49,500		
Pluto	2,300		

a.   How many times bigger is 24 centimeters than 0.20 millimeters? These are the diameters of Earth for the two scale models you created.

b.   Using your answer to question 5a, what would be the distance between the sun and Pluto on this larger scale? Come up with a way to explain or model this distance.

c.   Why is it challenging to make a scale model of the solar system that includes the distances between planets and the sun and the sizes of the planets?

The Sun

Question: How can we use energy from the sun to generate electricity?

In this Investigation, you will:

1. Measure the power output of a photovoltaic cell.
2. Determine the efficiency of a photovoltaic cell.

You have learned that the sun produces 3.9×10^{26} watts of energy every second. Of that amount, 1,386 watts fall on a square meter of Earth's atmosphere and even less reaches Earth's surface. This energy can be used to generate electricity without producing pollution or dangerous wastes. Photovoltaic (PV) cells convert sunlight *directly* into electricity and are used to run small appliances such as calculators and outdoor light fixtures. Many PV cells can be wired together to form *panels* that can be used to run larger devices such as irrigation pumps, radar stations, and even refrigerators. How much power does a PV cell produce? How efficient is a PV cell at converting the sun's energy into power?

1   Setting up

1. Gather the following materials: PV cell, electric motor with fan, wires, circuit grid, digital multimeter, protractor.

2. Measure the length and width of your PV cell (do not include the base) and calculate its area in square centimeters. Record this value.

3. Build a circuit with the PV cell and the electric motor with fan on the circuit grid. Use the wires to make connections.

4. Bring this setup outside into direct sunlight.

5. Set the circuit grid on level ground and hold it so that the sun casts no shadow over it.

6. Vary the angle of the electric circuit board by tipping one end of it up or down. Record your observations of what happens to the speed of the fan at different angles.

7. Record the angle at which you get the fastest fan speed.

a. How does changing the angle of the PV cell affect the speed of the fan?

b. At which angle is the fan's speed the fastest?

c. Why do you think the angle of the PV cell affects the speed of the fan?

SET UP

PV Cell

Wires   Electric motor and fan

Sun's rays

Measure angle

2   Measuring electrical quantities in the circuit

1. Readjust the angle of the electric circuit board until the fan's speed is its fastest. Record the angle.

2. Replace the fan with a 5-ohm resistor.

3. Use the digital multimeter to measure **voltage** across the resistor. Record the voltage.

4. Disconnect the circuit at point A and measure **current** in the circuit. Record the current.

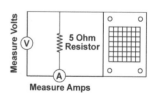

Measure Volts
5 Ohm Resistor
Measure Amps

3   # How efficient is your photovoltaic cell?

In this part of the Investigation, you will determine how much of the energy that is reaching your PV cell is being converted into **power**. To do this, you will use your data from Parts 1 and 2.

a. $\frac{a}{b}$ Use the formula below to calculate the **power output** of your PV cell in watts/cm^2.

$$\frac{\text{voltage} \times \text{current}}{\text{area}} = \text{watts/cm}^2$$

Record your result.

b.   Multiply your result by 10,000 to convert the value to watts/m^2. Record your result.

The amount of the sun's energy that reaches the edge of Earth's atmosphere is known as the **solar constant**. While the solar constant varies slightly, the average value is 1,368 watts per square meter (W/m^2). To visualize this amount of energy, imagine the energy of thirteen 100-watt light bulbs spread over a single square-meter surface.

How much of this energy actually reaches Earth's surface on a sunny day? This amount varies according to the time of year. The following values are estimates for how much energy reaches Earth's surface on a sunny day, according to the time of year:

- 1000 watts/m^2 on a sunny summer day.
- 900 watts/m^2 on a sunny autumn or spring day.
- 700 watts/m^2 on a sunny winter day.

Depending on the time of year, one of the values above is the *power input from the sun* that is converted into electrical energy by your PV cell.

c.   Calculate the efficiency of your photovoltaic cell using the formula below.

$$\% \text{ efficiency} = \left(\frac{\text{power input from the sun}}{\text{power output of your photovoltaic cell}} \right) \times 100$$

Record your result.

d.   Most PV cells have efficiencies between 5 and 20 percent. How does yours compare?

4   ## Applying your knowledge

a.   Besides angle, what other factors do you think will affect the energy output of your PV cell?

b.   PV cells are found on satellites, space probes, and the space shuttle. Do you think the power output of your PV cell would be greater or less just beyond Earth's atmosphere? Explain your answer.

c.   With your group, design and conduct an experiment that addresses one of the questions below. Prepare a lab report that explains your hypothesis, procedure, data analysis, and conclusions.

- How does the *distance from a light source* affect the power output of a PV cell?
- How does the *color of light* affect the power output of a PV cell?
- How does *temperature* affect the power output and efficiency of a PV cell?

Question: What are stars made of?

In this Investigation, you will:

1. Explain why spectroscopy is an important tool of astronomers.
2. Identify elements that are the most common in a main sequence star.

With the exception of the sun, stars appear as mere specks of light in the night sky. Through a technique called **spectroscopy**, astronomers are able to analyze the light emitted by stars to determine their temperature, chemical composition, and even how fast they are moving. In this Investigation, you will learn how to analyze light using spectroscopy to determine which elements are present in different light sources. You will then analyze the light emitted by a main sequence star (the sun) to determine its chemical composition.

1   Using the spectrometer

A **spectrometer** splits light into a spectrum of colors and displays the different colors of light along a scale. The scale measures the wavelengths of different colors of light in nanometers (nm).

Safety Tip: Never look directly into any light source—especially the sun!

Hold the spectrometer so that the printed side is facing upward. In a well-lighted room, hold the spectrometer so that one eye is looking through the diffraction grating and the other eye is closed. You should see a scale, as illustrated below. The bottom scale measures wavelengths in nanometers. You should also notice colors at various places inside the spectrometer. This is caused by light entering the spectrometer from different sources.

Notice that the plastic disk that is attached to the diffraction grating can be turned. Looking into the spectrometer, rotate the disk until you see colors in a horizontal line to your left. The colors should appear between the two lines of numbers on the scales.

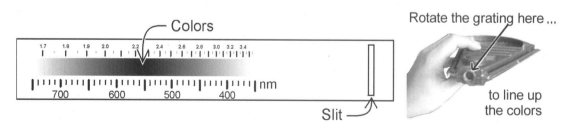

a. While looking through the eyepiece, point the slit of the spectrometer directly at an incandescent bulb. Use colored pencils to show where the different colors of light appear in on the spectrometer scale.

b. Blue light has the highest energy and red light the lowest. Based on your observations with the spectrometer, what is the relationship between wavelength and amount of energy?

2

Using a spectrometer to identify elements in a fluorescent light

1. Use the spectrometer to examine a fluorescent light source (most likely the ones that illuminate your classroom). This time, you will see lines (called **spectral lines**) of different colors instead of a smooth spectrum like you observed with the incandescent light.

2. You should see a green line at 546 nanometers on the scale. If the green line is not at 546 nanometers, ask your teacher to calibrate the spectrometer for you.

3. Use colored pencils to sketch the lines you observe. Be very precise in your sketch by placing the lines you see in the *exact* positions on the scale below.

|ᴵ|ᴵᴵ|ᴵᴵᴵ|ᴵᴵᴵ|ᴵᴵᴵ|ᴵᴵᴵ|ᴵᴵᴵ|ᴵᴵᴵ|ᴵᴵᴵ|ᴵᴵᴵ|ᴵᴵᴵ|ᴵᴵᴵ|
700   600   500   400

4. Identify the wavelength of each spectral line, from left to right, then fill in Table 1.

Table 1: Spectral lines produced by a fluorescent light

Line number	Spectral line color	Spectral line wavelength (nm)
1		
2		
3		
4		

What do the lines mean?

When elements are heated until they are hot enough to emit light (like those elements that make up stars), they produce characteristic spectral lines. Each element produces a pattern of spectral lines that is like a fingerprint. Shown to the right are some examples of the spectral lines produced by four different elements. Each line has a specific wavelength (these values are not shown in the diagram).

The light produced by a fluorescent source is created when electric current is passed through a gas inside of the tube. This gas, which is made of only one element, absorbs energy, and emits light.

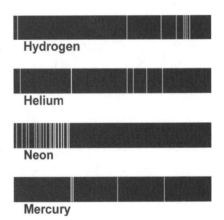

a. The light produced by the fluorescent tube you observed contains only one element. Compare the spectral lines you observed with the ones shown in the diagram above. Which element does it contain?

b. Fluorescent tubes have special instructions for disposal and must not end up in a landfill. Based on your spectral analysis of the gas inside the tube, why is this so?

c. Stars are made up of more than one type of element. When astronomers use a spectrometer to analyze the light produced by stars, they observe the combined spectral lines of all of the elements present in the star. What specific information would an astronomer need to know in order to determine which elements are present in a star?

3

Analyzing light from different sources

Identify five different light sources to observe with the spectrometer. Examples include gym lights, street lights, security lights, monitor screens, plant growing lights, and glow sticks. Write the types of light sources in the first column of Table 2. Follow the steps below for each light source.

1. Use the spectrometer to analyze the light emitted by the light source.
2. Use colored pencils to draw the position of each spectral line in column 2 of Table 2.
3. Record the wavelength, in nanometers, of each spectral line in the third column of Table 2.
4. Table 4 on the next page lists the values, in nanometers, of the spectral lines produced by various elements. Use these values to identify the elements found in each light source you observed and write them in the last column of the table.

Table 2: Spectral lines produced by different light sources

Light source	Spectrometer scale (nm)	Position of each vertical line (nm)	Elements present
	700 600 500 400		
	700 600 500 400		
	700 600 500 400		
	700 600 500 400		
	700 600 500 400		

a. If one light source displays more spectral lines than another, does that mean that it contains more elements? Explain your answer.

b. Which light source contains the greatest variety of elements?

c. Which light sources contain only one element?

4   Analyzing the light from a star

So far, the light sources you observed contain only a few elements. However, stars' atmospheres contain many elements and are much more complex.

1. Use the spectrometer to analyze the light of our closest star—the sun. Do not point the spectrometer directly at the sun. Instead, point it at reflected sunlight, off a cloud, for example, or a patch of blue sky.

2. Record in Table 3 the color and value, in nanometers, of each spectral line you observe.

3. Use Table 4, shown below, to identify the elements present in the sun's atmosphere and record them in the third column of Table 3.

◆ **Safety Tip: Do not point the spectrometer directly at the sun. Point it only at reflected sunlight. NEVER look directly at the sun!**

Table 3: Analyzing light from the sun

Spectral line color	Spectral line wavelength (nm)	Element present

Table 4: Spectral lines and elements present

Spectral line (nm)	Element present	Spectral line (nm)	Element present
393	calcium	527	iron
397	calcium	546	mercury
405	mercury	577	mercury
434	hydrogen	579	mercury
436	mercury	589	sodium
486	hydrogen	590	sodium
517	magnesium	656	hydrogen
517	iron	687	oxygen

a. Explain why the sun's light produces more spectral lines than the light sources you observed in Parts 2 and 3.

b. Where do elements in the sun's atmosphere come from? Explain your answer in detail.

c. The sun is a main sequence star. If you could analyze the light from a much older star, what would you expect to see? Justify your answer using your knowledge of the star life cycle.

Galaxies and the Universe

Question: How do we measure the distance to stars and galaxies?

In this Investigation, you will:

1. Use a solar cell and electric meter to measure brightness at various distances from a light source.
2. Discover the mathematical relationship between apparent brightness and distance.

The **apparent brightness** of any light source depends on the distance from which it is being observed, and how much light it actually emits (its **absolute brightness**). When astronomers know the values for absolute and apparent brightness for a star or galaxy, they can calculate the distance to these objects. In this Investigation, you will discover the mathematical relationship between how bright a light source appears and the distance from which it is observed. You will then understand how astronomers are able to use light to measure the distances to faraway stars and galaxies.

1 ## Setting up the experiment

For the experiment, you will use a 100-watt light bulb as a light source. You will measure the brightness of the light source at various distances from the light bulb using a solar cell and electric meter.

Set up the experiment as shown in the diagram, then answer the questions below.

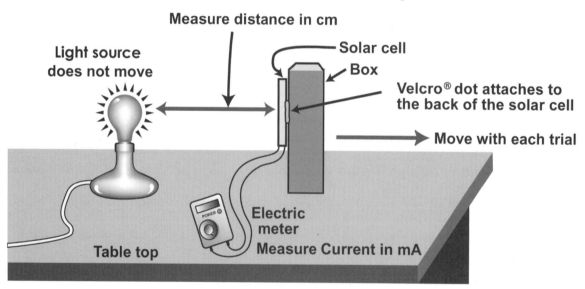

a. Does this experiment measure the *absolute brightness* or the *apparent brightness* of the light source? Explain your answer.

b. Is the power rating of the light source (100 watts) a measure of the light bulb's *absolute brightness* or *apparent brightness*? Explain your answer.

c. What effect do you think increasing the distance will have on your measurements of brightness?

2   ## Doing the experiment

1. Turn on your light source and turn off the overhead lights in the classroom.
2. Place the solar cell exactly 10 centimeters from the light bulb. Make sure the solar cell is directly facing the light bulb and is not at an angle.
3. Make sure the electric meter is set to measure current in milliamps (mA).
4. Measure the light's brightness in mA and record your results in Table 1.
5. Measure the brightness at 10-centimeter intervals and record your data in Table 1.

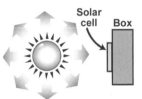

View from above

Solar cell is directly facing the light bulb

Table 1: Brightness and distance data

Distance (cm)	10	20	30	40	50	60	70	80	90	100
Brightness (mA)										

3   ## Analyzing your data

Make a graph of brightness versus distance. Plot brightness on the *y*-axis and distance on the *x*-axis.

a. Is your graph increasing or decreasing from left to right?
b. Describe the shape of the curve on your graph. Have you seen a curve like this before?
c. Is there a mathematical relationship between brightness and distance from your graph? Explain your answer.

4   ## $\frac{a}{b}$ Inverse relationships

From your graph, you can tell that the brightness of the light bulb *decreases* as the distance *increases*. When one factor increases as another decreases, it is called an **inverse relationship**. In this case, we can say the brightness varies inversely with distance. This can be shown as a mathematical relationship using the variables *B* for brightness and *D* for distance, where:

$$\text{Brightness} \longrightarrow B = \frac{1}{D} \Big\} \text{ Inverse of distance}$$

Your graph shows an inverse relationship between brightness and distance, but can you tell from the curve exactly by how much brightness will decrease as distance increases? Here are three possible mathematical relationships:

$$B = \frac{1}{D} \quad \text{or} \quad B = \frac{1}{D^2} \quad \text{or} \quad B = \frac{1}{D^3}$$

The first equation says the brightness is inversely related to the distance. The second equation says the brightness varies with the inverse of the distance *squared*.

a. What does the third equation state?
b. Assuming that the correct equation is one of the three above, how could you figure out which is the correct one?
c. Which equation do you think is the correct one? Explain your reasoning.

5   ## Identifying the correct inverse relationship

To figure out which equation is correct, you will need to further analyze your data from Part 2.

1. Enter your distance data from Table 1 into the first row of Table 2 below. You will need to convert centimeters to meters. The first two values are done for you.
2. Calculate 1/D and enter the results in the second row of Table 2. The first two are done for you.
3. Calculate $1/D^2$ and $1/D^3$ and enter the values in rows three and four of Table 2.
4. Enter your brightness data from Table 1 into the fifth row of Table 2.
5. Make the following three graphs:

    Graph 1: *Brightness vs. 1/D*

    Graph 2: *Brightness vs. $1/D^2$*

    Graph 3: *Brightness vs. $1/D^3$*

Table 2: Analyzing your distance and brightness data

Distance (cm)	10	20	30	40	50	60	70	80	90	100
Distance (m)	0.10	0.20								
1/D	10	5								
$1/D^2$	100	25								
$1/D^3$										
Brightness (mA)										

6   ## Reaching a conclusion

a.   Which graph identifies the correct inverse relationship between brightness and distance? Explain your choice.

b.   Write down the correct formula for the relationship between brightness and distance.

c.   Test your formula by following these steps:

(1) Choose a distance for which you did not measure brightness (for example, 45 centimeters).

(2) Calculate brightness using your formula. This is your *predicted brightness*.

(3) Move the solar cell to the distance you chose and measure the brightness of the light. This is your *actual brightness*.

(4) Calculate your percent error using the following formula:

$$\left(\frac{\text{predicted brightness - actual brightness}}{\text{predicted brightness}} \right) \times 100 = \text{percent error}$$

d.   Your actual brightness should be fairly close to your predicted brightness. What are some possible reasons for differences between predictions and measurements in this experiment?

7 | **Applying your knowledge: How bright would the sun appear on Pluto?**

You have learned that the average distance of Earth from the sun is 150 million kilometers. This is also defined as 1.0 astronomical unit (AU). Using the relationship between apparent brightness and distance that you discovered in this Investigation, we can determine that the brightness of the sun from Earth is equal to 1.0 solar brightness units (SBU):

$$\text{Brightness of the sun from Earth} = \frac{1}{(1.0 \text{ AU})^2} = 1.0 \text{ SBU}$$

Use what you have learned in this Investigation to complete Table 3 below. Then answer the questions.

Table 3: Apparent brightness of the sun from the planets

Planet	Average distance from the sun (AU)	Apparent brightness (SBU)
Mercury	0.37	
Venus	0.72	
Earth	1.0	1.0
Mars	1.5	
Jupiter	5.2	
Saturn	9.5	
Uranus	19.2	
Neptune	30.0	
Pluto	39.5	

a. How much brighter is the sun viewed from Mercury compared with its brightness viewed from Earth?

b. How much fainter is the sun viewed from Pluto compared with its brightness viewed from Earth?

c. CHALLENGE! Alpha Centurai is 4.1×10^{13} km from Earth. How bright would the sun appear in SBU from Alpha Centurai? (Hint: You must first convert kilometers to astronomical units.)

8 | **Using light to measure distances to stars and galaxies**

$\boxed{\frac{a}{b}}$ In the Investigation, you determined that the apparent brightness of a light source decreases as the distance increases. However, the brightness of the light source also depends on how much light it actually emits (its absolute brightness). The inverse square law of brightness shows the relationship between apparent brightness (how bright an object appears from a certain distance), absolute brightness (how much light an object actually emits), and distance:

Inverse square law   Absolute brightness

$$\text{Apparent brightness} \rightarrow B = \frac{L}{4\pi D^2}$$

Constant (4 x 3.14)   Distance

a. Which variables would an astronomer need to know in order to determine the distance to a faraway galaxy or star? Describe how an astronomer could determine each variable.

b. In the diagram to the right, which galaxy is the farthest from Earth? Explain your reasoning.

B = 3.0
L = 18.0

Galaxy A

B = 6.0
L = 9.0

Galaxy B